INSIDER'S
BASEBALL

INSIDER'S BASEBALL

The Finer Points of the Game, As Examined
by the Society for American Baseball Research

L. Robert Davids
Editor

with a Foreword by
Bill James

Charles Scribner's Sons
New York

Library of Congress Cataloging in Publication Data

Main entry under title:
Insider's baseball.
1. Baseball—United States—Addresses, essays, lectures.
I. Davids, L. Robert.   II. Society for American Baseball
Research.
GV863.A1I57   1983   796.357'0973   82-42657
ISBN 0-684-17905-9

1 3 5 7 9 11 13 15 17 19   F/C   20 18 16 14 12 10 8 6 4 2

Printed in the United States of America.

Contents

Foreword

Bill James

I joined the Society for American Baseball Research (SABR) in 1975, one of a series of steps that I needed to cross the bridge and enter the private fantasyland (twenty-four baseball hours a day) that I am now privileged to inhabit. Most of the people whose work is collected here were there before me, going about their obsession. If the Baseball Writers Association of America (BBWAA) is an organization of those to whom baseball represents a way of making a living, SABR is an organization of those to whom baseball is a way of life.

To go through these articles, for me, is like walking around a room shaking ideas and exchanging hands with forty-plus old friends, and not only because many of the people who have contributed to this long-overdue collection are, in fact, friends of mine. An introduction, you say? Very well . . . meet SABR, an organization heading into its second decade, with over a thousand members, heading toward two thousand. Meet Bob Davids, the guiding force behind SABR from its beginnings and the editor of this book. I don't believe that I know anybody who has worked harder, or longer, to create anything than Bob Davids has worked to create, preserve, and strengthen SABR. Meet Bill Borst, St. Louis publisher. Bill revives the memory of Helene Britton, the nearly forgotten woman who once owned a St. Louis baseball club. Meet Mil Chipp, statistician of the San Diego Padres, in the process of separating inside-the-park home runs from the indistinct masses of four-base hits. Meet Eddie Gold, whose memory embraces warmly every detail of each and every Cub inning and season. Eddie's "Baseball Rhyme Time" is a classic in the history of self-indulgent literature. (I keep intending to have a copy framed.) Meet Ernest Infield. Actually, I don't think I know Mr. Infield, and he doesn't have an article in this collection, but you've got to admit it's the best name for a baseball fanatic that you'll ever hear. Meet Pete Palmer, head of SABR's stat analysis committee, whose disheveled gaze belies a command of details and an impressive ability to produce and organize work. I estimate that I have owed Pete a letter 97.284 percent of the time for the last six years. The formula for this is . . . well, never mind. Meet Emil Rothe, a retired school administrator with a great dignity about him and a long list of published articles.

In passing through each of us, baseball becomes a different game. These men share a deep and intensely personal love of the game that breaks it down like forty-plus mirrors and reflects it out to the world a new game. These images of the game will seem strange, almost bizarre, to those who know baseball only by the clichés into which journalism unrecognizably renders it, morning by morning. These are not the sterile, one-dimensional images of the game produced by men foolish enough to adopt the position that they must remain uninterested in the results so that they can report accurately on the games.

There are many differences between what I do for a living and what these people have done because they wanted to do it, but there is one paramount similarity. One of my goals in writing is never, ever, to tell the reader anything that he already knows. These pages pour forth a profusion of fresh and fascinating details covering more than a century of the Pastime and representing probably as many years spent in libraries reading microfilm. How many hours has Ray Gonzalez spent reviewing the career of Lou Gehrig? How many hours did John Tattersall spend analyzing Henry Aaron's home runs? It's hard to imagine, but I'd bet nobody in this book would want any of those hours back. Beisbol, as Chico would say, has been bery, bery good to all of us.

Preface

L. Robert Davids

The Society for American Baseball Research (SABR) was established at Cooperstown, New York, August 10, 1971, with sixteen baseball historians, statisticians, and fans participating in the organization meeting. The society grew steadily from that humble beginning and gathered into its midst such authorities on the national pastime as Fred Lieb, John Tattersall, Leonard Gettelson, Harold Seymour, David Voigt, Bob Broeg, Seymour Siwoff, and Allan Roth. Today most of the leading sportswriters and broadcasters are members. In early 1983, SABR membership was more than 2,500, including about 100 members in Canada and 25 others spread around the world.

One of the objectives in organizing SABR was to provide a forum for the exchange of historical and statistical information among members, as well as to disseminate this information to the public. The primary vehicle for the latter is the *Baseball Research Journal,* which has been published annually by the society since 1972. The journal has carried articles by the members on a wide range of subjects and much research that has not been previously published. Most of this material was generated in the various SABR research committees: biographical research, minor leagues, Negro leagues, statistical analysis, baseball records, collegiate baseball, and ball parks.

What new information has the society uncovered and published in the past ten years? Here are some examples:

- The dates and circumstances of Ty Cobb's 35 steals of home
- All the pitchers who struck out Joe Sewell in his career
- The game ambidextrous Tony Mullane pitched with both hands
- A black player who pitched in the Pacific Coast League in 1916
- The list of Lou Gehrig's 15 career steals of home versus Lou Brock's one
- The fact that Sam Crawford hit 50 of his 97 home runs inside the park
- A 17-game streak of runs batted in by an obscure player with the 1922 Chicago Cubs
- Willie Mays' record of 22 home runs in extra innings— and the fact that Elroy Face gave up 21 in overtime
- Regulation major league games played since 1900 in such places as Grand Rapids, Michigan; Fort Wayne, Indiana; Dayton, Ohio; and Providence, Rhode Island.

Some fans may consider this type of information to be baseball trivia. Members of the society look upon it more as significant historical information that bolsters the concept of baseball as the national game.

Nearly fifty articles from SABR publications of the past ten years have been selected for inclusion in this anthology. The society appreciates the opportunity provided by Scribners to publish this volume for a broader segment of the American sports-loving public. We hope you find the articles interesting and enlightening.

INSIDER'S
BASEBALL

Baseball's Greatest Games

Frederick G. Lieb

In addition to the fact that 1976 was the nation's bicentennial, it was a big year for celebration in each of America's major baseball organizations. The venerable National League, born in New York, February 2, 1876, celebrated its proud centennial. Its once upstart junior, the American League, accepted congratulations on surviving 75 tempestuous seasons.

Over the course of the past century and then some, baseball fans have attended thousands of games and have seen even more ball players. In the parade of games, which particular game stood out above all others? It had to be a contest of vital concern to the game's statistics, but even more it had to be a contest that ranged the full gamut of human emotions, that evoked intense partisan loyalty and the deepest of hatreds, that involved bribery, a threat of mayhem, and even a suicide of a major league executive. All of these things were wrapped up in the emotions of one game.

For my number one game of the past 100 years I must pick a contest played at the old New York Polo Grounds early in the present century. It was a postseason play-off between John McGraw's scrappy New York Giants and Frank Chance's brilliant, wily Chicago Cubs, winners of 116 NL games in 1906 and 107 in 1907 and strong contenders with New York and Pittsburgh for the 1908 pennant.

Of course, picking the greatest game must depend a lot on personal opinion or prejudice—also on how many games you have seen or know about. I am sure that by picking the 1908 Cub–Giant play-off game as number one, some of the younger fans will say, "The old geezer picks a game we know nothing about. We haven't even heard of it."

Fans today can only guess at the heated atmosphere in which this game was played. It came at a time when baseball still was undisputed king of American sports. Spring and summer, baseball received more than three-fourths of the space in the nation's sports pages. It yielded somewhat to college football in the fall, but in winter, baseball still got a third to a half of the space allotted to sports.

Golf and tennis then were largely amateur events, getting real space only when they had their annual championships. Pro football was played mainly in Ohio and western Pennsylvania. College football centered around Yale, Harvard, and Princeton in the East and Michigan and the University of Chicago in the Middle West. Basketball was a lesser sport played by high schools and colleges between the football and baseball seasons. Big championship boxing matches were fought in mining towns in Nevada and other out-of-the-way places, not in major cities.

As a consequence, the baseball world championship and the two major league pennants were the most cherished sports prizes. A lot of people did not go to ball games by today's standards, but those of the sporting fraternity knew all the players and what they did from day to day. The 1908 play-off was not a ball game between respected opponents, such as the Reds and Red Sox in the 1975 World Series, but a war between the cities of New York and Chicago—the cities, the teams, and the followers. All over the country, fans backed either the Cubs or the Giants, with the majority supporting Frank Chance's well-oiled machine.

The hatreds and ill feeling had all started with an earlier Chicago–New York game, at the Polo Grounds on September 23, 1908. At the time the top contenders—the Giants, the Cubs, and the Pirates—were running almost neck and neck. In this particular game, the score was 2–2 in the New York half of the ninth inning. There were two out, Harry "Moose" McCormick was the Giant runner on third base, and Fred Merkle, a rookie, was on first base, when little Giant shortstop Al Bridwell smacked a clean single over second base, permitting McCormick to score the apparent winning run. The crowd surged onto the playing field, as that was the quickest way to the exits leading to the trolley cars and the Sixth Avenue El trains.

However, things still were happening on the ballfield. Artie Hofman, the skillful Cub center fielder, fielded Bridwell's hit and threw in the general direction of second base. The alert Cubs had observed that young Merkle, instead of running down to second base after Bridwell's hit, had dashed off to the center field clubhouse. New York's iron man, Joe McGinnity, struggled with shortstop Joe Tinker for the ball thrown in by Hofman. McGinnity, suspecting that the Cubs were after a force play on Merkle at second, won possession of the ball and threw it deep into the left-field bleachers.

Then there was another odd development. Floyd Kroh, a second-string Cub pitcher, rolled another ball on the ground from the Cub bench to Johnny Evers, standing at second base. Johnny claimed a force play on Merkle, and umpire Hank O'Day, standing near the bag, called Merkle out, nullifying McCormick's run.

The Cubs were ready to go to bat in the tenth inning, but by this time most of the twenty thousand people who had watched the game were on the playing field. The Giants' management made no effort to clear the field, and Charley Murphy, the Chicago club owner, immediately called for a 9–0 forfeit victory. However, Giant president John T. Brush and manager John McGraw ridiculed the antics of the Cubs after Bridwell's "winning hit" and insisted their team had won fairly on the playing field. They dismissed Merkle's failure to tag second as not being relevant. When the winning run is scored, they contended, "that's the end of the game."

As Merkle's failure to touch second became more and more damaging to the Giants' cause, he became "Bonehead" Merkle, an unfair nickname that followed him to the end of his career. However, I always have felt that McGraw was partly to blame. A fortnight before the Merkle play in New York, Evers had tried the same play in the ninth inning of a game the Cubs lost in Pittsburgh. The umpire-in-chief was Hank O'Day. As the winning Pittsburgh run was scoring from third base, a young player named Warren Gill also failed to tag second with two out. When Evers and Chance argued that the side had been retired by a force play on Gill, O'Day said, "I had my back turned to the play, and did not see it. But if such a play comes up in the future, I will look for it, and call it accordingly." With this warning from O'Day, McGraw should have drilled all of his players, especially the youngsters, to be sure to touch the bag ahead in all situations.

League president Harry Pulliam ruled the September 23 game a 2–2 tie and ordered that it be replayed the day following the last game of the schedule if it were needed to determine the winner. The league board of directors supported Pulliam in this decision, but it was stubbornly fought by John Brush, who still considered the game of September 23 a Giant win and stated that "neither Pulliam nor the board of directors could steal this victory from the Giants."

The National League ended its regular season on October 3 in the West and on October 7 in the East, as there then was Sunday ball only in Chicago, St. Louis, and Cincinnati. When the western clubs finished on the Sunday, the Cubs were 98–53 and the Giants were 95–53. They still had three games to play with Joe Kelley's Boston Braves. Kelley had been a teammate of McGraw's on the Baltimore NL champions of 1894–95–96. One Boston win in the three games would have killed off the Giants' chance to get into a play-off, but the Giants swept all three games without using their ace, Christy Mathewson, by scores of 5–1, 5–1, and 8–1. Both top contenders now were 98–55, and the October 8 game therefore was not only a replay of the Merkle game but also the play-off for the pennant.

Jim Johnstone and Bill Klem were assigned as the umpires. While Klem was walking on Madison Avenue near his hotel the night before the big game, a man emerged from one of the brown-front houses with a fat roll of bills in his hands, saying to Klem, "The Giants mustn't lose tomorrow." Klem pushed him away and said, "Get away from me, you bum."

As Klem walked through one of the subterranean passages under the old wooden Polo Grounds stands the next day, he again was approached by the man with the big roll of bills. Again, he muttered, "Take these, Bill; the Giants mustn't lose." "Get out of my way; you stink," said Klem.

Of course, Klem was not to be corrupted. He was an umpire who regarded his craft as something almost sacred. An investigation after the play-off game came up with a statement that the attempted briber was a part-time trainer and early osteopathic doctor to the Giants named "Doc" Cramer. The National League ruled that Cramer would be barred for life from all National League parks.

Most of the seats at the Polo Grounds then were unreserved, and crowds gathered around the Harlem field as early as daybreak. Though the game was scheduled for 3 P.M., the New York police closed the gates to all but holders of reserved-seat tickets at 1:30, and even those with reserved seats had difficulty in getting in. They jammed Eighth Avenue and streets near the Polo Grounds. Some of the most daring somehow scaled the fence and climbed into the center-field bleachers.

Others produced some sort of battering ram and knocked several boards loose in the center-field fence. Fans poured through the gap in the fence until some of the grounds crew, aided by New York firemen, repelled the freeloaders with fire hoses.

When it came time for the Cubs to take infield practice, Chance led his players onto the playing field, but the Giants continued with their batting practice. McGinnity, who was batting out fungoes, refused to yield his position at the plate. It was then that McGinnity and Chance had their confrontation. There was some pushing, and both men swung. It later came out that this was all according to Giant plans. The strong McGinnity was supposed to pick a fight with Chance, and work him over to the point that he would be unable to play. It didn't work, however, because Chance protected himself. And then in the game he whacked out two doubles and a single and drove in two runs.

Even though McGraw had rested Mathewson through the three-game series with the Braves, the big right-hander was overworked and tired. He already had won 37 games for the Giants in 1908. That morning he told his wife, "Jane, my arm is as heavy and stiff as a board. I've got to tell McGraw I can't work, and to pitch Hooks Wiltse or Red Ames." However, when Matty told McGraw of his ailments, the Little Napoleon replied, "You've simply got to pitch, Matty. Sore or lame arm, you still are the best I have. I wouldn't entrust this game to anyone else." So Big Six was the Giant starter.

Chance's starting pitcher was his left-hander, Jack Pfiester. He was a Giant hoodoo and was called Jack the Giant Killer because of his ability to beat New York. But this day he did no Giant killing. He got in trouble in the very first inning, when the Giants picked up an early run and should have had more. Chance quickly turned to his old reliable, Mordecai Brown, to silence the Manhattan bats. The former coal miner gave up only four hits and one run the rest of the way.

The Cubs struck hard against Mathewson in the third inning, when they did all their scoring. Joe Tinker led off. Though he was only a .260 hitter, Joe was Christy's most difficult out. He started the victory ball with a triple over Cy Seymour's head. Kling quickly brought Tinker home with a single to left. Brown sacrificed Kling to second, but Sheckard lifted an outfield floater for the second out.

Then came an unhappy ten minutes for New York's beloved Matty. He made a mistake by walking Johnny Evers, and then Frank Schulte and Frank Chance crashed successive doubles, bringing in Kling, Evers, and Schulte—four runs for the inning.

The Cubs spent the rest of the game in defending their lead. Mathewson allowed no further scoring in his next four innings, and Wiltse pitched runless ball in the eighth and ninth.

New York fans had one last time to shout. They almost raised the roof of the old wooden grandstand when in the seventh the Giants filled the bases with none out on singles by Devlin and McCormick and a base on balls to Bridwell. But the promising inning flickered out with only one run. A limping Larry Doyle (he was just recovering from a broken leg) batted for Matty and raised a dinky little foul to catcher Kling. Devlin scored on Tenney's sacrifice fly, but the crowd gave a cry of despair when Tinker threw out Herzog for the third out. After this tough inning, Brownie retired the Giants in order in the eighth and ninth innings.

The Cubs won the game 4–2, making it three straight flags, and went on to beat Detroit in the 1908 World Series, four games to one. But it didn't end the bitterness, backbiting, and vicious criticism of league president Harry Pulliam, who had disallowed what the Giants considered a legitimate 3–2 victory and made possible the play-off defeat and the loss of the pennant.

The NL and the Giants both had offices in the St. James Building at 26th Street and Broadway. The two offices became hostile camps. Pulliam was booed when he walked along Broadway or attended the theatre or sporting events. "I won the 1908 National League fairly and honestly on the ball field, but was skeedaddled out of it in the league's head office," McGraw protested, and his fellow members of the Lambs Club all felt the same way.

Pulliam took this sharp criticism through the winter of 1908–09, but when it carried into the 1909 season he fretted and worried. His physician in New York told him to take a trip to Atlantic City, to forget all about baseball, and let John Heydler, the league secretary-treasurer, run the everyday duties of the office. On July 4, 1909, in a fit of despondency, Pulliam took his own life by firing a bullet into his brain in his Atlantic City hotel room.

I am sure many fans will be surprised that I did not pick as my first choice the final game of the 1951 NL play-off series between the New York Giants and Brooklyn Dodgers at the Polo Grounds. I'll admit that this game, known as the Bobby Thomson home run game, was more spectacular in itself. However, in my mind, it did not have the intriguing background, the intense rivalry, or the lasting ramifications.

I don't mean to minimize the Giant–Dodger rivalry, which was substantial in the New York area. In 1951, the Giants, managed by Leo Durocher, trailed Brooklyn by 13½ games in mid-August, but thanks to a 15-game winning streak in September, they tied the Bums on the last day of the season. This necessitated a three-game play-off. The Giants won the first game in Ebbets Field 3–1, but the Dodgers stormed back with heavy artillery at the Polo Grounds, winning 10–0 behind Clem Labine.

In the third game, also played in New York, it was a 1–1 pitching duel for seven innings between Sal Maglie of the Giants and Don Newcombe, the Brooklyn ace. However, the Dodgers apparently tore the game apart with three runs in the eighth, and they began counting their World Series dollars.

Newcombe hastily retired the Giants in the second half of the eighth. Three runs behind in the ninth, the Durocher cause looked rather hopeless. Don had yielded only four hits up to this point, but there was a glimmer of hope when Alvin Dark led off the Giant ninth with an infield hit. Another single by Don Mueller sent Dark to third. After Monte Irvin popped out, Whitey Lockman doubled to left, scoring Dark. Mueller suffered an ankle injury sliding into third and was replaced by Clint Hartung.

At this point, Dodger manager Chuck Dressen had to make an important decision—to let Newcombe stay in the game or to bring in one of several hurlers warming up in the bullpen. He decided to yank Don, and he signaled for Ralph Branca, who a few years before had been Brooklyn's top hurler. Ralph did little pitching that day. He served one called strike to Bobby Thomson, but the Staten Island Scot drove the next pitch high into the left-field bleachers.

It was "the shot heard round the world," as the score quickly changed from 4–2, Brooklyn, to the dramatic final count of 5–4, New York. It was one of the historic blows of the first 100 years of big league baseball.

If the fan is a pitching nut, he may prefer the double no-hitter on May 2, 1917, between Cincinnati's right-handed Fred Toney, the "man-mountain of Tennessee," and the equally large lefty of Chicago, Jim "Hippo" Vaughn. In the regulation nine innings, neither of these heavyweights gave up the semblance of a hit at Wrigley Field. The break came in the tenth inning, when the weak-hitting Larry Kopf opened with a roller to the right side that got between two former New York Giants, Larry Doyle at second and Fred Merkle at first. Vaughn then disposed of Greasy Neale with an outfield fly to Cy Williams for the second out. But Williams then muffed Hal Chase's line drive, and Kopf streaked to third. With Jim Thorpe, the Indian football and track star at bat, Chase stole second. Thorpe hit a high chopper in front of the plate. Seeing he could not catch the speedy Thorpe at first, Vaughn threw home, which caught catcher Art Wilson off guard. The ball went through him, and Kopf scored for a 1–0 victory. Thorpe was credited with a hit and an RBI. Toney pitched another hitless frame for a 10-inning no-hitter.

Among the other great games, I would have to include the October 2, 1908, pitching duel between Addie Joss of Cleveland, who pitched a perfect game, and Ed Walsh of the White Sox, who fanned 15 while giving up only four hits. Joss won 1–0. Another contest involving a perfect game was Don Larsen's World Series gem against Brooklyn on October 8, 1956. Not to be forgotten was the strong lineup the Yankee hurler was facing that day—players like Robinson, Hodges, Snider, Furillo, Campanella, and Reese. Another outstanding World Series game was the one featuring the 1960 home run by Bill Mazeroski, which gave the Pirates the title over the Yankees.

Three All-Star games also have high spots on my list of out-standing games. First is the familiar 1934 contest in which the Giants' brilliant meal ticket, Carl Hubbell, struck out Ruth, Gehrig, Foxx, Simmons, and Cronin in succession. But with Mel Harder's fine relief pitching, the American Leaguers still pulled it out 9–7 at the expense of Van Mungo and Dizzy Dean.

The second midsummer classic I have fond recollections of is the July 8, 1941, game, which young Ted Williams broke up with a three-run homer to give the AL a 7–5 win. I can still see Ted dancing around the bases with all his youthful exuberance when he hit that homer in Detroit.

An All-Star homer dearer to NL fans was one hit in old Comiskey Park, Chicago, on July 11, 1950. At that time the AL had won 12 games to the NL's 4, and it looked as though the usual pattern would be followed, with the AL leading 3–2 after eight innings. The late Arthur Daley, then the sports columnist for the *New York Times* and a NL partisan, said sadly in the Chicago press box, "No matter what the National League does, it just doesn't seem possible for it to win any of these games."

Hardly had he made the remark when Pittsburgh slugger Ralph Kiner tied the game with a homer into the left-field stands. Five innings later, Red Schoendienst hit another four-bagger in the same general area to give the Nationals a 4–3 win. It marked the end of AL domi-nance in All-Star play. From that time on, the NL dominated to the extent that the junior circuit won only six games in more than a quarter century. The 1950 game was the turning point.

In conclusion, I should be allowed one sentimental choice, or so it may seem. Actually, this was a historic game in that it virtually assured the Yankees of their first pennant. It was a contest between the World Champion Cleveland Indians and the challenging New Yorkers on September 26, 1921. It was the last meeting of the two clubs for the season, and it followed a 20–5 thrashing which the crew of Miller Hug-gins took the day before.

A sellout crowd of forty thousand packed the Polo Grounds to see Babe Ruth hit two homers and a double and George Burns hit a triple and three singles to lead the Yankees to a come-from-behind 8–7 vic-tory. There was great tension and pressure, particularly in the ninth inning, when the Indians loaded the bases. Yankee club president Jake Ruppert couldn't take it and retreated from the press box. He missed the most dramatic play of the game as the count went to 3 and 2 on batter Steve O'Neill. Barely able to see the tricky underhand delivery of Carl Mays in the evening dusk, O'Neill fanned on a pitch that was almost in the dirt. From the yelling of the crowd, Ruppert knew his club had triumphed. That put the Yanks a game and a half up, a lead they held for the rest of the final week of the season. It gave them the right to meet their landlords, the Giants, in the historic 1921 World Series.

Considering the way the Yankees dominated the American League and baseball in general over the next forty-odd years, the September 26, 1921, triumph over the Indians merits inclusion among the outstanding games of the past 100 years.

Mantle Is Baseball's Top Switch-Hitter

Robert C. McConnell

In spite of Pete Rose's 44-game hitting streak in 1978 and his achievement of more than 3,000 hits in his career, Mickey Mantle has been selected as the greatest switch-hitter in baseball history. In a survey conducted by the Society for American Baseball Research, Mantle was ranked first by 215 of the 302 researchers who cast ballots. In total points, the Yankee outfielder was well out in front with 780½, followed by Rose with 519½, Frank Frisch with 398, and Max Carey with 26.

The survey, conducted because of the increased emphasis on switch-hitting in recent years, also included selection of an all-time all-star team of switch-hitters. Mantle was a near unanimous choice (missing on one ballot) for one of the outfield positions. The others were filled by Max Carey and Reggie Smith. Going around the infield, the winners were James "Ripper" Collins, first base; his former manager and teammate on the Cardinals, Frank Frisch, second base; Rose (who also received 63 votes for the outfield), third base; and Maury Wills, shortstop. The catcher was Ted Simmons and the pitcher Early Wynn.

Rose and Frisch, both aggressive, talented players who hit for a higher average than Mantle, lost out to the Yankee star because of the latter's great slugging ability. Mantle revolutionized the art of switch-hitting by belting 536 home runs in his career. This was a quantum jump beyond the 135 hit by Collins in his career. Mantle shattered all assumptions that no player could hit that hard from both sides of the plate.

After Mantle retired, Reggie Smith has moved in as the leading long ball hitter among those who bat both ways. At the end of the 1982 campaign, he had 314 round-trippers, the great majority of which were hit from the left side. Other switch-hitters now active who are hitting with considerable power include Ted Simmons, Ken Singleton, and Eddie Murray.

Before Mantle switch-hitters made little contribution in the home run, slugging, and RBI departments. In 1942, for example, the leading home run hitter among switch-hitters was Roy Cullenbine with six. In 1920, at the start of the lively ball era, when Ruth hit 54 home runs, Frisch and Wally Schang led the switch-hitters with four each. Schang, incidentally, was one of the first batters known to have hit two homers in one game, one right and one left. Playing with the Athletics in a game against the Yankees at Shibe Park on September 8, 1916, Schang hit a grand slam homer into the right field stands off right-hander Allan Russell in the first inning and then hit a solo shot to the scoreboard in center in the second off southpaw Slim Love. The incident was not publicized at the time because of an unusual circumstance. So much rain fell that day that reporters, assuming that the game could not possibly be played, did not go to the park. For schedule reasons, Connie Mack insisted that the game be played, and it was, late in the afternoon, in a sea of water and in front of fewer than 100 people.

Switch-hitters made their primary contribution as players by getting on base and then scoring runs. Rose, Frisch, and Carey are among those who did it by getting hits; Tommy Tucker, who was a pretty fair hitter, had an extra talent in getting hit by pitches (more than 200 times in his career). A large number had an unusual talent for receiving bases on balls. This included not only Mantle, who was a great threat with the bat, but little Miller Huggins, who led the NL four times in walks, and Donie Bush, who led the AL five times. Others who led or who had outstanding walk totals included Lu Blue, Roy Cullenbine, Augie Galan, Jim Gilliam, Ken Singleton, and Roy White the one-time teammate of Mantle. In 1947, when Cullenbine was with the Tigers and accumulated a team record of 137 walks, he had a stretch of 22 consecutive games, from July 2 through July 22, in which he received one or more bases on ball. This is a major league record.

It is also a switch-hitter who holds the career record for fewest times grounding into double plays. Don Buford hit into only 33 double plays in 4,553 at bats or once every 138 times at the plate. His frequency rate is lower than that of all left-handed batters, including Lou Brock, Joe Morgan, and Richie Ashburn, who have that extra step advantage. Augie Galan, another ambidextrous batter, played the full schedule for the Cubs in 1935 and never grounded into a double play.

While acknowledging that switch-swinging has no bearing on stolen bases, we feel compelled to point out that those who bat both ways seem to excel on the basepaths. Take, for example, such aggressive base runners as Max Carey, Frank Frisch, George Davis, Bob Bescher, Donie Bush, Walter Wilmot, Miller Huggins, Augie Galan, Jim Gilliam, Don Buford, Sandy Alomar, and Maury and Bump Wills.

Switch-hitters also seem to strike out less; that is, with the exception of Mantle. Of the more than 30 major leaguers who have fanned more than 1200 times in their careers, only one (Mantle) is a switch-hitter. Only two switch-batters led their leagues in season strikeout totals: Mantle in the AL, and Bob Bescher in the NL.

To call attention to the increased use of switch-hitters, all we have to do is recall the 1965 Los Angeles Dodgers' infield of Wes Parker, first base; Jim Lefebvre, second base; Jim Gilliam, third base; and Maury Wills, shortstop. A recent example to illustrate the emphasis on switch-hitting is the 1977 batting race in the National League. Dave Parker won the crown, but of the top 11 batters in the league, five were switch-hitters: Garry Templeton, .322; Simmons, .318; Rose, .311; Reggie Smith, .307; and Lenny Randle, .304. Competing against these five were three left-hand swingers and three right-hand hitters. Ironically, these five switch-swingers were outhit by another, Ken Singleton in the American League, who hit .328.

Also emerging from this group is one of the great triple hitters in modern times, Garry Templeton, who led with 18 in 1977, 13 in 1978, and 19 in 1979, the highest NL total in many years. No NL batter has ever led three years in a row in this category. In 1979, Templeton also established a new major league record by collecting 100 or more hits both left-handed and right-handed. Willie Wilson equaled this unusual mark for Kansas City in 1980. He went on to win the AL batting crown in 1982.

Mickey Mantle, selected by the Society for American Baseball Research as baseball's greatest switch-hitter

Top Season Records, Switch-Hitters

Year	Department	Season Leader and Club	Total
1962	At bats	Willie Wilson, Kansas City	705
1922	Runs	Max Carey, Pittsburgh	140
1973	Hits	Pete Rose, Cincinnati	230
1980	Hits	Willie Wilson, Kansas City	230
1978	Doubles	Pete Rose, Cincinnati	51
1893	Triples	George Davis, New York (NL)	26
1961	Home runs	Mickey Mantle, New York (AL)	54
1956	Total bases	Mickey Mantle, New York (AL)	376
1957	Walks	Mickey Mantle, New York (AL)	146
1897	RBI	George Davis, New York (NL)	131
1889	Batting	Tommy Tucker, Baltimore (AA)	.375
1956	Slugging	Mickey Mantle, New York (AL)	.705

Top Ten Switch-Hitters (through 1982)

At Bats

Pete Rose	12544
Max Carey	9363
Frank Frisch	9112
George Davis	9027
Red Schoendienst	8479
Mickey Mantle	8102
Don Kessinger	7651
Maury Wills	7588
Kid Gleason	7445
Larry Bowa	7314

Home Runs

Mickey Mantle	536
Reggie Smith	314
Ken Singleton	222
Ted Simmons	209
Eddie Murray	165
Roy White	160
Pete Rose	158
Tom Tresh	153
Rip Collins	135
Ken Henderson	122

Runs

Pete Rose	1995
Mickey Mantle	1677
George Davis	1546
Max Carey	1545
Frank Frisch	1532
Donie Bush	1280
Red Schoendienst	1223
Jim Gilliam	1163
Lu Blue	1151
Reggie Smith	1123

RBIs

Mickey Mantle	1509
George Davis	1432
Frank Frisch	1244
Pete Rose	1164
Reggie Smith	1092
Ted Simmons	1087
John Anderson	976
Ken Singleton	945
Tommy Tucker	932
Duke Farrell	912

Top Ten Switch-Hitters (through 1982) (Continued)

Hits

Pete Rose	3869
Frank Frisch	2880
George Davis	2683
Max Carey	2665
Red Schoendienst	2449
Mickey Mantle	2415
Maury Wills	2134
Reggie Smith	2020
Dave Bancroft	2004
Kid Gleason	1951

Strike Outs

Mickey Mantle	1710
Ken Singleton	1103
Pete Rose	1022
Reggie Smith	1030
Ken Henderson	763
Don Kessinger	759
Roy White	708
Tom Tresh	698
Max Carey	695
Maury Wills	684

Total Bases

Pete Rose	5292
Mickey Mantle	4511
Frank Frisch	3937
George Davis	3678
Max Carey	3609
Reggie Smith	3439
Red Schoendienst	3284
Ted Simmons	3012
Ken Singleton	2808
Roy White	2685

Walks

Mickey Mantle	1734
Pete Rose	1358
Donie Bush	1158
Ken Singleton	1126
Lu Blue	1092
Max Carey	1040
Jim Gilliam	1036
Miller Huggins	1002
Augie Galan	979
Roy White	933

Doubles

Pete Rose	697
Frank Frisch	466
George Davis	442
Red Schoendienst	427
Max Carey	419
Ted Simmons	374
Reggie Smith	363
Mickey Mantle	344
Augie Galan	336
John Anderson	326

Batting Average

Frank Frisch	.316
Pete Rose	.308
Mickey Mantle	.298
George Davis	.297
Rip Collins	.296
Garry Templeton	.296
Eddie Murray	.295
Tommy Tucker	.292
John Anderson	.292
Ted Simmons	.291

(Continued)

Top Ten Switch-Hitters (through 1982) (Continued)

Triples		Slugging Average	
George Davis	167	Mickey Mantle	.557
Max Carey	159	Eddie Murray	.502
Frank Frisch	138	Rip Collins	.492
John Anderson	126	Reggie Smith	.489
Pete Rose	126	Ted Simmons	.453
Duke Farrell	123	Ken Singleton	.444
Lu Blue	109	Frank Frisch	.432
Tom Daly	103	Roy Cullenbine	.432
Dan McGann	102	Pete Rose	.422
Walter Wilmot	91	Augie Galan	.419

The 1892 Split Season

The 1981 split season, which resulted from a player strike lasting two months in the middle of the year, calls forth comparisons with the only other split season in the majors, that of 1892 in the National League. The main differences, of course, were that the 1892 break was planned and that there was no hiatus between the halves. However, there are some similarities, which become apparent in a brief review of the 1892 situation.

Major league baseball had been through a trying experience with the players' revolt of 1890, which resulted in the one-year operation of the Players' League and then the collapse of the American Association (AA) after the 1891 season. The National League picked up four AA cities and expanded from 8 teams to 12 for the 1892 season. Consideration was given to adopting a first half and a second half of the season based on an apparently successful experiment in the Eastern League in 1891. The *Reach Guide* for 1893 described it this way:

> To add to the novelty which a 12-club league might have, the season was divided into two championships, the first to end on July 15 and the second to terminate late in October. At the same time the complement of championship games was

increased from 140 games to 154. So the season began two weeks early and ended ten days later than in 1891. The result was that the opening games were played in weather which was far from being inducive to enthusiasm and that fact threw a damper upon the year's sport from the beginning.

Attendance was down in many cities and particularly in New York, where the Giants got off to a bad start. A real financial crisis developed. The 12 clubs had assumed a debt of $125,000 to cover the 4 clubs dropped in the consolidation, and a sinking fund had been created requiring 10 percent of gross receipts to go to the general treasury. That figure had to be increased to 12½ percent.

At a meeting in New York in late June, club representatives decided to make a sweeping reduction in salaries all along the line for the remaining half of the season. The player salaries had increased until they had become "in general most unreasonable. The wars of 1890 and 1891 had forced salaries nearly 100 percent above what they had been in 1888–89." The players were now informed that their salaries were cut 30–40 percent. Any player refusing to take the cut was to be unconditionally released. Pitcher Charlie Buffinton of Baltimore was one, and his major league career ended right there. Tony Mullane of Cincinnati also quit for the season. Even so, only Pittsburgh and Cleveland made expenses; all other clubs lost money, including Boston, which won the first half by a few games over Brooklyn.

Many clubs reorganized on financial grounds for the second half, which followed without delay. Cleveland, which had finished fifth in the first half, won the second half on the strength of Cy Young's fine pitching. He was 36 and 10 over the full season and led in winning percentage, shutouts, and ERA. Boston, led by hurlers Jack Stivetts and Kid Nichols, who each won 35 games, finished a close second. The Beaneaters had the best record overall. The *Reach Guide* gave this background:

At the close of the second championship, the Cleveland club, winner of the second series, was extremely anxious to meet the champions of the first series, the Bostons, in a series of firsts. But the Bostons expressed an unwillingness to play any such games. They alleged that an impression prevailed among baseball patrons in their city that their team had not tried to win the second series in order that they might, in that way, secure the financial benefit which would arise out of a subsequent struggle for the Championship of the United States. The officials of the Boston club wanted to refute such an insinuation or belief by foregoing any postseason games with the Clevelands, and so decided not to meet the Clevelands in the final games.

But the league insisted that such a series take place and it did. A nine-game play-off was agreed upon to decide the championship. Three games were scheduled in Cleveland, three in Boston and three in New York, if necessary, to decide the winner. The series opened in Cleveland on October 17, and almost 6,000 turned out to witness a great 11–inning, 0–0 pitching duel between Boston's Jack Stivetts and Cleveland's Cy Young, which was halted by darkness. The next day a crowd of almost 7,000 saw Boston nip the home club 4–3, with Harry Staley beating John Clarkson. Clarkson, incidentally, had spent the first half of the season with Boston and pitched for Cleveland in the second half.

On October 19, Boston won another one-run contest, 3–2 (Stivetts over Young), before 6,000. After a day off the teams moved to Boston, where, on October 21, Kid Nichols blanked the Spiders 4–0 before a gathering of 6,547. Boston won its fourth straight the following afternoon, 12–7 (Stivetts over Clarkson), wiping out an early 6–0 Cleveland lead. Only 3,466 witnessed the contest. After a Sunday rest, Boston won 8–3 (Nichols over Young) on October 24 for its fifth straight and a sweep of the series. The final game drew the smallest crowd of the series, with only 1,812 showing up on a cold day. Boston fandom showed little interest in the majors' first play-off champs. Nevertheless, as a reward for winning the championship, the Boston directors gave the team $1,000 to split up among the 13 players. Center fielder Hugh Duffy was the batting star, collecting 12 hits in the 6 games, including 2 doubles, 2 triples, and a home run.

It was not a very successful season. As the editor of the *Reach Guide* stated, "The clubs have this year acknowledged their error in both the double championship and the lengthened season by abolishing both. This year [1893] there will be one continuing season beginning late in April and ending about the first of October."

The really important change, however, was in the playing rules. In 1893 the pitching distance was increased from 50 feet to 60 feet 6 inches, with the pitcher being required to work off a plate instead of a pitcher's box. This resulted in increased hitting, and it proved to be the magic that lured the fans back to the ball parks.

Here are the club records for the 1892 split season.

First Series			Second Series		
Boston	52–22	.703	Cleveland	53–23	.697
Brooklyn	51–26	.662	Boston	50–26	.658
Philadelphia	46–30	.605	Brooklyn	44–33	.571
Cincinnati	44–31	.587	Pittsburgh	43–34	.558
Cleveland	40–33	.548	Philadelphia	41–36	.532
Pittsburgh	37–39	.487	New York	40–37	.519
Washington	35–41	.461	Chicago	39–37	.513
Chicago	31–39	.443	Cincinnati	38–37	.507
St. Louis	31–42	.425	Louisville	33–42	.440
New York	31–43	.419	Baltimore	26–46	.361
Louisville	30–47	.390	St. Louis	25–52	.325
Baltimore	20–55	.267	Washington	23–52	.307

Comiskey Park
George W. Hilton

Inevitably, the deeds done in ball parks receive more publicity than the stadiums themselves. Comiskey Park is where Luke Appling and Billy Pierce went to greatness and Chick Gandil to infamy, but the architect's name is all but unknown. This is lamentable, for the park has long been admired for its spaciousness and symmetry, and recently it has succeeded to the honor of being the major leagues' oldest active ball park.

When the Chicago White Sox were founded in 1900, only the Philadelpia club of the National League had a ball park of permanent concrete and steel construction, and then only for a limited area of 5,500 seats. Every other franchise operated with a wooden grandstand and bleacher. Charles A. Comiskey, upon moving the St. Paul club of the Western League to Chicago to become the White Sox in 1900, was confronted with the necessity of building a park quickly. The wooden stadium he had used as manager of the Players' League's Chicago club in 1890 had been a good example of the older class of park. It had enjoyed a fine location at Wentworth Avenue, on one of the major streetcar lines running south from the central business district. This park, however, had been demolished, and Comiskey was unable to acquire the land on which it had stood. Consequently, he leased the

23

Comiskey Park, the home field of the Chicago White Sox, which was officially opened on July 1, 1910, and is the oldest ball park still in use

grounds of the Chicago Cricket Club, at 39th Street between Wentworth and Princeton avenues, and built a single-deck wooden grandstand of about 15,000 capacity. During the first decade of the White Sox' history, Comiskey repeatedly stated that he would build a permanent park of steel and concrete as soon as he was able to pay cash for land and the building.

The White Sox were a great initial success, quickly winning the loyalty of the South Side's industrial population. Their NL rivals, later known as the Cubs, still played on the West Side, which was becoming a slum of foreign-born population with limited interest in baseball. The White Sox capped their early successes by winning the 1906 World Series from the Cubs. Comiskey in this period made enough money to be able to buy land for his projected permanent ball park. He was still unable to acquire the former PL site at 35th and Wentworth, but on February 1, 1909, he announced the purchase for $100,000 from the estate of Chicago's first mayor, John Wentworth, of the lot immediately to the west at 35th Street and Shields Avenue. The lot was 600 square feet, reportedly the largest in the major leagues. Comiskey was strongly of the opinion that first-class baseball required an ample playing area so that fielders could roam widely, runners could demonstrate themselves on extra-base hits, and home runs should be fully earned.

Design of the park was entrusted to a relatively obscure Chicago architect, Zachary Taylor Davis (1872–1946). Davis, a graduate of the nearby Armour Institute (now the Illinois Institute of Technology), had executed many of the two- and three-story walk-up apartment buildings characteristic of Chicago and had designed St. Ambrose Church at 47th Street and Ellis Avenue. Later he was to do the courthouse at Kankakee, Illinois, and, in collaboration with Gustave Steinbach, the Quigley Memorial Chapel and educational buildings of the downtown campus of Loyola University of Chicago. The Comiskey Park commission established Davis as a specialist in ball parks. Later he was architect of Wrigley Field, Chicago, and Wrigley Field, Los Angeles.

Davis was reported to have traveled to all of the other recent major league ball parks and to have been most impressed with Forbes Field, Pittsburgh, which had opened in 1909. Davis adopted the Pittsburgh stadium's plan of a double-deck grandstand between first and third bases with detached single-deck pavilions beyond. The design, shown in an accompanying illustration, was an obvious embodiment of Daniel H. Burnham's "city beautiful" concept of classical building set in parklike surroundings. The Roman façade, which resembled Shibe Park and several of the other new steel and concrete parks of this period, was never applied. No explanation of the change was ever made, but presumably Comiskey, exercising his well-known passion for economy, had Davis redesign the exterior with an ordinary brick façade with a motif based on repetition in the bays of a block letter *C*. Consequently, the park emerged aesthetically as an undistinguished example of modern architecture.

An elderly Chicago architect, Karl Vitzthum, in an interview with Dick Hackenberg of the *Chicago Sun-Times* in 1965, reported a further consequence of Comiskey's habitual nickel-nursing. Vitzthum, once a young architect on Burnham's staff, was apparently engaged to work out some of the engineering details of the stadium. He stated that it was he, rather than Davis, who made a tour of the ball parks in Cleveland, St. Louis, and Pittsburgh in preparation for executing the design. He reported that Ed Walsh, the White Sox' leading pitcher, accompanied him and was responsible for the park's generous outfield dimensions. Vitzthum reported that on his return he endeavored to interest Comiskey in a cantilevered grandstand, free of posts. Such a design would have been unique among ball parks, but Comiskey, upon discovering that cantilevering could add as much as $350,000 to the cost of the park, vetoed the idea and ordered the architects to proceed with a conventional design of vertical steel-beam supports.

The ball park was built in great haste in early 1910. Ground was broken about February 15, and by mid-March the foundation was nearing completion. Symbolizing the team's attachment in its early years to the South Side Irish population, Davis laid a green brick by the main entrance on St. Patrick's Day, March 17, to initiate the building of the superstructure. The contractor was George W. Jackson, a friend of Comiskey's.

The design called for 35,000 seats—6,400 in the boxes, 12,600 in the grandstand, and 16,000 in the pavilions and bleachers. The bleachers were wooden, apparently built in the expectation of eventual removal for permanent stands. Comiskey, who had made his success in the American Association and American League on 25-cent admissions, was careful to provide a mix favorable to the cheaper seats. The distances, as Comiskey and Walsh wanted, were ample: 362 feet on each foul line and 420 feet to center. Investment in the park was variously reported between $500,000 and $750,000.

The park was ready for play by midseason of 1910. The seats, which were narrow, straight-back, and cramped, were installed in June. Comiskey, who had taken personal pride in the 1902 transfer of the Milwaukee Brewers to St. Louis, arranged for the Browns to open the new stadium on July 1, 1910. The engraved invitations read "White Sox Park," although the stadium was known as Comiskey Park, at least by 1913. Ed Walsh, whose heroic pitching for the White Sox had contributed so mightily to the building of the ball park, pitched the first game, but lost to the Browns 2–0. The crowd was 24,900 paid and an estimated 28,000 total. Initially, the park was thought to have a curse of ill luck, for four White Sox pitchers were injured in the first five games. The injuries were minor ones stemming from loose sod, a problem that quickly resolved itself.

In the decade from the opening of the new stadium to the revelation of the Black Sox scandal in 1920, the White Sox had the most successful period in their history, including the world's championship of 1917 and the pennant of 1919. The park witnessed three consecutive World Series, because the Cubs leased it for their home games in the 1918 classic. The only major change in the park in this period was the expansion of the bleachers to raise the capacity to 41,000. The largest crowd in the original configuration of Comiskey Park was 43,825 in the 1925 City Series.

The 1920s in one sense were an unlikely time for Comiskey Park to be expanded. The Black Sox scandal had plunged the team into the second division, and beginning in 1925 the team performed the unmatched feat of finishing fifth four years consecutively. Nonetheless, in the mid-1920s Comiskey decided upon replacing the wooden bleachers with permanent steel and concrete stands.

This addition to Comiskey Park was a "house that Ruth built" no less than Yankee Stadium was. The existing stands were entirely adequate for the crowds that the White Sox of the 1920s drew, but the mania for Babe Ruth was at its peak, and the crowds the Yankees attracted warranted greater capacity. The City Series also was a major attraction in Chicago, drawing to the two ball parks a double set of fans.

Accordingly, Comiskey commissioned Davis to draw up plans for double-decking the pavilions along the right- and left-field lines, with an extension of the double-decked stands around the outfield, closing the park with a small, high bleacher in dead center. Davis also closed the open areas between the original stands and the pavilions by adding two small seating areas (Sections 16 and 35) of fourteen seats in width. Comiskey had long since acquired the old Players League grounds between the stadium and Wentworth Avenue and was able to build the stands in the right-field area out to the east.

To the north, however, Comiskey Park fronted 34th Street, which, though unpaved and mainly unused, was a public thoroughfare. North of 34th Street was a small municipal park. Thus, although Comiskey Park has always been notable for its symmetrical playing field, Davis was unable to provide symmetry in seating: in the lower deck in right field he designed thirty-one rows, but in left field he could provide only nineteen. In the upper decks, he was able to design twenty rows in both. Relatively high and with a steep pitch, the outfield stands proved to have excellent sight lines, making attractive what in most ball parks are unpopular seats. In contrast, the lower deck seats in the former pavilion area are relatively unsatisfactory. As in most parks at the time, these seats directly face the outfield, with no canting toward the plate. Thus, the sight lines toward the infield are oblique and through posts and are frequently obscured by one's fellow fans.

Oddly, and probably irrelevant to Davis's intentions, Comiskey Park makes an excellent football field. With the normal north–south placing of the gridiron, the asymmetry of the right- and left-field stands gives the park a higher capacity along the sidelines, and the sight lines in the former pavilion areas are entirely appropriate to football. Comiskey Park was the home of the Chicago Cardinals for many years. It was there on Thanksgiving Day of 1929 that Ernie Nevers scored a record 40 points in a historic Cardinal victory over the Chicago Bears of George Halas and Red Grange, 40–6.

Comiskey undertook the expansion of the park immediately after the 1926 City Series. Concrete had already been poured for some of the foundation, and the stands were erected during the winter. Not all of the seats had been installed by the time of the home opener on April 20, 1927, but in a good indication of the purpose of the extension, fans were assured that the entire facility would be ready for the Yankees' first visit in May. Davis's plan had been for a capacity of 55,000, but the Chicago Fire Department intervened and held seating to 52,000. Nonetheless, the seating of the new stands had the flat backs and close proximity of the earlier portion. Lou Gehrig hit the first homer into the new pavilion on May 7. It was a grand slam off Ted Lyons. The large crowd included Vice-President Charles G. Dawes.

With his new stands Comiskey remained true to his principle that good baseball requires a big field. The new dimensions were 352 feet down each foul line and a heroic 440 feet to center field. The walls were 9 feet high to the right- and left-field stands. Consequently, Comiskey Park was to be a pitchers' park in which home runs were honestly earned. One of the most effective features of the design was the 70-foot height of the outfield stands. Hitting a ball onto the roof or entirely over it required a drive with a ground-to-ground distance of at least 474 feet. This was possible but could never be common. The feat was achieved with about the frequency of pitching no-hit games, and in similar fashion made players memorable who might otherwise have been undistinguished. Buddy Bradford joined Ruth and Foxx in hitting one out of Comiskey Park, just as Bob Keegan joined Ed Walsh and Bob Feller in pitching a no-hitter there.

The prospect of seeing a ball hit out or of seeing a no-hitter pitched was an incentive to come to the park; a fan who had seen either was a man of status among his friends. After the 1934 season the infield was moved out 14 feet to provide Al Simmons with a better shot at the fences, but the experiment was ended when Simmons left a year later. Similarly, inside fences in left and right fields were tried in 1949 and 1969–70, but they were then abandoned. Since 1949 a fence has reduced the center-field distance, currently to 400 feet. To their credit— and that of the management—Bill Melton in 1971 and Dick Allen in 1972 won the AL home run championships with the park's 1927 foul lines. Ironically, Sherm Lollar remains the player who has hit the most homers at Comiskey Park—66.

Had Comiskey anticipated the events of the 1930s, it is doubtful that he would have expanded the stadium. The team lost its hold on fifth place and began contending with the Red Sox for last place in 1929. Ruth became older and lost some of his appeal at the gate. The Cubs— on the North Side since 1916—began a pattern in 1929 of winning pennants at three-year intervals through 1938, and were contenders annually. The Great Depression was abroad in the land, and the White Sox attendance sank to a low of 233,198 in 1932—a figure for which the old 39th Street park would have sufficed. In 1930 the man arrived who was to be for the White Sox statistically—and more important, emotionally—what Walter Johnson had been to the Senators or Ty Cobb to the Tigers: Luke Appling. But not until the mid-1930s did the enthusiasm for him begin to make itself felt at the gate.

With the improvement in the team after Jimmy Dykes's assumption of the managership in 1934 and the simultaneous upturn in national business conditions, attendance rose beyond half a million in 1937. Comiskey had died in 1931; his heirs, with the help of the long-time general manager, Harry Grabiner, had brought the team through the most difficult years. After a poor 1938 season, in which the team finished sixth, the management in 1939 decided upon night baseball. In 1910 Comiskey had stated that the park was designed for the eventual installation of lights for "hippodromes and night baseball." Davis's design easily adapted itself to installation of light towers, and the first night game was played, fittingly, against the Browns on August 14, 1939. For the 1941 season the management replaced the grand-stand seats in the original stands with wider, curved-back models, which were vastly more comfortable. For 1947 the original movable box seats were also replaced with curved-back fixed seats. The changes, together with the blocking off of the center of the bleachers for better visibility by batters, reduced the official seating capacity to 46,550.

Except for isolated games, Comiskey Park's capacity after 1927 was not really utilized until after World War II. The arrival of Negro players and the upturn in the team's fortunes in 1951 increased attend-ance to annual levels of over a million from 1951 to 1965, with the exception of 1958. Attendance reached its all-time high in 1960 at 1,644,460. Bill Veeck, whose control of the team coincided with the 1959 pennant, promoted attendance with his usual avidity and wrought several changes in the park. Believing strongly that the park was a good structure and that it was located in a neighborhood far better than its reputation indicated, Veeck painted the park white—obscuring Davis' green brick, alas—knocked the bricks out of the left-field wall to provide a picnic area with a view of the game, and installed the famous exploding elements on an electric scoreboard that had been installed by the Comiskey management in 1951.

The park necessarily has had a large number of minor changes. Office space, washrooms, vending machines, storage areas, and even a bottling plant gave the area under the stands an anarchic character that helped create a bustling atmosphere totally appropriate to a ball park. Inevitably, the park developed odd features. Beneath the three stairways leading from the lower deck to the upper, ladies' rooms are located behind home and first; one men's room is behind third.

All in all, the park has survived essentially in its 1927 state. Arthur Allyn, who succeeded to the team ownership in 1961, considered covering the entire stadium with a dome but never executed his plan. He also considered replacing Comiskey Park with a new ball park for the Sox and Cubs as part of a three-stadium complex on the site of Dearborn Station. This project, together with various municipal plans for a multipurpose stadium, perished quietly. Comiskey Park's closest brush with the wrecker came in 1969 when Arthur Allyn arranged terms for sale of the White Sox to Milwaukee interests. Instead, the team passed into the hands of his brother, John Allyn, who kept the team at its traditional stand. The current management has generally reverted to the name White Sox Park, even though the stadium is owned by a subsidiary of the White Sox called the Comiskey Park Corporation. Remarkably, the park's all-time record attendance, 55,555, was achieved as recently as May 20, 1973.

There are three types of good architecture: seminal buildings that initiated a new style of architecture, such as Louis H. Sullivan's Carson-Pirie-Scott department store in Chicago; buildings that are distinguished examples of the architecture of a particular time, such as the United States Capitol; and buildings that gain esteem through long acquaintance and effective service to their purpose. Comiskey Park is a fine example of the last category. It is best seen from the upper deck in either the right- or left-field stands. There one can appreciate the fine proportions of the stands and the graceful curve behind home plate. More important, the narrow seats and straight backs remind one of Comiskey's famous preoccupation with economy, but the ample dimensions of the field below testify to his respect for baseball and his regard for the surroundings in which it is played.

The Base-Out Percentage: Baseball's Newest Yardstick

Barry F. Codell

Is the batting average the most important morsel of information concerning a player's offensive ability? It most assuredly is not. It is baseball's most misleading number. It has pacified and fooled generations of players, fans, managers, sportswriters, and broadcasters, masquerading as the sport's grandest garment when in reality a player's batting average is more like a certain emperor's clothes.

What is the matter with the batting average? Let's begin with the fact that it considers a home run the same as a single. That it pretends no player has ever drawn a walk. That a player hitting into a double play has made one out. That nothing happened when a bunt advanced a man or a fly ball brought a runner home. After hiding such integral parts of the game, the batting average cannot proclaim itself an honest indicator of anything but the durability of its own cliches.

How about the offshoot of the BA—the slugging average? Doesn't it take total bases from hits into account? Yes, but then it loses all credibility by disregarding outs made while batting, which enables long-ball hitters to produce outs at a rapid clip and still maintain their slugging averages with a once-in-a-great-while long hit—for example,

Player A, 1 HR, 4 ABs, 1.000 SA; Player B, 2 2Bs, 4 ABs, 1.000 SA, although Player A has made three outs and Player B two.

The base-out percentage, on the other hand, is baseball's most complete and informative offensive statistic. Its simplicity may be startling, yet it accounts for everything a player accomplishes individually whenever his team is at bat. It can be computed in seconds and kept track of easily. Its roots are in the nature of the game itself—the struggle of all batters to attain as many bases as possible while attempting to avoid being put out. Unlike any other statistic, it takes each plate appearance into consideration. In doing this, it reveals abilities and flaws previously unaccounted for and destroys common myths about player success. It is a true barometer of what a player has accomplished during the season and his career.

The base-out percentage is founded on the simple theory that a batter may embark on two journeys after completing a plate appearance: (1) back to the dugout or, more pleasurably, (2) that magic trek around the bases.

Bases are of the highest importance, competing with outs for the production of the sport's gold—runs. The object of the game is circling the bases before the third out is made. To attain the highest number of bases while compiling the fewest number of outs is each batter's dream. To build the highest ratio of bases to outs is his desire. And consciously or not, the batter has always been trying to improve his percentage of bases to outs. This is where the base-out percentage (BOP) comes in.

The BOP is figured in this manner. *Bases* are derived by adding total bases, walks, times hit by pitch, stolen bases, sacrifice hits, and sacrifice flies. *Outs* are totaled by adding "outs batting" (at bats minus hits), sacrifice hits, sacrifice flies, times caught stealing, and double plays grounded into. Bases are then divided by outs. The result is the base-out percentage.

Chronicling the base-out percentage is easy. And the results are astounding. To see the base-out percentage in action, let's sample the 1982 records of two players whose offensive reputations are made on the traditional batting average—Steve Garvey of the Dodgers and Julio Cruz of the Mariners:

	G	AB	R	H	TB	2B	3B	HR	RBI	BA	SA
Garvey	162	625	66	176	261	35	1	16	86	.281	.418
Cruz	154	549	83	133	189	22	5	8	49	.242	.344

The batting average and slugging percentage give Garvey a huge offensive edge in the traditional listings. The base-out percentage does not stop there, however. Consider these additional, less publicized facts:

	BB	HP	SB	SH	SF	OB	CS	GDP
Garvey	20	1	5	5	9	449	3	10
Cruz	57	3	46	6	2	416	13	6

Julio Cruz is known as a waiter, and Steve Garvey is affectionately called a free swinger. In other words, in search of extra bases Garvey hits away, avoiding the base on balls, and makes many more outs. While he may make more bases this way—261 total bases to Cruz's 189, or 72 more bases—this is lessened by the BB column—20 walks to Cruz's 57, or 37 *less* bases. And by his inability to draw a walk, Garvey has made *more* outs with his free and dubious swinging than Cruz did by waiting for his pitch and remembering a walk is as good as a hit. The walk, of course, may sometimes be more damaging physically and mentally to opposing hurlers.

This is not all. Garvey has grounded into 10 DPs. This is overlooked in his batting average but accounts for ten extra outs. Cruz was more able to avoid the DPs, hitting into only six.

Further, Garvey did not appreciably aid his team on the base paths. He stole five bases and was caught three times. Cruz stole 46 bases and was caught only 13 times, a better and more profitable percentage.

All told, the comparison totals:

	Bases	Outs	BOP
Garvey	301	476	.632
Cruz	303	443	.684

The base-out percentage is a far cry from the batting average and slugging average. It shows Cruz had the more effective 1982 season.

Let's look at a few more 1982 examples.

	BA	SA	BOP
Pena	.296	.435	.647
Porter	.231	.402	.741
Herndon	.292	.480	.749
Lemon	.266	.447	.795
White	.298	.469	.672
Bernazard	.256	.396	.729
Dawson	.301	.498	.870
Morgan	.289	.438	.935
Buckner	.306	.441	.735
Driessen	.269	.421	.801

The BOP does not void anything a player does offensively. A sacrifice is counted as a base gained *and* an out made. (And when, lords of baseball, will a hit-behind-the-runner ground out be credited as a sacrifice?) A hit by pitch is a base. For the first time a stolen base is reflected in a percentage. And, equally, a time caught stealing is accounted for. What Eddie Stanky used to call intangibles—not hitting into DPs, sacrificing, waiting out a pitcher—are rightfully rewarded in the base-out percentage.

The lure of baseball has in great part come in the weighing of players' statistics, analyzing the different offensive departments to which each batter contributes. The base-out percentage offers a clear picture of what a player has accomplished. An .800 percentage means that for each 1,000 outs, a player has made 800 bases. A BOP of over .700 would be above average. A manager who chooses a player who makes 60 bases for each 100 outs (.600 BOP) over one who totals 75 bases (.750 BOP) may do so at the peril of his team's run-scoring capacity.

The base-out percentage shows familiar players in a new light. California's Reggie Jackson is indeed more than a Mr. October, with a fine career mark of .910. And what about Pete Rose? For all his base hits, his lifetime BOP stands at .770.

There were three 1.000 or over "BOPers" in 1982, meaning these players had more bases than outs. They were Baltimore's John Lowenstein (1.105), Philadelphia's Mike Schmidt (1.043), and Oakland's Rickey Henderson (1.029). The unheralded Lowenstein becomes Baltimore's second season leader in this category. Frank Robinson's 1966 Triple Crown season translated to a 1.114 percentage.

The current lifetime BOP leader is Mike Schmidt, nearly matching base for out during his brilliant career (3,997 bases, 4,001 outs, .999 BOP).

Because of sketchy caught stealing and double play compilations from baseball's past, complete BOPs for some of the all-time greats are incalculable. But calculating BOP just on the basis of batting and not including running shows the awesome abilities of such immortals as Babe Ruth (1.428), Lou Gehrig (1.252), Jimmie Foxx (1.170), and Hank Greenberg (1.124).

With current players such as Julio Cruz successfully using the BOP in contract negotiations, players and fans may soon see the base-out percentage as the game's foremost statistic.

Career Leaders, Base-Out Percentage, Active Players
(1,000 or more bases, through 1982)

Player	Bases	Outs	BOP
Mike Schmidt	3997	4001	.999
Rickey Henderson	1431	1497	.956
Joe Morgan	6213	6560	.947
Reggie Jackson	5395	5930	.910
Willie Stargell	5300	5948	.891
Fred Lynn	2527	2839	.890
Gene Tenace	3021	3424	.882
George Brett	3072	3533	.870
Reggie Smith	4583	5336	.859
Andre Thornton	2214	2579	.858
Carl Yastrzemski	7498	8819	.850
Jim Rice	2953	3486	.847
Greg Luzinski	3579	4246	.843
Otto Velez	1168	1391	.840
Eddie Murray	2118	2529	.837
Rod Carew	4950	5923	.836

Career Leaders, Base-Out Percentage, Past Stars
(3,000 or more bases)

Player	Bases	Outs	BOP
Ted Williams	6951	5547	1.253
Mickey Mantle	6472	5901	1.097
Willie Mays	8043	8062	.998
Frank Robinson	7312	7622	.959
Henry Aaron	8672	9125	.950
Duke Snider	5009	5281	.948
Richie Allen	4494	4772	.942
Eddie Mathews	5982	6474	.924
Harmon Killebrew	5840	6410	.911
Norm Cash	4522	5124	.883
Bobby Bonds	4814	5487	.877
Al Kaline	6179	7123	.867
Minnie Minoso	4355	5052	.862
Jimmy Wynn	4481	5313	.843
Billy Williams	5857	6969	.840
Frank Howard	4108	4892	.840
Rocky Colavito	4019	4812	.835
Boog Powell	4234	5189	.816
Orlando Cepeda	4835	5953	.812
Ron Santo	5070	6280	.807
Ernie Banks	5728	7261	.789
Tony Oliva	3655	4640	.788
Roberto Clemente	5392	6890	.783

Ladies and Gentlemen, Presenting Marty McHale

Lawrence S. Ritter

Damon Runyon once wrote a story about me, saying this fellow McHale, who is not the greatest ballplayer that ever lived, is probably the most *versatile* man who ever took up the game. This was in the 1920s, after I had left baseball. So Johnny Kieran of the *New York Times* asked Babe Ruth about it, knowing he and I had been on the Red Sox together. Johnny said, "Marty played in the big leagues, he played football in college, he was on the track team, he was on the stage, he wrote for the *Wheeler Syndicate* and the *Sun*, he was in the Air Service"—and so forth. He went on listing my accomplishments until the Babe interrupted to say, "Well, I don't know about all those things, but he was the best goddamn singer I ever heard!"

You see, I sang in vaudeville for twelve years, a high baritone tenor—an "Irish Thrush," they called it then, and *Variety* called me "The Baseball Caruso." But even before vaudeville, before baseball even, I used to work in a lot of shows around Boston and made trips down to Wakefield, Winchester—minstrel shows, usually—and sometimes these little two-act sketches.

So when I joined the Boston club, a bunch of us—Buck O'Brien, Hughie Bradley, Larry Gardner, and myself—formed the Red Sox Quartette. After a while Gardner gave it up and a fellow named Bill

Lyons stepped in. This Lyons was no ballplayer, but Boston signed him to a contract anyway, just to make the name of the act look proper. We were together three years, and when we broke up I was just as well satisfied because it was quite an ordeal keeping the boys on schedule. They just couldn't get used to that buzzer that tells you you're on next. They'd be a couple of minutes late and think nothing of it, but you can't *do* that in vaudeville, you know—you're *on*.

I did a single for about another three years, which was not very good—just good enough so that they paid for it—and then Mike Donlin and I got together. Now, you may not remember Mike, but he was— well, he was the Babe Ruth of his day. "Turkey Mike," they called him, because when he'd make a terrific catch or something he'd do a kind of turkey step and take his cap off and throw it up like a ham, a real ham; but he was a great one, he could live up to that stuff in the field or at the bat. His widow gave me some of his souvenirs: a gold bat and ball that were given to him as the most valuable player in 1905, some cufflinks, and a couple of gold cups, one from the Giants and the other from the Reds. He hit over .350 for both of them.

Mike and I were together for five years, doing a double-entendre act called "Right Off the Bat"—not too much singing, Mike would only go through the motions—and we played the Keith-Orpheum circuit: twice in one year we were booked into the Palace in New York and that was when it was the Palace, not the way it is now! They had nothing but the big headliners. When Mike left for Hollywood, I went back to doing a single. He made a bunch of pictures out there, and that's where he died.

Which did I like better, baseball or vaudeville? Well, I'd call it about fifty-fifty. The vaudeville was more difficult, the traveling. Sure, you had to travel a lot in baseball, but you always had somebody taking care of your trunk and your tickets and everything; all you had to do was get your slip, hop onto the train, and go to bed. When you got to the hotel your trunk was there. In vaudeville you had to watch your own stuff. I used to say to Mike, you're the best valet I know, because he was always on time with the tickets and had our baggage checks and everything all taken care of, right on the button all the time.

Of course, Mike and I wouldn't have been such an attraction if it hadn't been for baseball, so maybe I ought to tell you how I came to sign with the Red Sox in 1910. First of all, Boston was almost my home-town—I grew up in Stoneham, that's nine miles out, and if you took a trolley car and changed two or three times, you could get to the ball park. Which I'd done only once—I only saw one big league game before I played in one, and Cy Young pitched it; I wasn't really a Red Sox fan. But here comes the second reason for my signing: they gave me a *big* bonus. How big? Two thousand dollars, and back then that was money!

You see, that year for Maine University I had thrown three consecutive no-hitters, and the scouts were all over. I had a bid from Detroit, one from Pittsburgh, one from the Giants, and another from the Braves. And there was sort of a veiled offer from Cincinnati, which is an interesting story.

This Cincinnati situation—Clark Griffith was down there managing, and when I reported to the Red Sox, which was in June, following the end of the college term, his club was playing the Braves, over at Braves Field across the tracks from the Huntington Avenue park. Now, the Red Sox were on the road when I and some other college boys reported. We had signed, but the Red Sox didn't want us with them right away: they had to make room for us, they could only have so many players. So I remember that Griffith came over to the Red Sox park one morning to watch the boys work out. The clubhouse man told us we were all being watched—like you'd watch horses, you know, working out each morning, and he said if we wanted to stay with the club, better take it easy and not put too much on the ball and so on. See, the club usually asks waivers on the newcomers immediately upon reporting to see if anybody else is interested in them, and if so they can withdraw the waivers after a certain time.

I remember very definitely—I went out there and I was pitching to the hitters and I put everything I had on the ball, because after looking over that bunch of Red Sox pitchers I could see there was not much chance for a young collegian to crack that lineup.

At any rate, Griffith must have put in some claim, you see, because two days later I was on my way to Chicago to join the Red Sox. They had withdrawn the waivers. I joined them in Chicago and we went from there to Cleveland. I remember my pal Tris Speaker hurt his finger in Chicago and he was out for a few days, and Fordham's Chris Mahoney, who was an outfielder, a pitcher, and a good hitter, took his place.

He and I weren't the only college boys on that team, you know: Bill Carrigan, Jake Stahl, Larry Gardner, Duffy Lewis, Harry Hooper . . . even Speaker went to—not the University of Texas, but Texas Polyclinic, Polytechnic or something of that kind out there; only went for two years, but he went. And Ray Collins and Hughie Bradley, too. Buck O'Brien, he came the next year, he said, "I got a degree, I got a B.S. from Brockton." He said B.S. stood for boots and shoes, meaning that he worked in a factory.

Now on this day in Cleveland, we had Chris Mahoney playing right field, Harry Hooper moved over to center, and Duffy Lewis stayed

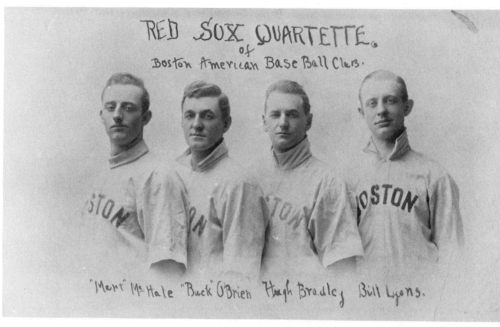

The Boston Red Sox Quartette, second edition, minus Larry Gardner

in left, and Patsy Donovan put me in to pitch my first game in the big leagues against Joe Jackson and those Cleveland boys.

I wasn't what you'd call sloppily relaxed, but I wasn't particularly nervous, either. You see, I was one of the most egotistical guys that God ever put on this earth: I felt that I could beat anybody. I struck out ten of those Naps, including Jackson. The first time he was up, I had Joe two strikes, no balls, and I did something that the average big league pitcher would never do. Instead of trying to fool him with a pitch, I stuck the next one right through there and caught him flat-footed. He never dreamed I'd do that.

So the next time up there the same thing happened. He hit a foul, then took a strike, and then Red Kleinow, an old head who was catching me, came out for a conference. He said, "What do you want to pitch him, a curve ball?" And I said, "No, I'm going to stick another fast one right through there."

He said, "He'll murder it." Well—he did! Joe hit a ball that was like a shot out of a rifle against the right field wall. Harry Hooper retrieved it in *left* center!

Yes, I had ten strikeouts, but I lost the ball game. It was one of those sun-field things: a fellow named Hohnhurst was playing first base for Cleveland and, with a man on first, he hit a long fly to left-center field. Harry Hooper, who was in center this day, was dead certain on fly balls, but when Speaker was out there, as Harry said afterwards, he used to let Speaker take everything within range. Harry said he and Duffy Lewis didn't exactly get their signals crossed, but they were not sure as to who was going to take the ball.

Finally Duffy went for it, and just as he made his pitch for the ball, the sun hit him right between the eyes and he didn't get his hands on the thing and the run, of course, scored, and Hohnhurst, the fellow who hit the ball—he got himself to second base. Ted Easterly got a single on top of that, and anyway, the score ended up four to three. That was it.

I was supposed to be a spitball pitcher, but I had a better overhand curve, what they called a drop curve—you'd get that overspin on it, and that ball would break much better than a spitter. I had what they call a medium-good fastball, not overpowering but good enough, and if you took something off your curve and your spitter, your fastball looked a lot better. For my slow one, the changeup as they call it now, I tried a knuckler but never could get any results with it, so I stole Eddie Karger's slow-breaking downer. He and I used to take two fingers off the ball and throw it with the same motion as we used for the fastball.

They still have those fellows today that throw spitters, but it doesn't make much difference—because even when the spitter was legal in my day, in both leagues you couldn't pick six good spitball pitchers. You'd take a fellow like Ed Walsh with the White Sox, the two Coveleskis, Burleigh Grimes, and the left-handed spitter in the National League, who has since lost both legs, Clarence Mitchell.

Now, Clarence was a good spitball pitcher, but Walsh was the best. He worked harder at it, had a better break, had better control of it, and he pitched in more ball games than any pitcher in either league over a period of years.

Eddie Cicotte, he was with us in Boston, you know, he was going with a spitter for a while. He used to throw that emery ball, too, and then he developed what we call the "shine" ball. He used to have paraffin on different parts of his trousers, which was not legal, and he would just go over all the stitches with that paraffin, making the other part of the ball rougher. It was just like the emery situation, but in reverse, and an emery ball is one of the most dangerous, not like the spitter, which can be controlled. But Cicotte's main pitch was the knuckleball, and he used that to such an extent that we called him Knuckles.

Joe Wood was with the Red Sox when I joined them, too. Now there was a fellow who could do nearly everything well. He was a great ballplayer, not just a pitcher, he was a good outfielder, he was a good hitter, he was a good baseman, he would run like blazes, he used to work real hard before a ball game, he was just a good all-around ball-player and a great pitcher. And he was a fine pool player, too, and billiards. He could play any kind of a card game and well; also he was a good golfer. I think that he could have done nearly everything. If he were playing football he'd be a good quarterback.

Joey was a natural—and talking about egotistical people, there's a guy who had terrific confidence, terrific. Without being too fresh, he was very cocky, you know. He just had "the old confidence."

I wasn't with Boston the year they won the World's Championship and Joey won those thirty-four games and then three more against the Giants, but I was at the Series and wrote a story about that final game. I saw the Snodgrass muff—he was careless, and that happens. But right after that he made a gorgeous running catch.

Earlier in that game Harry Hooper made the best catch I ever saw. I hear from Harry twice a year or so; he lives in California, and he's got plenty of the world's goods. Harry made this catch—he had his back to the ball—and from the bench it looked like he caught it back-handed, over his shoulder. After I sent my story to him, he wrote to me. "I thought it was a very good catch, too," he said, "but you were wrong in your perspective. When I ran for that ball, I ran with my back toward it and you guys with your craning necks were so excited about it, when I ran into the low fence"—you see the bleachers came up from a low fence in Fenway—"the fence turned me around halfway to the right and I caught the ball in my bare hand." Imagine!

In 1913 I joined the Yankees—they weren't called the Highlanders anymore—and then three years later I went back to the Red Sox. Bill Carrigan, who was the Boston manager then, said, "Now that you're seasoned enough you can come back and pitch for a *big league* team." The Yankees in those days were a terrible ball club. In 1914 I lost six-teen games and won only seven, with an earned-run average under three. I got no runs. I would be beaten one to nothing, two to nothing, three to one, scores like that. You were never ahead of anybody. You can't win without runs. Take this fellow who's pitching for the Mets, Roger Craig, what did he lose—twenty-two, something like that? What did he win—five? One to nothing, two to nothing, terrible.

When I got to New York, Frank Chance was the manager, a great guy. He had a reputation as a really tough egg, but if you went out there and worked and hustled and showed him that you were interested in what you were doing he would certainly be in your corner, to the extent that he would try and get you more money come contract time.

I have a watch, one of these little "wafer" watches, that Chance gave me in 1914 after I guess about the first month. I had won a couple of games for him, one of them was the opening game against the World Champion A's, and one day, just as a gesture, he said, he gave me this watch.

Frank and I were such good friends that late in 1914, when we were playing a series in Washington, after dinner, one evening he said, let's take a little walk. So we went out to a park across from the hotel and sat down. "I'm going to quit," he said. "I can't stand this being manager, can't stand being the manager of this ball club."

He said, "We're not going to get anyplace. I've got a good pitching staff"—and he did have a good pitching staff—"but you fellows are just batting your heads against the wall every time you go out there, no runs." The owners wouldn't get him any players, see, and he said, "I just can't take it—I'm going to quit."

He had already talked it over with the front office in New York and one of the reasons he took me out to the park was that he had told them which men he thought they should keep, and I happened to be one of three pitchers along with Slim Caldwell and Ray Fisher, and he said I know that you'll be working in vaudeville next winter and I would advise you to get yourself a two- or three-year contract, if you can, before you leave New York on your tour, which was very good advice —which advice I didn't take. I was too smart—you know how it is, very smart—so Mike Donlin and I went out on the Orpheum circuit that winter after opening at the Palace.

So Mike, before we left New York, he said, you better go over to the Yankee office and get yourself signed in before we leave for Chicago. He said, you never can tell what's going to happen. I, being very, very smart, I said, "No, I'll be worth more money to them in the spring than I am now after the publicity we will get in vaudeville this winter."

But I was wrong, because during the winter, while we were in Minneapolis at the Orpheum theatre, Devery and Farrell sold the team to Ruppert and Huston. I'm quite sure I could have made a deal with Frank Farrell for a two- or three-year contract before leaving, but as I say, I wasn't very smart.

When we got back East Bill Donovan (that's Bill, not Patsy) had been appointed manager of the Yankees, and he was not in favor of anybody having a long-term contract. I didn't even last out the year with him.

It seemed every time I pitched against Washington I had Walter Johnson as an opponent, or Jim Shaw, either one. Griffith, he used to . . . I don't know . . . I had an idea he didn't pitch them against Caldwell. It seemed that every time Slim pitched, the team would get him three or four runs—though he didn't need them, he was a great pitcher.

Was Johnson as great a pitcher as they say? Let me tell you, he was *greater* than they say. He was with one of the worst ball clubs imaginable, not quite as bad as the old Yankees but almost as bad.

When I got out of the Air Service, after the war—you see, I quit baseball on the fourth of July, I think, in 1917 and went into the Air Service—when I came out I went to work for the *New York Evening Sun*. I wrote articles, and the *Sun* used to run them every Saturday. The Wheeler Syndicate used to sell them to—wherever they could sell them, Boston, Philadelphia, Newark, anywhere they could, you know, and I used to get five, two, four, eight dollars apiece for them, and one of the stories that I wrote was about Walter Johnson.

I wrote one about Joey, too, and about Cicotte, and Mathewson, oh, so many of them. In the story about Johnson, I wondered what would have happened if he had been pitching for the Giants, who could get him five or six runs nearly every time he started, and I'm wondering if he'd *ever* lose a ball game. I found out from Joe Vila, who was the sports editor for the *Sun*, that Matty didn't care very much for that.

Matty was a very good friend of Mike's, and so was McGraw, who was my sponsor into the Lambs Club. He was a Jekyll and Hyde character. Off the field he was very affable, but the minute he'd get in uniform, he was one of the toughest guys you'd ever want to know. Mike used to tell me a lot of inside information, which of course helped me when I was writing these stories.

Do you know about the movie Speaker and I made? In 1917, just before I went into the Service, we produced a motion picture of the big stars in both major leagues. We had $80,000 worth of bookings for the picture, and then they declared baseball during the war not essential, so all the bookings were canceled. We sold the rights to the YMCA to use it in the camps all over Europe, in the ships going over and back, and in the camps here.

After the war was over I showed the film to my friend Roxy, God rest him, and he took the thing over and showed it at the Rivoli and the Rialto and down to Fifth Avenue, and then I happened to come into Wall Street to work as a stockbroker—in 1920 I started my own firm, which I still run today—and I forgot all about the film.

It was put in the morgue someplace up at the Rialto or the Rivoli, and the YMCA lost their prints somewhere over in France, but I had left in the tins some cuts and outtakes of the shots of—well, Speaker, Hooper, Ruth, Wood, Matty, and Johnson and all, and I still have them. I showed the clips only about two years ago at the Pathé projection room one day and they still look pretty good.

The game's a lot different today from what it was when I played. The biggest change—and the worst one, in my opinion—is the home run. Now, let's first talk of the fellow going up to the plate. Seventy-five percent of the time he goes up there with the thought of hitting the ball out of the ball park, and it's not too difficult to do, because they have moved the ball park in on him. Now in right field and center field and left field, you've got stands. They used to have a bleacher, way out, in the old days, but the only home run you'd get would be if you hit it between the fielders. "In grounds," they'd call it, a home run in grounds: if a ball got in between those fielders and if you had any speed, they wouldn't be able to throw you out. Today, if you hit a good long fly it's in one of these short stands.

In the old days they juiced up the ball some, but when they talk about the dead ball—there *never* was any dead ball that I can remember. I've got a couple of scars on my chin to prove it. I saw Joe Jackson hit a ball over the top of the Polo Grounds in right field—*over the top of it* —off one of our pitchers, and I have never seen or heard of anyone hitting it over since, and that was around 1914–15, in there.

Today's ball is livelier, no doubt of that. They are using an Australian wool now in winding the core of the ball. In the old days they used wool, but not one that is as elastic as this wool. The bats are whippier, too. But the principal reason for all these homers is the concentration of the hitter on trying to hit the ball out of the park.

The fielding today? Well, any of these boys in the big leagues today could field in any league at any time. I think the better equipment has more to do with the spectacular play. You take this here third baseman up with the Yankees—Clete Boyer—he's terrific, just terrific. Larry Gardner, who played third on the Boston team with me, he was a great third baseman, and he had that "trolley wide throw" to first, but Larry was not as agile as Boyer. I think Boyer is a little quicker. But, if you want a fellow to compare with Boyer, take Buck Weaver of that Black Sox team. He would field with Boyer any day, and throw with him, and he was a better hitter. He would be my all-time third baseman.

Players of my age, give them the good equipment, and they would be just as good or better. Now, you take a fellow like Wagner—I don't mean the Wagner we had with the Red Sox, but the Pirates' Wagner, Honus Wagner, who came to see us in Pittsburgh at the theatre, and he took up the whole dressing room with that big can of his. There was one of the most awkward-looking humans you ever saw, but he made the plays, without the shovel glove. And Speaker—could a big glove have made him any better?

As an outfielder, Speaker was in a class by himself. He would play so close to the infield that he'd get in on rundown plays! Then the next man perhaps would hit a long fly into center field, and he would be on his bicycle with his back to the ball—not backing away, he'd turn and run—and you'd think he had a radar or a magnet or something because just at the proper time he'd turn his head and catch the ball over his shoulder.

Those fellows, Speaker, Lewis, and Hooper, they used to practice throwing, something that you don't see anymore. Those fellows would have a cap down near the catcher and they'd see who would come closest to the cap when they'd throw from the outfield. They all had marvelous arms. Nobody would run on them and I think that most of the people who ever saw them play would say there was no trio that could compare with them.

Mike and I, in our act, we used to do a number called, "When You're a Long, Long Way From Home." In it I used to do a recitation, and the last two lines were, "When you're on third base alone, you're still a long, long way from home." It was serious, about life being like a game of baseball. Times have changed—a boy can't peek through a knothole in a concrete fence—but that's still true.

Dean Was Ruthless with Aging Babe

Babe Ruth and Dizzy Dean, two of baseball's most colorful performers, faced each other in only two games, May 5 and 19, 1935. Dean was then in his prime with the Cardinals, whereas Ruth was forty and was closing out his career with the Boston Braves. Diz clearly had the upper hand, holding the Babe hitless in six trips in the two games, both of which he won.

The May 5 game, before 30,000 anxious fans in Boston, was the more exciting. Dean walked Ruth in the first, and in the fourth worked the count on the Bambino to one ball and two strikes. Diz, with a wide grin on his face, then waved his outfielders back to the fences. He reared back and steamed a fast one down the middle. The huge crowd was stunned into silence as Ruth swung mightily and missed. This was frosting on the cake for Dean, because, in his first time at bat, he had hit a screaming line drive over Ruth's head and into the left field stands for a home run. It was a big day for Dean as he blanked the Braves 7–0.

The Trading Record
Bill James

Since the invention of the hook, fishermen have entertained one another with tales of the big one that got away. Baseball men are not so lucky: they *know* how big the one was that got away. To the San Francisco Giants, the outfield that got away (Bobby Bonds, Garry Maddox, and George Foster) is no tall tale. It is a fact regrettably well established. But not, until now, well measured.

How do you tell what constitutes a good trade? While it is obvious, for example, that the Cardinals' 1964 trade of Ernie Broglio for Lou Brock was a spectacular success, we have never been able to express that fact by any simple, succinct mathematical statement. How could we? To fill the void, I have developed a method of scoring a trade that attempts to reduce all of the contributions of the players exchanged to a single ratio.

Each player's season is evaluated in accordance with 17 rules, 6 applying to pitchers and 11 to nonpitchers. For example, Lou Brock's contributions to the 1964 Cardinals are evaluated at 12—3 points for games played (103), 4 for batting average (.348), 3 for slugging average (.527), 1 for home run percentage (2.9), and 1 for stolen bases (33)—but reduced to 10 because Brock batted less than 500 times for the Cardinals. Ten points is an above-average total for a full season and an exceptional total for 103 games. Brock earned no points for defense, though they are available. Meanwhile, Ernie Broglio is credited with 2 points for his wins total (4) and 2 for other reasons, but when adjustments are made for his ERA and activity level, he winds up with a rating of only 1 point for his contributions to the Cubs' success in the 1964 season.

A full explanation of how the rating-point system works would leave us no space for anything else, so we will move on. The system makes no claims to precision but attempts to sort out *levels* of performance with a consistency convincing to the point of being, in a general way, undeniable. Take, for example, the 1972 National League. The MVP, Johnny Bench, was rated at 16, the same rating given to Billy Williams (37 HR, 122 RBI, .333) and Cesar Cedeno (22, 82, .320, with 55 SB). Two other players, Joe Morgan (16, 73, .292, 58) and Steve Carlton (27–10) rated even higher, at 17. Obviously, there is some question about who should rate 16 and who 17, as Bench, at 16, won the big award. But there is no doubt whatsoever that, in naming Bench, Williams, Cedeno, Morgan, and Carlton, we have listed a group of players who ranked (for that season) at the very top of the league's stars.

Similarly, were we to take the players who ranked at 12 (Willie Stargell, Jose Cardenal, Jon Matlack), we would have a list of players who were, while still excellent ballplayers, undeniably not in the class of the 16s and 17s. The players listed at 8 include Burt Hooton (11–14), Joe Torre (.289), and Tim Foli (.241, with good defensive stats at SS), still undeniably not in a class (that year) with Stargell and Cardenal but still clearly better than such players, rated at 4, as Ernie McAnally (6–15), Bobby Valentine (.274, as a utilityman) or Steve Garvey (.269, in half a season at third), who, in their turn, still made a much larger contribution that such 0-value players as Jim York (0–1, 5.25 ERA) and Bob Fenwick (0, 4, .180).

Armed with a system for evaluating seasons, the next task is to sort out the ground rules of a fair trade-evaluation method. Question one is, "What constitutes a 'trade'?" "Curt Motton for cash and two players to be named later," for example—is that a trade or a sale? I decided not to rate any transactions involving cash, except for those listed as "sold in exchange for."

Question two is, "What is a fair rating period?" One year is obviously not enough, but you can't go back every season and update the records of trades made ten or fifteen years ago. You have to stop somewhere. I decided on five years as an acceptable period. There are trades for which this is misleading, of course, such as the George Foster trade, but as a general rule five years is quite enough for the direction of the result to be well established. There were many other ground rules needed, but only two other important enough to explain here. If a player is traded again within his five-year rating period, then the points he accumulates with his new team are credited to the team that acquired him in the original trade, as they will be counted against that team when the player is traded out of the system. If, on the other hand, the player is later sold, drafted, released, becomes a free agent, or is reassigned in a minor league transaction, then the count stops.

To see how these rules work, let us examine one trade in detail. In the winter of 1965, the Cincinnati Reds committed one of the most visible blunders in trading history when they exchanged their superstar outfielder, Frank Robinson, to the Baltimore Orioles for pitchers Jack Baldschun and Milt Pappas and outfielder Dick Simpson. Robinson's contributions to the Orioles over the following five years were assessed at 16, 13, 8, 14, and 14 points, a total of 65. Simpson played for the Reds, occasionally, for two seasons; his accomplishments were measured at 1 point in 1965 and 0 in 1966. From then on he was traded to four teams in two years, contributing two more points for a total estimated value of 3. Baldschun made no measurable contribution to the Reds in two seasons before returning to the minors, where he somehow became the property of the expansion Padres. His future major league success, such as it was, is irrelevant to the Reds and is not credited to them. Milt Pappas, the main bait for Robinson, pitched for the Reds for two full seasons; his value was considered at 5 in 1966, 8 in 1967, and 0 in 1968 before he was traded to Atlanta, where he earned an additional 5 and 3 points in two seasons. In midseason, 1970, he was sold to Chicago, and that stops the count. His total value: 21 points. The final score on that trade: Baltimore 65, Cincinnati 24. The final log on the Brock trade: St. Louis 54, Chicago 8.

To provide a basis for analysis, I rated every major league player for every season between 1963 and 1972 and every significant trade that I could find record of between the close of business 1962 and June 15, 1973. Many players, of course, also had to be rated for the 1973–77 seasons. A few points from the complete study will serve to illustrate the general accuracy, and marginal inaccuracy, of the player-rating system. First, the correlation between team total rating points and team wins is .92 (Pearson product/moment), indicating a very close relationship. Second, of the twenty MVPs in those years, ten were rated as high as any player in the league, while five others missed by only one or two points. One MVP, Ken Boyer of the '64 Cardinals, won with a rating of 11, although Willie Mays rated 5 points higher, at 16. However, if you added to the system a 2-point bonus for playing on a pennant winner and a 4-point bonus for leading the league in RBIs, it would nominate seventeen of the twenty MVP correctly. Fourteen of the

seventeen Cy Young winners and sixteen of the twenty top rookies were
also the highest-rated players available for the awards.

Finally, the results. What were the best trades of the period (or,
from the other side, the worst)? Number one on the lopsided list was
the October 1970 trade between Detroit and Washington. Bob Short,
then owner of the Senators, had come to baseball following a largely
successful run as owner of the Los Angeles Lakers, and his experience
in basketball had led him to greatly overestimate what star value would
mean to a baseball team. Denny McLain, for his part, had become a
superstar by age 24, and it had led him to greatly underestimate the
value of a reasonable training program. The results were enough to put
an end to 70 years of baseball in the nation's capital; Joe Coleman
(45 points), Eddie Brinkman (36), and Aurelio Rodriquez (34) went
to Detroit in exchange for Denny McLain (5), Elliott Maddox (9), and
two 0-value players, a final count of Detroit 115, Washington 14, for
101 points given away in a single trade, the worst (or best) exchange
of the period.

Close behind it is the 1971 trade in which Houston traded Cincinnati several championships, in the form of Joe Morgan, whose 86 points
in the rated period are easily the highest of any player traded. The Reds
also got Geronimo (40), Billingham (37), Menke (8), and Armbrister
(1) for Lee May, Helms, and Stewart. Houston actually got a lot of
talent out of the deal, as both May and Helms rated well for several
years, but it didn't compare to the talent that they traded away. Final
Score: Cincinnati 172, Houston 79.

Rating behind these trades are, in order, Gaylord Perry and Frank
Duffy for Sam McDowell (92–5); Nolan Ryan and others for Jim
Fregosi (83–4); Ken Singleton, Tim Foli, and Mike Jorgensen for
Rusty Staub (126–48); Amos Otis plus for Joe Foy (83–6); and Randy
Hundley and Bill Hands for Lindy McDaniel and Don Landrum
(91–19).

That's right—the Mets made three of those trades in two years.
The Mets have, as their fans well know, traded themselves out of contention by giving away half of the American League's All-Star team in
fruitless attempts to find a third baseman or power hitter.

But for consistency and durability in the Monty Hall giveaway
game, no one can begin to touch the astonishing series of coups pulled
off by the San Francisco Giants. They made 25 rated trades in the
1963–72 period, almost all of them bad, for a sum total of 270–717, a
deficit of 447 points, enough to win three pennants without help and
enough to turn seven last-place teams into pennant winners. That may
seem extreme, but consider what would happen to a last-place team if
essentially you gave them the best years of Hundley and Hands, Perry

and Duffy, plus Matty Alou (his trade was 8–57), Orlando Cepeda (22–50), Stu Miller and John Orsino (10–51), Ron Hunt (0–27), George Foster, and several others. The series of trades by which they rid themselves of Maddox, Bonds, Ontiveros, Falcone, and Speier have not yet come up for review.

The best of traders? The Kansas City Royals, easily. Although they existed for only half of the rated period and made only thirteen rated trades, five of them bad ones, they pulled off such "godfather" bargains as the Amos Otis deal (83–6), the Lou Piniella for two non-prospects exchange (43–7), Cookie Rojas for a minor leaguer (39–0), the Freddie Patek steal (69–14), John Mayberry for Jim York (52–2), Hal McRae plus for Richie Scheinblum plus (48–6), and others at 32–3 and 10–0, for a net gain of 225 points. They traded a bunch of journeymen into a championship team.

Since we measure the best by the bulk gain, not the ratio, the accomplishment is made more and not less impressive by the short span of time in which it was accomplished. But it is true that many of the other organizations have had "gain" periods when they traded well but have forfeited the gains during other managements. Two other manage-ments could challenge the Royals' record. The Cubs during the Durocher years made the Hundley deal, plus Fergie Jenkins and Adolfo Phillips for two old pitchers (88–29) and Jim Hickman and Phil Regan for Ted Savage (55–2). The Orioles during the Harry Dalton years pulled off more heists than the Dalton Gang, topped by the Mike Cuellar caper (74–12) and the Robinson deal.

Having computed all this, the question now becomes, what can we do with it? Well, first of all, we could make it more accurate, and more complete. The rating system I have devised is a good one, but by no means perfect. Second, we could use it, I would hope, to evaluate trad-ing strategies. Beyond saying that one should trade with San Francisco whenever possible, I really haven't reviewed my own data with an eye to such strategic questions as, "What kind of risk are you really taking in trading an established player for a hot prospect?" and "Is it a solid strategy to try to trade for a star player coming off a bad year?" and "How safe is it to trade an everyday player for a pitcher?"

This method is simply a tool, and a rather crude one at that. I'm not saying we would learn anything by analyzing these questions, but we couldn't get any more stupid. We have a possible method here of getting answers. Unlike ballplayers and managers, general managers have never had a record to contend with before. Now, the record book has one more chapter.

Pitching for the
Red Sox—Ted Williams
Tom Hufford

The use by Baltimore of two nonpitchers on the mound in a 24–10 loss to Toronto on June 26, 1978, served as a reminder that there have been a sizable number of regular players who have taken a fling at pitching. If the pitching staff is depleted or overworked, the manager may go this route in a game that is obviously lost, as was the case between the Orioles and the Blue Jays. Outfielder Larry Harlow did not fare well, giving up five runs in ⅔ of an inning. Catcher Elrod Hendricks, an eleven-year veteran and part-time coach, did much better, giving up only one hit and no runs in 2⅓ innings.

A surprising number of well-known players with long service at a regular position have taken a turn on the hill, for various reasons. Sometimes it was expediency; sometimes it was an emergency; sometimes it was an opportunity to really see if the player could pitch; and sometimes it was a late season stunt. It might be of interest to elaborate on some of these occasions.

Ty Cobb, for example, pitched in three official games, giving up 6 hits and 2 runs in a total of 5 innings. Two of these outings came in season-ending games against the St. Louis Browns in which the opposing pitcher was his chief batting rival, George Sisler. Of course, Sisler had better credentials as a hurler, having been a part-time pitcher in 1915–16, once winning a 1–0 victory over Walter Johnson. On Septem-

Ted Williams

ber 1, 1918, Sisler pitched a scoreless frame against the Tigers and, facing Cobb, hit a double and scored the only run off him in the two innings. On October 4, 1925, Cobb pitched a perfect inning, and Sisler was not scored on in two innings. Both Cobb and Sisler were managers of their respective teams as well.

Another manager who took to the mound was Lew Fonseca of the White Sox in 1932, but this was out of frustration with his hill corps rather than as a stunt. The date was September 23, and the opposition team was the Cleveland Indians. Young Ed Walsh was batted out by the Tribe, but the White Sox had nearly closed the margin, trailing 8–6 in the fifth. However, Bill Chamberlain, the third Chicago pitcher, gave up five runs in the sixth before he could get anyone out. In disgust, Manager Fonseca yanked him and went to the mound himself. There were two Indians on base, but they died there as the new hurler got Frank Pytlak to foul out, Wes Ferrell, the rival pitcher, to fly out, and Johnny Burnett to ground out.

Fonseca admitted many years later that this was one of his prouder moments, but he decided to quit while he was ahead and had Chad Kimsey pitch the rest of the game.

Manager Joe Cronin of the Red Sox never inserted himself as a pitcher but was not averse to sending in regular players. On August 24, 1940, the Tigers were leading the Red Sox 11–1 in the first game of a twin bill at Boston when Cronin called in the left fielder Ted Williams to pitch in the eighth. The *Boston Globe* said it was in response to repeated requests over the season from the young outfielder, who that day could do nothing at bat against Tommy Bridges. According to the reporter: "The appearance of Williams on the mound marked Joe Cronin's annual insult to his regular mound corps, as well as another exhibition of the Sox skipper's eye for showmanship. He did it a year ago with Jimmie Foxx and two years ago with Doc Cramer." (Foxx actually has one major league win to his credit.)

Ted handled himself pretty well. Frank Croucher led off with a single, but when Bridges tried to bunt him to second, Williams grabbed the ball and retired the lead man with a bullet peg. In the ninth Pinky Higgins and Hank Greenberg singled, and one run scored when Charlie Gelbert at third juggled a double play grounder. Ted's big moment came when he fanned Rudy York on three pitches—the Tiger first baseman had previously knocked in five runs with a homer, double, and two singles.

The Red Sox had an interesting lineup that game. When Williams went to the mound, he was replaced in left field by pitcher Jim Bagby, who shared the outfield with Dom DiMaggio and Doc Cramer. Cronin played short, Bobby Doerr second, and Lou Finney was at first while Jimmie Foxx was the starting catcher. But Double X was also scheduled to catch the second game, so he departed before Ted took to the hill. It ruined a chance for baseball's greatest home run battery, but from a historical standpoint all was not lost. Joe Glenn was behind the plate for Williams, and he was the same journeyman backstop who caught the last game pitched by Babe Ruth when he beat the Red Sox in 1933. Glenn never made it into a World Series with the Yankees, but he did have the distinction of catching two of baseball's greatest hitters.

Another pitcher–outfielder exchange took place on the last day of the 1952 season in the National League. That was the year Stan Musial was leading Frankie Baumholtz of the Cubs in the batting race. On the mound were Paul Minner of the Cubs and Harvey Haddix of the Cards. When Baumholtz came up in the first inning, Musial, a pitcher many years before in the minors, went to the mound from center field. Haddix shifted to right field and Hal Rice went to center. Baumholtz, who was a left-handed swinger, batted right against Stan and lined the ball to Solly Hemus at third, who made an error on the play. Haddix then returned to the mound and Musial to center field. Paul Minner shut out the Cards 6–0. Musial had one hit and ended the season at .336; Baumholtz went hitless and ended at .325.

The most recent example of a regular player's actually winning a game took place in 1968. Rocky Colavito was playing his final year in the majors and volunteered to help out the Yankees in a period when they were besieged with a series of doubleheaders compounded by a 19-inning game. In the first game of a twin bill against the Tigers on August 25, 1968, Rocky pitched 2⅔ innings of scoreless ball in a period when the Yanks rallied and went ahead to win 6–5. Colavito got the victory. Ten years before, the strong-armed outfielder had pitched three scoreless innings for Cleveland, so his ERA stands at 0.00 for the two games.

Colavito pitched very well compared to most of the other spot per-formers. Others who showed a flash of talent included Jimmie Foxx, a wartime fill-in for the Phils who had a nifty 1.59 ERA; George Kelly, who had one good outing for the Giants in 1917; and Myril Hoag, who gave up no runs in three brief stints. After Hoag left the majors he had good success as a twirler in the lower minors.

Of those who might like to forget that they ever appeared on the mound, the names of Red Kress, Mark Koenig, Vic Davalillo, and Larry Biittner could be cited. Davalillo never retired a batter in two outings, and Larry Biittner of the Cubs, who did strike out three batters in the one inning he pitched in 1977, also got banged for six runs, compiling an ERA of 54.00. As might be expected under the circumstances, the primary characteristic of most of the one-time hurlers was wildness. Their walks outnumbered their strikeouts by a substantial margin.

Listed below are some other notable long-service stars who for one reason or other got into a box score or two as a hurler. The list includes two, Cesar Tovar and Bert Campaneris, who did it while playing all nine positions in one game. Two others, Bus Mertes and Jack Rothrock, did it while playing all nine positions in one season. Most of the hurlers pitched only one inning or so, but in 1942, his last season, outfielder Hank Leiber of the Giants pitched in one game, went the route, and lost.

Substitute Hurler	G	IP	H	SO	BB	ERA	W–L
Eddie Ainsmith	1	⅓	2	0	0	54.00	0–0
Matty Alou	1	2	3	3	1	0.00	0–0
Sal Bando	1	3	3	0	0	6.00	0–0
Jake Beckley	1	4	9	2	1	6.75	0–0
Bert Campaneris	1	1	1	1	2	9.00	0–0
Hal Chase	1	⅓	0	0	0	0.00	0–0
Ty Cobb	3	5	6	0	2	3.60	0–0
Rocky Colavito	2	5⅔	1	2	5	0.00	1–0
Roger Cramer	1	4	3	1	3	4.50	0–0
Alvin Dark	1	1	1	0	3	18.00	0–0
Vic Davalillo	2	0	2	0	2	81.00	0–0
Jimmy Dykes	2	2	2	0	1	4.50	0–0
Lew Fonseca	1	1	0	0	0	0.00	0–0
Jack Fournier	1	1	0	0	0	0.00	0–0
Jimmie Foxx	10	23⅔	13	11	14	1.52	1–0
Barney Friberg	1	4	4	1	3	4.50	0–0
Gary Geiger	1	2	2	2	1	9.00	0–0
Jack Graney	2	3⅓	6	1	0	5.40	0–0
Granny Hamner	7	13⅓	21	5	8	5.40	0–2
Elrod Hendricks	1	2⅓	1	0	1	0.00	0–0
Jim Hickman	1	2	2	0	0	4.50	0–0
Myril Hoag	3	4	3	0	1	0.00	0–0
Harry Hooper	1	2	2	0	1	0.00	0–0
George Kelly	1	5	4	2	1	0.00	1–0
Dave Kingman	2	4	3	4	6	9.00	0–0
Mark Koenig	5	16	18	9	19	8.44	0–1
Ed Konetchy	3	16⅔	19	6	7	4.32	1–1
Ralph Kress	4	9⅓	13	6	6	12.54	0–0
Eddie Lake	6	19⅓	20	7	11	4.19	0–0

Substitute Hurler	G	IP	H	SO	BB	ERA	W–L
Hank Leiber	1	9	9	5	5	6.00	0–1
Duffy Lewis	1	1	3	1	0	18.00	0–0
Pepper Martin	2	4	2	0	2	2.25	0–0
Sam Mertes	1	7⅔	6	0	0	1.17	1–0
Terry Moore	1	1	0	1	0	0.00	0–0
Stan Musial	1	0	0	0	0	0.00	0–0
Cookie Rojas	1	1	1	0	0	0.00	0–0
Jack Rothrock	1	1	0	0	0	0.00	0–0
Germany Schaefer	2	1	3	0	0	18.00	0–0
Tris Speaker	1	1	2	0	0	9.00	0–0
Cesar Tovar	1	1	0	1	1	0.00	0–0
Bobby Veach	1	2	2	0	2	4.50	0–0
Hans Wagner	2	8⅓	7	6	6	0.00	0–0
Ted Williams	1	2	3	1	1	4.50	0–0

Pitching Contrasts—Jim Palmer and Jeff Schneider

On Wednesday, August 12, 1981, in the first game of a twin bill against Kansas City at Baltimore, Jim Palmer, on the mound for the Orioles for the first time since the long players' strike, pitched six innings and left the game trailing 3–0. Those six innings gave Palmer a total of 3,575.1 innings pitched in the majors in 493 games without ever throwing a grand slam home run. Palmer was replaced by Dave Ford, who could retire only two men in the seventh inning and gave way to Jeff Schneider, a twenty-seven-year-old southpaw who was making his major league debut. Schneider got the dangerous George Brett to fly out to end the inning. But before he could retire a batter in the eighth inning, he had given up a bases-loaded home run to Frank White, and the Royals went on to a 10–0 win. So what no major league batter could do to Palmer in 3,575.1 innings in 493 games, one did to rookie Schneider in one-third of an inning in his first big league contest!

Al Kermisch

The First Negro in Twentieth-Century Organized Baseball

William J. Weiss

In the last two decades of the nineteenth century, some 55 Negro players saw service in leagues in organized baseball. After 1898, however, the doors to the major leagues and to the National Association of Professional Baseball Leagues were closed to Negroes, although there were no rules anywhere prohibiting them from playing. It is, of course, possible that a light-skinned Negro of mixed racial background may have passed, to use the expression of the time.

Thus the first documented instance of a Negro playing in organized baseball in the twentieth century was Jackie Robinson, who was signed by the Brooklyn Dodgers and who made his debut with Montreal of the International League in 1946, right? Wrong!

Exactly thirty years earlier, in 1916, a Negro named Jimmy Claxton pitched for the Oakland Oaks in the Pacific Coast League—briefly, to be sure, but he was there. Jimmy was a well-known baseball figure in the Pacific Northwest and in 1969 was elected to the Tacoma–Pierce County Hall of Fame. Claxton was a baseball player for more than forty years.

James E. Claxton was born in 1892 at Wellington, British Columbia, on Vancouver Island off the west coast of Canada. His family moved to Tacoma, Washington, when he was three months old, and he always considered that city to be his hometown. His mother was Irish and English, his father was Negro, French, and Indian.

As chronicled by Tacoma *News-Tribune* sports editor Dan Walton in a 1964 column, "Jimmy began playing baseball as a left-handed catcher with the Roslyn town team as a 13-year old. He held the job for five years. He started pitching in 1912 with the Chester team, near Spokane, and fanned 18 in his first game." Walton went on to say:

His travels took him to such teams as the Tacoma Giants; Sellwood of the Portland City League; Good Thunder, Minn.; Homestead in the Stevens County League; Shasta (Calif.) Limiteds; the Lincoln Giants of the Los Angeles Winter League; the Seattle Queen City Stars; Mukilteo of the Snohomish County League; the Chicago Union Giants; the Tacoma Longshoremen; Eureka, S.D.; the Cuban Stars of the Negro American League; the Nebraska Indians and many way points.

He had a 20–1 record with the Chicago Giants the season they played 43 barnstorming games against the House of David, he won 20 games in 20 starts at Edmonds, managed and pitched Roslyn to three titles in four years in the Central Washington League, and had Luis Tiant, Sr., as a fellow left-hander with the Cuban Stars in 1932.

How did he get to the Pacific Coast League in 1916? "I got off to a real good start as a southpaw pitcher with the Oakland Giants in a Colored League in the spring of 1916," Jimmy told Walton.

A fellow named Hastings, a part-Indian from Oklahoma, I believe, followed every game we played. He introduced me to Herb McFarlin, secretary of the Oakland Coast League club, and told him I was a fellow tribesman. I was signed to an organized baseball contract, but the manager was against me and did everything to keep from giving me a fair chance.

I had been with Oakland about a month when I got a notice that I was released. No reason was given, but I knew. They tried to get out of paying me, but I had my contract and the notice of release. They had to come through with the money.

After forty-eight years, Claxton's memory was a little off as to the time he spent with the PCL club, but otherwise research indicates he was correct.

The *San Francisco Chronicle* for Sunday, May 28, 1916, reported,

ZEE-NUT
SERIES
1916
CLAXTON
OAKS

Jimmy Claxton, photographed for a Zeenut candy card in 1916 while making a brief appearance with Oakland in the Pacific Coast League

"Claxton, the Indian pitcher who works from the port side and hails from an Indian reservation in Minnesota, will make his PCL debut [today]." Being a Sunday, the Oaks were playing a morning–afternoon doubleheader with visiting Los Angeles, then managed by Frank Chance and fielding such players as Harl Maggert, Johnny Bassler, and Harry Wolter.

Claxton started the first game, pitched two-plus innings, allowed four hits and three runs, two of them earned. He walked three, struck out none. Jimmy left the game with the Oaks trailing 3–0 but got off the hook when his teammates tied the score in the fourth. The Angels won the game 5–4.

Claxton finished the second game that afternoon, pitching one-third of an inning, giving up no runs or hits and walking one batter. Los Angeles won that contest handily, 10–5.

The press was reasonably kind in the next day's editions. The *Chronicle* stated, "Klaxton [some incorrectly spelled his name with a K], the Indian youngster who made his PCL debut, was obviously nervous and cannot be fairly judged by his showing."

The *San Francisco Call* reported, "Klaxton, the Indian southpaw recently nailed by the Oaks from an Eastern reservation, stepped into the box for the first time yesterday morning. The Redskin had a nice windup and a frightened look on his face, but not quite enough stuff to bother L.A. He lasted two innings. However, he may do better in the future."

Unfortunately for Claxton there was to be no Pacific Coast League future. His name next appeared in the press on June 3, when his outright release was announced.

The *Call* reported it in a rather mattter-of-fact manner. "Elliott [Oaks' manager Harold "Rowdy" Elliott] has given the gate to George Klaxton, the Indian southpaw recently secured from an Eastern reservation. Klaxton appears to have a lot of stuff, but he's not quite ripe for this company. He's a free agent and will probably make a stab to secure a job in the Western League."

The *Chronicle*, however, had a little different twist to the story. In his 1964 interview with Walton, Claxton indicated he always suspected that a "supposed friend" had tipped off Oakland officials that he was part Negro.

The *Chronicle*'s story, signed by sports editor Harry B. Smith, said, "George Claxton, the Indian pitcher who was signed by Elliott, has been handed his release. According to Rowdy, the heaver had nothing on the ball and he couldn't afford to bother with him. Claxton pitched last year, according to reports, with the Oakland Giants, but Manager Rowdy declared that he appeared at the Oakland headquarters with an affadavit signed before a notary showing him to be from one of the reservations in North Dakota."

The commentary was somewhat different after it became known Claxton was part Negro!

Despite his very brief Pacific Coast League trial, Claxton did have enough ability as a pitcher to say that had he been born thirty to forty years later, he might well have made the majors. For example, in 1919, in what the Oakland *Tribune* called "the greatest semi-pro game ever put on here," Claxton pitched the Shasta Limiteds to the Northern California championship by beating Best Tractors 2–1 on a five-hitter. His mound opponent that day was Johnny Gillespie, who three years later was pitching for Cincinnati. Best's first baseman and cleanup hitter was Babe Danzig, former Red Sox and PCL performer, and their catcher, Andy Vargas, later played several years in the Coast League.

Claxton must have been a pretty fair hitter, too. The box score for that 1919 game shows him batting fourth and, while the game was still a scoreless tie, drawing an intentional walk to load the bases.

Claxton was still pitching once a week at the age of fifty-two, in fast semipro company. According to a nephew, he pitched, and won, a two-hitter when he was sixty-one. He died in Tacoma on March 3, 1970, at the age of seventy-eight.

Claxton's timing might not have been the best in that he was born too soon to be a major league player, but it was uncanny in another context. Believe it or not, Jimmy Claxton was the first Negro player who ever appeared on a baseball trading card.

From 1911 to 1939 a candy company in San Francisco issued the famous "Zeenut" cards, once the longest continuous series of baseball cards printed. (The Zeenut record was recently surpassed by Topps.) Claxton may have been with the Oaks for just one week, but he happened to be there when the photographer was around taking the pictures for the 1916 set of Zeenut cards, and his card was issued with all the rest that year.

The Matron Magnate
Bill Borst

Despite the women's liberation movement of the 1970s, some professions have remained sacrosanct. The country appears light-years away from having a woman president. Baseball, with its archconservative leanings, has virtually negated the active role of women within its sacred domain.

It is ironic that both of these bastions of male chauvinism fell prey to female influence during the years surrounding World War I. As President Wilson lay in his bed, the victim of a stroke, his wife, Edith, unofficially acted in his stead for over a year. A few years earlier, Helene Britton had become the sole owner of the St. Louis Cardinals, at the death of her uncle Stanley Robison.

Mrs. Britton's father, Frank DeHaas Robison, and his brother Stanley had purchased the Cardinals from G. A. Gruner in 1898. In addition to owning the Cardinals, the Robisons owned the Cleveland Spiders, also an NL entry. Baseball had been quite profitable for the Robisons in Cleveland. Their transportation lines carried many of the fans to and from the ball park. They expected to capitalize on the St. Louis market in a similar fashion.

In 1899 they shifted many of Cleveland's star players, including

Jesse Burkett and Denton "Cy" Young, to St. Louis, completely decimating the Spiders. As a result, the Spiders set an all-time single-season record for diamond futility. With nothing but fringe players and upgraded minor leaguers, they finished the season with a 20–134 record— a winning percentage of .129. The team had become such a civic disgrace that they were forced to play most of their games on the road for fear of bodily harm from the few frustrated fans who saw them play. In St. Louis, the Robisons won 84 games, finishing a modest fifth under manager Patsy Tebeau.

The Robisons devoted most of their energies to their St. Louis team, as the Spiders quietly folded at the end of the season. They altered the pallid image of the Browns by changing the trim of the uniforms from Von Der Ahe's brown to a cardinal red. This change gave rise to their current name of Cardinals. Frank served as president of the club until his death in 1905. Sole ownership then went to Stanley Robison, who succeeded his brother as president. In 1911 he contracted blood poisoning and died in Cleveland on March 27, at the age of fifty-four.

The bulk of the Robison estate, valued at $400,000, went to Frank's daughter, Helene Schuyler Britton, the attractive wife of a Cleveland printer. Mrs. Britton was thirty-two at the time of her uncle's death. She had misgivings about assuming ownership, but amid some of the "tricky baseball men of that period" she did overcome her initial reluctance and became a very active owner, involving herself with a passion in league affairs.

During the first two years of her ownership, Edward A. Steininger, the president of the E. A. Construction Company, and then for a brief time in 1912, James C. Jones, her attorney, acted as president *pro tem.* Helene Britton contented herself with being the "man" behind the title. Though she often delegated the voting to her representatives, Mrs. Britton attended all of the league's annual meetings, held at the Waldorf-Astoria Hotel in New York, from 1911 to 1916. She listened attentively to all of the league proceedings, and her answers were generally sharp and straight to the point. She always sat in the first row for the meetings and for the group picture that was shot each year. Her very presence at these meetings irritated the likes of Charlie Ebbets of the Dodgers, Harry Hempstead of the Giants, and William Baker of the Phillies. Most of her baseball colleagues resented the petticoat rule that earned her the title of the "matron magnate."

Helene Britton was a warm and charming person who was affectionately known as a Lady Bee to members of the press. Though she was a socialite, known for her lavish parties at her Lindell Boulevard mansion in the heart of Millionaires' Row, she found time to support actively the women's suffrage movement that was sweeping the nation at the time.

When her father and uncle had owned the team, it was usually mired deep within the second division. St. Louis then belonged to the Browns of Robert Hedges. During the first year of her ownership, the Cardinals rose to fifth place. What was more important was that the team ledgers showed a net profit of $165,000, which she used to pay off some of the franchise's accumulated debts. She was so pleased with the team's progress, both on the field and at the gate, that she rewarded her field manager, Roger Bresnahan, "the Duke of Tralee," with a lucrative five-year contract. This moment of generosity proved to be a very costly and unwise decision for Mrs. Britton.

As a star catcher with the New York Giants, Bresnahan had learned his manners in the John McGraw School of Etiquette. The Duke was fond of using every expletive known to the human ear. He was not the type to mince his words, even in front of his female boss. A serious rift developed between Bresnahan and the Cardinal owner that festered until his dismissal at the end of the 1912 season. He resented the fact that Mrs. Britton "interfered" with his management of the team on the field. After the Cardinals had blown a game in Chicago, Bresnahan exploded when questioned about his strategy during the loss. "No woman can tell me how to play a ball game!" Bresnahan's Irish temper drove Mrs. Britton to tears. The Irishman also resented the maneuvering of the team's scrappy little second baseman, Miller Huggins. Mrs. Britton was quite fond of Huggins, which led Bresnahan to believe that the "little snake is after my job."

Bresnahan won a $20,000 settlement from the Cardinals out of court for the remainder of his five-year contract. He then proceeded to manage the 1913 Cubs. In 1913 Mrs. Britton replaced Jones as president with her husband, Schuyler, though she still continued to exercise most of the real authority.

At the conclusion of the 1914 season, it became apparent that Mrs. Britton had become disenchanted with the administrative aspects of the game. Most observers believed that she wanted to sell her interests. At the winter meeting in New York, her fellow owners attempted to force the issue once and for all. At first they attempted to soften her up with a pretty floral bouquet, delivered to her room. But the seven male chauvinists were not dealing with a typical woman of the early twentieth century. Helene Britton was a woman far ahead of her time. She was well aware of their ploy to force her out.

Mrs. Britton deeply resented their efforts to force her to sell. Behind closed doors they had conspired to auction off her team to a buyer, presumably, Phil Ball of the rival Federal League. She was aware that it was a "woman against men" situation, and, as Sid Keener of the *St. Louis Times* reported, "she stood toe-to-toe with them and won the fight." She thoroughly disagreed with their chief selling point: that "it would be for the good of the game for her to get out of baseball." Refusing to part with the club, she rightfully revoked her selling option and declared to the press, "I have not sold the Cardinals and I'm not going to sell the Cardinals." She returned to St. Louis, still in possession of Robison Field and the St. Louis Cardinals.

Her husband, Schuyler Parsons Britton, was an affable man who presented a perfect public image for the Cardinals. He mingled quite well with the press, who affectionately called him Skip. Yet he continued to listen dutifully to the wishes of his wife. On one occasion she suggested that the game needed some added attraction to bring more women to the ball park. She wisely realized that if more ladies were present, a larger group of men would also attend, even if the team was not doing so well. She was an early advocate of ladies day many years before the idea became popular among baseball promoters. She felt that "we just have to prevail upon more members of the fair sex to come out and see the Cardinals play!" She suggested to Schuyler that he arrange for a male singer to entertain between each inning. When they finally agreed on a successful candidate, he was so excited about singing before crowds that ranged from 5,000 to 20,000 people that he agreed to sing for nothing. One observer noted that "every day he parades in front of the bleachers, singing at the top of his voice into a large megaphone." Britton added band music that turned Robison Field into a "baseball cabaret." The experiment worked, and more women *and* men attended Cardinals' games.

In the 1914 Christmas edition of *Reedy's Mirror,* an internationally circulated St. Louis periodical, the editor and publisher, William Reedy, described Schuyler Britton in flowery terms. The article commended him for his nobility of character in presenting his players with an incentive bonus at the end of the past season. In March of 1914, Britton had gone on record by promising his players a flat 20 percent increase in their salaries if they finished third or better. The offer "acted like magic," as the Cardinals won 81 games to finish in third place. Britton had lived up to his promise and had gladly paid their bonuses.

Publisher Reedy found this to be truly amazing, considering that the Cardinals were already the highest paid team in the league, though they were far from the best team in the league. Reedy regarded Britton's overt act of generosity in serious contrast to the "taint of monopolistic greed and denigration which has blurred baseball's escutcheon during the past few years. . . ." Reedy editorialized that the game of baseball would rise to "unparalleled popularity" if all owners were "as honest and fair-minded" as Schuyler Britton, who possessed a "puritanic soul." Even though in the past he had placed his confidence in men who were "rapscallions at heart," and at a cost of a "pretty penny" (his wife's money), Britton had never relinquished his "trust in his fellow man."

There is great evidence that Reedy's saccharine portrayal of Helene Britton's husband was far from an accurate one. While he kept up his convivial image for the press and idealists like Reedy, his private life was in turmoil. Persistent rumors implied that there was a great deal of marital discord at 4215 Lindell. The everyday strains of having his wife looking over his shoulder at his every move became intolerable for the "Cardinal front." Perhaps it was pride or the lack of a positive self-image. Whatever the case, Schuyler Britton began a strong flirtation with the bottle. He began to stay out to all hours of the night with extreme regularity. As his wife's divorce petition testifies, their marriage was emotionally terminated in the early morning hours of November 7, 1916. Britton had returned home around 2 A.M., only to find that his wife had locked him out of their mansion. In a drunken rage he almost broke down the door. When she finally did admit him, she testifies that he "nearly set fire to the house" with his careless use of a cigar. After a heated argument, Britton packed some of his things and left, never to come back. Later that morning Helene Britton assumed the title of president of the Cardinals, making her the first woman to openly hold such a title in the annals of baseball history.

With her own life now in a shambles, and with her two children to think about, she lost her enthusiasm for baseball. In a private meeting with Jones, her lawyer, and Miller Huggins, who had replaced Bresnahan as the Cardinal manager after the latter's rift with the woman owner, Helene Britton quietly stated that she wanted "to get out of baseball." She told only them because she reasoned that they might be interested in buying the club themselves. Huggins was very interested in her proposition. He made a "verbal promise" to purchase the team but was unable to come up with enough money to meet Mrs. Britton's asking price of $375,000, which included Robison Field.

Jones was equally interested. He recruited a fan syndicate from the city's prominent businessmen that formed an army of stockholders. The project was promoted as an exercise in civic duty. Any buyer could purchase from $50 to $10,000 worth of stock. W. E. Bilheimer, a St. Louis insurance man, introduced the idea of a Knot Hole Gang. With each fifty dollars worth of stock purchased went one bleacher seat that was opened up free of charge for the city's youth. Bilheimer cited the city's rising rate of juvenile delinquency in the campaign. He believed that his plan would serve as a useful antidote to juvenile crime. Later Branch Rickey picked up on this idea and endeared thousands of youngsters to the Cardinals for life.

Helene Britton disappeared from the Social Register in St. Louis after the sale of the club. She later married Charles S. Bigsby, an electrical appliance distributor, who died in 1935. Helene Britton Bigsby died at the age of seventy-one on January 8, 1950, in the Philadelphia home of her daughter, Mary R. Britton. Her body was returned to Cleveland for burial. Thus ended the story of baseball's matron magnate.

A Major League Game in Grand Rapids?

Many fans and researchers recall that the Brooklyn Dodgers, to stimulate gate receipts, played seven games in Jersey City in 1956 and in 1957. For the same reason, the Chicago White Sox played nine games in Milwaukee in 1968 and eleven in 1969. That was in the period when Milwaukee did not have a team in either league.

Before 1900 it was considered good promotion to play a game in a neutral city to stimulate attendance late in the season. As John Tattersall has pointed out, the first major league grand slam homer was hit by Roger Connor in Albany, N.Y.—in a game between Troy and Worcester.

Since 1900 the neutral field contest has been more rare. The primary reason for leaving the home park was to escape Sunday baseball restrictions. In the period 1902–05 Cleveland played "home" games in Canton, Columbus, and Dayton, and in Fort Wayne, Indiana; Detroit played in Columbus, Toledo, and in Grand Rapids, Michigan; and the New York AL club played in Newark, N.J. The Boston NL club played in Providence, R.I. All these were regulation games.

These were not crucial games, but they provided an opportunity for additional fans to see such great stars as Cy Young, Nap Lajoie, Willie Keeler, Ed Delahanty, Jesse Burkett, Sam Crawford, Jimmy Collins, and Addie Joss. These games also added a certain dimension in that George Mullin, for example, was the only major leaguer to win a game in Grand Rapids and Roger Bresnahan was the only player to hit a major league home run in Dayton. Weak-hitting Hobe Ferris of Boston was able to homer in both Canton and Columbus, Ohio.

The Durable Dodger Infield

W. R. Schroeder

Garvey, Lopes, Russell and Cey
The Dodger infield that came to stay
Nothing flashy, but steady and true
Dating way back to Seventy-Two

No, there'll never be a real poem written about these four players, but they do deserve some recognition as the major league team infield that played together the longest. In 1981 they finished their ninth season as Los Angeles regulars, with Steve Garvey at first, Davey Lopes at second, Bill Russell at shortstop, and Ron Cey at third. This is a remarkable achievement considering that players get traded, released, injured, and shuffled to other positions.

Certainly the Dodger quartet, in spite of its longevity, is not the most famous infield. The Chicago Cubs of 1906–10 had, of course, a more publicized, but less deserving, infield of Frank Chance, Johnny Evers, Joe Tinker, and Harry Steinfeldt, the latter having gained some notice in recent years as the answer to a familiar trivia question. This combination was broken up in 1911, when Steinfeldt was traded to the Boston Braves.

Connie Mack had his famous $100,000 infield of Stuffy McInnis at first base, Eddie Collins at second base, Jack Barry at shortstop, and Frank "Home Run" Baker at third base, but this group lasted for only four years, 1911–14. In 1915, Collins was traded to the White Sox, and Baker sat out the season. This was a very classy infield and would now be valued at considerably more than it was some seventy years ago.

The Detroit infield of 1933–37 had a couple of big names, with Hank Greenberg at first base and Charlie Gehringer at second. They were grouped with Billy Rogell at short and Marv Owen at third. They helped lead the Tigers to the AL pennant in 1934 and 1935. The keystone of this infield—Gehringer at second and Rogell at short— did not miss a game for three years, from August 1932 to August 1935. In 1934 the four infielders knocked in a total of 462 runs. All but Greenberg played the full schedule, and he missed only one game. He was not so fortunate in 1936, when he was out almost the full season with a broken wrist. Greenberg was back in 1937, but the next year the quartet was broken up when Owen was traded to the White Sox.

The Brooklyn Dodgers of 1948–52 had a pretty enterprising infield with Gil Hodges at first, Jackie Robinson at second, Pee Wee Reese at short, and Billy Cox at third. The fielding at the corners was about the best in the National League. It was not the most stable group by position because Cox also played a little at short and Robinson played some at first and third and also in the outfield when Jim Gilliam came up in 1953.

In 1968–72 the Baltimore Orioles had Boog Powell at first, Dave Johnson at second, Mark Belanger at short, and Brooks Robinson at third. Powell fielded surprisingly well in spite of his bulk, while Johnson won three Gold Gloves, Belanger two, and Robinson five in this five-year period. The great fielding combination was broken up when Johnson was traded to Atlanta for the 1973 season.

The infield with the longest service prior to the Dodgers of 1973–81 was the Chicago White Stockings of 1883–89. It started out with player-manager Cap Anson at first, Fred Pfeffer at second, Tom Burns at short, and Ned Williamson at third. In 1886 Burns shifted to third, and Williamson moved to short in an apparently smooth transfer that lasted through 1889. Williamson, nearing the end of his career, played with Chicago in the Players' League in 1890.

All four of the current Dodger infielders came up through the L.A. farm system, playing with Spokane and/or Albuquerque. However, they never played together at any one time in the minors. Russell and Garvey came up to the Dodgers first in 1969, with Bill playing in the outfield and Steve making pinch-hitting appearances only. In 1970 Russell again played in the outfield, and Garvey filled in at third and

The Dodger infield of Ron Cey, Bill Russell, Davey Lopes, and Steve Garvey displays a Los Angeles team poster in April 1980

second. In 1971 Russell played second, the outfield, and short, and Garvey played third, but not full time. The next year Russell was the regular at short, and Garvey played 85 games at third, where he made a league-leading 26 errors. Ron Cey, who had come up just briefly in 1971, played 11 games at third at the end of the 1972 season. Davey Lopes, the oldest of the quartet, was the last one up, playing 11 games at second at the tag end of 1972. That same season Garvey also played three games at first base.

In 1972 the Dodger infield was Wes Parker at first; Lee Lacy, Bob Valentine, and Jim Lefebvre at second; Russell at short; and Garvey and Valentine at third. Most of these positions were up for grabs in 1973. Parker retired, and Bill Buckner moved in from the outfield to take his place. In midseason Garvey started playing first, and Buckner went back to the outfield. Lacy started at second but shortly lost out to Lopes. Cey soon became the regular at third, and Russell retained his shortstop position. Although all four had played in the Dodger infield late in 1972, the first box score to show Garvey, 1B, Lopes, 2B,

Russell, SS, and Cey, 3B, was on June 13, 1973, and the next one was on June 23. In the last half of that season they were regulars at those positions. They continued that way through the 1981 season.

Of course, there were times when injuries laid off one or the other. Russell, who had played the full 162-game schedule at short in 1973, was out almost two and a half months with injuries in 1975 and wound up playing only 83 games at short. In 1980, Bill missed most of the last month of the season with a broken finger. In 1976, Lopes went on the disabled list at the start of the season and got into only 100 games at second plus 19 in the outfield. Garvey was the steady player, taking part in essentially the full schedule at first base from 1975 through 1981 and having some excellent batting seasons as well.

Cey, although he never batted .300, had some good power seasons, including 1977, when he hit 30 homers and knocked in 110 runs. Lopes, the premier base stealer with the best theft percentage in the majors, surprised everyone by hitting 28 homers in 1979. The Dodger field captain for part of this period, Lopes was a Gold Glove winner at second base in 1978. Garvey won Gold Gloves at first base from 1974 to 1977. It also should be pointed out that Cey tied a league record in 1979 with only nine errors at third.

Each of these four infielders played in three or more All-Star games. They played as a unit in four Championship Series and in four World Series—1974, 1977, 1978, and 1981. In 1981 they won the Series by defeating the Yankees. That final game, on October 28, 1981, ended the long-lasting infield unity, for after the season ended Lopes was traded to Oakland.

Here is a listing of the number of games each played at his position from 1972 through 1981.

Player	Pos.	1972	'73	'74	'75	'76	'77	'78	'79	'80	'81
Garvey	1B	3	76	156	160	162	160	161	162	162	110
Lopes	2B	11	135	143	137	100	130	147	152	140	55
Russell	SS	121	162	160	83	149	153	155	150	129	80
Cey	3B	11	146	158	158	144	153	158	150	157	84

The Split Century
Arthur R. Ahrens

The days of the classic umpire–ballplayer feuds are long gone and, in all probability, will never return. The present generation of fans does not realize what it has missed, having never witnessed the likes of such umpire baiters as Cap Anson, John McGraw, Joe Medwick, and Leo Durocher. Only Earl Weaver, manager of the Orioles through 1982, has served as a significant reminder of times that once were.

Although not primarily remembered as such, another notorious umpire baiter in his own way was Henry "Heinie" Zimmerman, renowned Chicago Cub infielder of some 70 years ago.

As the National League season of 1913 opened, the great Zim was at the peak of his career, having batted .372 the year before to win most of the batting honors. He was to enjoy another highly successful season in 1913, but this time his umpire problems rather than his batting totals were to reach their all-time high.

Heinie went along smoothly until May 19, when umpire Charles Rigler ejected him in the fourth inning during a game at Philadelphia. After that incident, all was calm until Friday, June 6, when he was given the heave-ho in the fourth inning for cursing arbiter William Byron during a Cubs–Braves contest in Chicago. Remaining quiet for exactly one week, Zimmerman then became baseball's answer to a nihilist. In what must be a record of some sort, Heinie earned the dis-

tinction of getting tossed out of three home games in a five-day period
—June 13, 15, and 17. Here is the grim chronicle of Zimmerman's
epic verbal bouts with the men in black:

> June 13—In what is an apparent force of the Brooklyn
> Dodgers' Jake Daubert at third base, Daubert is ruled safe by
> umpire Malcolm Eason, after which, according to *Chicago
> Tribune* writer Sam Weller, "Heinie roared, being ordered
> out of the game quick as one could wink."
> June 15—Upon being called out when attempting to
> slide into home plate during the seventh inning of the Cub–
> Dodger game, Heinie curses plate umpire William Brennan
> and is promptly put out of the game.
> June 17—In the third inning of the Cub–Phillie contest,
> Zimmerman, perched on third base and hoping to score, is
> banished for hollering at Bill Klem after the latter calls Roger
> Bresnahan out on strikes.

By this time it appeared as if Zimmerman were on the verge of
getting chased off the diamond every time he appeared thereon. At
last, the following letter of desperation appeared in the *Chicago
Tribune* of June 19, 1913:

> To the Sporting Editor of the *Tribune:*
> I'm Irish and I haven't much use for the Dutch, but
> there's one Dutchman I think a whole lot of and that's Heinie
> Zimmerman. I think so much of him that I love to see him
> fight the other fellows. And, ah, there's the rub. Darn him,
> he doesn't play regular. He gets canned too often for fighting
> the "umps." It ain't fair for those who pay their money to
> see Zim swat the pill and it also ain't fair to the rest of the
> bunch.
> Now to come down to brass tacks: Here's a $100 bill
> split in two. Go give half to Heinie and if he stays in the game
> for two weeks—that is, if he doesn't get canned by an ump
> in that period of time, pass him the other half and a piece of
> sticking plaster to stick 'em together.
> Seriously, I want Zim to quit kicking. Two weeks of
> living with umps will do everybody a lot of good, Zim most
> of all.
> Please put a mask on my name, and sign:
>   A. "SPLIT" CENTURY

The *Tribune* sports staff did as instructed, giving half of the bill to Heinie and the other half to umpire Bill Klem, the ball field judge responsible for Zim's June 17th ejection. Upon hearing of the stipulations attached, Heinie boasted, "Say, just hand me that one-half and watch me get the other. I'm through fussing with the umpires anyway. It don't get you anything. I don't intend to be put out of the game again this year. From now on you'll see me as a model guy on the ball field." Finally, he added, "That $100 is just as good as mine."

But on June 20 Ring Lardner, then a sportswriter for the *Tribune,* brought up a thought-provoking question when he asked, "But suppose that Zim is canned before the expiration of two weeks. Will Mr. Century get his half back?" That very day Heinie was fined $200—no, not for breaking his truce with the umps—but for engaging in backtalk to his fiery manager, Johnny Evers. "If he had said to Chance what he said to me," Evers told Ring Lardner, "he would not play all season along."

"You're right, John," Lardner replied. "And we would have all been asked to chip in for a floral tribute." (It was an open secret in Chicago that Zimmerman and his former manager, Frank Chance, had not gotten along very well.) Lardner also commented that "Heinie would probably hit 1.075 if he played every other day and quarreled the rest of the time."

By June 22, the Split Century had become the number one conversation piece of every baseball fan in Chicago, and the city's gamblers, many of whom operated on the west side in the vicinity of the Cubs' ball park, were already laying 3–2 odds that Zim would win. One fan at the West Side Grounds gave Heinie half of a dollar bill under the same condition that Split Century had given him the half a hundred.

But the ordeal was no easy task for the Cub third baseman to endure. At the June 24 game in St. Louis Heinie began to exchange harsh words with umpire Hank O'Day; fortunately he held his tongue not a moment too soon and remained in the game.

The following morning, after the Cubs had pulled into Cincinnati, Zimmerman received a visit at the team's hotel from his former Cub teammates, Joe Tinker and Mordecai Brown, both of whom had been traded to the Reds during the winter of 1912–13. Tinker and Brown had heard of the Split Century affair but, thinking it to be some sort of hoax, demanded to see the bill for themselves. Upon being shown the half, Tinker, still believing the whole thing to be a joke, grabbed it from Heinie's hand and tore it in two. Zimmerman wrenched the precious certificate away before the Red shortstop could perpetrate further damage upon it, but as the *Tribune* correspondent noted, "now instead of one-half he has two quarters of a yellowback."

So, with a taped-up half of a gold certificate in his back pocket, Heinie sweated through the remainder of his good behavior probation. By July 2, 1913, he had lasted one week and six days without being exiled from a game. If he could play one more game without getting the ax, the reward would be his. That afternoon, in a game with Pittsburgh at Chicago's West Side Grounds, the grandstand held its breath as Heinie began to yell at umpire Ernest Quigley after the latter had ruled him out when he attempted to steal home. However, remembering the money, he managed to hold his temper and kept it in check for the rest of the game. The miracle had been completed—Henry Zimmerman had played two full weeks without having to take an early shower.

Bill Klem awarded him the other half of the split century while the fan who had given him half of the one-dollar bill came forward with the remaining portion, thus giving the great Heinie a total of $101 for his good conduct.

Said the boisterously jubilant infielder after the game, "I knew I could win that money after the first day. . . . I'm not going to say anything to an umpire that will give him cause to put me out of a game. I'm through bothering those guys. It doesn't get you anything." He then added, however, "Just the same, I think I was safe at the plate and couldn't help telling the umpire so," an indication that he would soon be back in his old form—which he was.

Iron-Man Pitching Performances
Leonard Gettelson

When reference is made to hurlers pitching both games of a double-header, the two who come to mind most readily are Joe McGinnity and Ed Reulbach. Iron Man McGinnity achieved this feat five times after 1900, including the winning of three twin bills for the Giants in the month of August 1903. His other two efforts were for the Orioles in 1901, and he split both times.

Reulbach of the Cubs is remembered, of course, because he was the only hurler to toss shutouts in both his efforts. On September 26, 1908, the Dodgers fell to him 5–0 and 3–0. But how good was his overall performance compared to that of the 23 others who since 1900 have won both games, or even the 14 others who pitched two complete games without winning both, or either? In the two games, Ed gave up a total of eight hits and five walks while striking out ten. Each of these efforts was bettered individually by other pitchers.

In fact, another Ed from Chicago, Big Ed Walsh of the White Sox, had a better overall performance in his twin triumph over the Red Sox just three days after the Reulbach victories. In the two games, he gave up only 1 run, 7 hits, and 1 walk while fanning 15, which is the top mark. The one walk was achieved by two other pitchers, including Grover Alexander twice.

Another great dual performance took place that same week when Ed Summers of the Tigers beat the Athletics 7–2 and 1–0 in ten innings on Claude Rossman's homer. This was a case of a pitcher getting better as he went along, as Summers gave up only two hits in that extra-inning game and did not issue a base on balls. He took on the extra duty because of his special ability to beat the A's. He had a string of seven straight wins over the Mackmen.

Who gave up the fewest hits in a twin bill? Fred Toney, the big right-hander of the Reds, on July 1, 1917, and Herman Bell, rookie of the Cardinals, on July 19, 1924. Toney gave up three hits and one walk in each game. He felt so strong after the first contest that he told his manager he would work the second game as well. His manager was Christy Mathewson, who had never pitched two games himself but who was grateful for Toney's offer, because the staff was severely depleted at the time. In fact, several days before, Hod Eller had pitched a doubleheader, winning one game.

Herman Bell was an unknown quantity for the Cardinals in 1924. He was not used much and was well rested. He did not give up a hit to the Braves until the eighth inning of the first game, and then went five in the second before he was touched. He gave up a total of six hits and two walks, and he moved right along—the times of the two games were 1:31 and 1:17. Bell won only three games that first season, and two came in this doubleheader.

Why do pitchers work both games of a twin bill? There are various reasons. We have already alluded to depleted pitching staffs and a special ability against the opposing club. McGinnity could do it because he had an easy underhand delivery. Ed Walsh was used to working hard under normal conditions. Doc Scanlan of the Dodgers did it more as a stunt on the last day of the 1905 season. George Mullin of the Tigers didn't think about it until he saw that the opposing pitcher in the second game was a green rookie. Mullin thought he would have an easy time of it, but it didn't turn out that way. Outpitched, he was lucky to win 4–3 with a Tiger rally in the ninth.

Did a pitcher ever work the second game after losing the first? Several times. On June 25, 1903, Wiley Piatt of the Braves lost to the Pirates 1–0 in a very well pitched game. In the second game he lost 5–3 and became the only hurler to lose two complete games in a day in this century. On July 21, 1918, the Athletics found themselves short staffed. John Watson, who pitched two doubleheaders for the club that summer, lost the first game to the Indians 3–2 in 11 innings. He still came back and pitched the second, a 5–5 tie called after 8 innings to let the A's catch a train. On August 31 of that year, he was roughed up by 12 hits in losing the first game, but he came back to shut out the Red Sox 1–0 on 1 hit in the second game. On August 13, 1921, while with the Braves, he finally won two games. Outside of McGinnity, he is the only hurler to have worked three doubleheaders in this century.

Kid Nichols pitched and easily won the first game for the Cardinals on September 11, 1904. He also worked the second game but was raked for 14 hits. He didn't withdraw, however, because he was also the manager of the Cards and didn't want to waste a new pitcher. And Carl Mays didn't neglect his hitting while pitching a doubleheader win over the Athletics in 1918. He collected 5 hits in 6 trips.

All the trivia experts know that in 1926 Emil Levsen of the Indians was the last hurler to pitch two complete-game victories in a doubleheader. But who was the last one to pitch two complete games? It was Jack Scott of the Phils, who did it on June 19, 1927. He won 3–1 and lost 3–0 against the Reds. At thirty-five, he was the oldest of the double-duty performers. Several have tried to do it in the past half century, and Don Newcombe of the Dodgers came closest on September 6, 1950. He beat the Phils 2–0 in the first game and was trailing 2–0 in the seventh of the nightcap when he retired. On July 20, 1973, Wilbur Wood started both games against the Yankees but was knocked out in each game, losing both.

It really isn't fair to talk about iron man pitchers who pitched two full games in one day without some reference to those who pitched 18 innings or more in the same game. After all, Joe Oeschger and Leon Cadore nearly pitched the equivalent of three games in one afternoon with their 26-inning 1–1 tie on May 1, 1920. And there have been 37 others who worked 18 or more innings in one game since 1900. Just like the twin bill hurlers, almost all of them were of an earlier generation. The last hurler to pitch as many as 18 innings was Vern Law of the Pirates on July 19, 1955, and he failed to get a decision, having left before the game was completed.

It is interesting to note that some of the same pitchers who pitched doubleheaders also worked in marathon games—Reulbach, Summers, Waddell, and Dixie Davis. Who performed best in the long games? Well, you have to give credit to Oeschger, who gave up only 9 hits and 1 run in 26 innings. However, Carl Hubbell pitched 18 shutout innings, giving up only 6 hits and no walks.

Shown below are the hurlers who won two complete games in one afternoon, those who pitched two complete games in one day, and those who pitched 18 or more innings in one game.

Pitchers Winning Two Complete Games in One Day (Post-1900)

Pitcher and Teams	Date	Scores	H	SO	BB
Joe McGinnity, Giants (vs. Braves)	Aug. 1, 1903	4–1 5–2	6 6	5 3	1 1
Joe McGinnity, Giants (vs. Dodgers)	Aug. 8, 1903	6–1 4–3	8 5	2 5	0 4
Joe McGinnity, Giants (vs. Phillies)	Aug. 31, 1903	4–1 9–2	5 6	4 9	3 1
Frank Owen, White Sox (vs. Browns)	July 1, 1905	3–2 3–0	4 3	3 0	3 0
Ed Walsh, White Sox (vs. Red Sox)	Sept. 6, 1905	10–5 3–1	9 5	5 5	4 1
Doc Scanlan, Dodgers (vs. Cardinals)	Oct. 3, 1905	4–0 3–2	3 9	8 5	2 0
George Mullin, Tigers (vs. Senators)	Sept. 22, 1906	5–3 4–3	11 9	4 5	1 2
Ed Summers, Tigers (vs. Athletics)	Sept. 25, 1908	7–2 1–0	6 2	1 6	3 0
Ed Reulbach, Cubs (vs. Dodgers)	Sept. 26, 1908	5–0 3–0	5 3	6 4	1 4
Ed Walsh, White Sox (vs. Red Sox)	Sept. 29, 1908	5–1 2–0	3 4	10 5	0 1
Ray Collins, Red Sox (vs. Tigers)	Sept. 22, 1914	5–3 5–0	12 4	3 0	1 1
Dave Davenport, Browns (vs. Yankees)	July 29, 1916	3–1 3–2	4 7	4 7	3 3
Bill Perritt, Giants (vs. Phillies)	Sept. 9, 1916	3–1 3–0	4 4	6 3	0 2
Al Demaree, Phillies (vs. Pirates)	Sept. 20, 1916	7–0 3–2	7 9	0 4	3 2
Grover Alexander, Phillies (vs. Reds)	Sept. 23, 1916	7–3 4–0	12 8	3 4	0 1
Fred Toney, Reds (vs. Pirates)	July 1, 1917	4–1 5–1	3 3	3 1	1 1
Grover Alexander, Phillies (vs. Dodgers)	Sept. 3, 1917	5–0 9–3	4 9	5 2	1 0
Bill Doak, Cardinals (vs. Dodgers)	Sept. 18, 1917	2–0 12–4	2 12	1 4	1 2
Carl Mays, Red Sox (vs. Athletics)	Aug. 30, 1918	12–0 4–1	9 4	2 3	0 2
John Watson, Braves (vs. Phillies)	Aug. 13, 1921	4–3 8–0	9 2	2 5	2 0

Pitchers Winning Two Complete Games in One Day (Post-1900)

Pitcher and Teams	Date	Scores	H	SO	BB
John Stuart, Cardinals (vs. Braves)	July 10, 1923	11–1	3	0	2
		6–3	10	0	2
Herman Bell, Cardinals (vs. Braves)	July 19, 1924	6–1	2	3	1
		2–1	4	2	1
Urban Shocker, Browns (vs. White Sox)	Sept. 6, 1924	6–2	9	1	1
		6–2	5	0	4
Emil Levsen, Indians (vs. Red Sox)	Aug. 28, 1926	6–1	4	0	1
		5–1	4	0	2

Other Pitchers Hurling Two Complete Games in One Day

Pitcher and Teams	Date	Scores	H	SO	BB
Joe McGinnity, Orioles (vs. Brewers)	Sept. 3, 1901	W 10–0	6	2	0
		L 1–6	9	2	4
Joe McGinnity, Orioles (vs. Athletics)	Sept. 12, 1901	W 4–3	7	2	3
		L 4–5	10	0	1
Wiley Piatt, Braves (vs. Pirates)	June 25, 1903	L 0–1	6	7	1
		L 3–5	8	5	2
Rube Waddell, Athletics (vs. Tigers)	Aug. 21, 1903	W 1–0	3	6	2
		L 1–2	8	7	3
Kid Nichols, Cardinals (vs. Reds)	Sept. 11, 1904	W 4–2	3	3	2
		L 5–8	14	0	2
Stoney McGlynn, Cardinals (vs. Reds)	June 3, 1907	W 1–0	5	3	2
		L 1–5	7	5	3
Dave Davenport, St. Louis Feds (vs. Buffalo)	July 31, 1915	W 1–0	4	8	0
		L 0–1	1	4	2
Rube Benton, Giants (vs. Dodgers)	Sept. 6, 1916	W 6–1	4	4	1
		L 1–2	10	5	1
Hod Eller, Reds (vs. Cubs)	June 19, 1917	L 1–2	6	6	2
		W* 6–2	7	2	0
John Watson, Athletics (vs. Indians)	July 21, 1918	L† 2–3	12	2	3
		T‡ 5–5	10	2	1
John Watson, Athletics (vs. Red Sox)	Aug. 31, 1918	L 1–6	12	1	5
		W 1–0	1	1	1
Carl Mays, Red Sox (vs. Yankees)	June 28, 1919	W 2–0	7	3	0
		L 1–4	7	5	2
Dixie Davis, Browns (vs. Red Sox)	Sept. 24, 1921	L 1–2	9	0	2
		W 11–0	6	2	0
Jack Scott, Phillies (vs. Reds)	June 19, 1927	W 3–1	6	0	1
		L 0–3	9	0	0

* 6 innings   † 11 innings   ‡ 8 innings

Pitchers Hurling 18 or More Innings in One Game

Date	Pitcher and Team	IP	H	R	SO	BB	Outcome
May 1, 1920	Joe Oeschger, Braves	26	9	1	7	4	Tie
May 1, 1920	Leon Cadore, Dodgers	26	15	1	7	5	Tie
Sept. 1, 1906	Jack Coombs, Athletics	24	15	1	18	6	Win
Sept. 1, 1906	Joe Harris, Red Sox	24	16	4	14	2	Loss
May 17, 1927	Robert Smith, Braves	22	20	4	5	9	Loss
July 17, 1914	Rube Marquard, Giants	21	15	1	2	2	Win
July 17, 1914	Babe Adams, Pirates	21	12	3	6	0	Loss
Aug. 1, 1918	Arthur Nehf, Braves	21	12	2	8	5	Loss
July 17, 1918	George Tyler, Cubs	21	13	1	8	1	Win
May 24, 1929	Ted Lyons, White Sox	21	24	6	4	2	Loss
July 4, 1905	Rube Waddell, Athletics	20	15	2	11	4	Win
July 4, 1905	Cy Young, Red Sox	20	13	4	9	0	Loss
Aug. 24, 1905	Ed Reulbach, Cubs	20	13	1	7	4	Win
Aug. 24, 1905	Tully Sparks, Phillies	20	19	2	6	1	Loss
July 17, 1918	Milt Watson, Phillies	20	19	2	5	4	Loss
Apr. 30, 1919	Joe Oeschger, Phillies	20	22	9	2	5	Tie
Apr. 30, 1919	Burleigh Grimes, Dodgers	20	15	9	7	7	Tie
May 24, 1929	George Uhle, Tigers	20	17	5	4	3	Win
July 21, 1945	Les Mueller, Tigers	19⅔	13	1	6	5	No decision
June 22, 1902	Jack Taylor, Cubs	19	14	2	6	1	Win
July 31, 1912	Otto Hess, Braves	19	14	7	3	8	Loss
Sept. 27, 1912	Eddie Plank, Athletics	19	12	5	10	6	Loss
May 24, 1918	Stan Coveleski, Indians	19	12	2	4	6	Win
May 3, 1920	Dana Fillingim, Braves	19	12	1	4	4	Win
Aug. 9, 1921	Dixie Davis, Browns	19	13	6	8	5	Win
June 22, 1902	Deacon Phillippe, Pirates	18⅔	14	3	6	3	Loss
June 17, 1915	George Zabel, Cubs	18⅓	9	2	6	1	Win (relief)
June 17, 1915	Jeff Pfeffer, Dodgers	18⅓	15	4	6	8	Loss
May 3, 1920	Sherrod Smith, Dodgers	18⅓	13	2	3	5	Loss
Aug. 17, 1902	Bill Donovan, Dodgers	18	14	7	13	7	Tie
June 24, 1905	Ed Reulbach, Cubs	18	14	1	6	6	Win
June 24, 1905	Jack Taylor, Cards	18	11	2	7	4	Loss
July 16, 1909	Ed Summers, Tigers	18	7	0	10	1	Tie
May 15, 1918	Walter Johnson, Senators	18	10	0	9	1	Win
May 15, 1918	Lefty Williams, White Sox	18	8	1	3	2	Loss
June 1, 1919	Jeff Pfeffer, Dodgers	18	23	10	6	3	Loss
May 14, 1927	Guy Bush, Cubs	18	11	2	5	8	Win
July 2, 1933	Carl Hubbell, Giants	18	6	0	12	0	Win
July 19, 1955	Vern Law, Pirates	18	9	2	12	3	No decision

Newly Discovered RBI Records

Seymour Siwoff

Runs batted in, now one of the most important measures of batting performance, were slow to be recognized by the major leagues. There were no official RBI records until 1920, and they were not carried in many box scores until ten years after that. It is not surprising, then, that a record such as "most consecutive games, one or more runs batted in" would be hard to pin down and might vary according to the latest research.

At one time Lou Gehrig was credited with an American League record of 10 consecutive RBI games, which he achieved twice in 1931 and once in 1934. Then further research showed that Babe Ruth and Al Simmons each had 11-game streaks in 1931. Then it was found that Red Sox playing manager Joe Cronin knocked in runs in 12 straight games in 1939 and that his star outfielder, Ted Williams, also had a 12-game string in 1942. In the National League, Mel Ott for many years was carried as the leader with an 11-game streak in 1929, but a few years ago it was discovered that Paul Waner had achieved a 12-game run in 1927.

The Elias Sports Bureau decided to research all the official records of runs batted in since they achieved that status in 1920 to see what great slugger had achieved the longest string of RBI games. It took considerable checking and rechecking, but we finally came up with a 13-game record holder in the AL and a surprising 17-game streaker in the NL.

They were two Chicago players of modest reputation—Taft Wright of the 1941 White Sox and Oscar Ray Grimes of the 1922 Cubs. They were good hitters, with lifetime records well over .300, but they didn't have very long careers and weren't regarded as particularly good run producers. Nevertheless, they did have legitimate streaks, which are of interest also because of some unusual aspects.

First, the thirteen-game streak of Taft Wright in 1941. The hefty White Sox outfielder was in his third season and playing his first full game of 1941 when the string was launched modestly on May 4 with an RBI single in four trips against Philadelphia. The streak became even more modest in the third, fourth, and fifth games, when Wright failed to hit in each contest yet was credited with an RBI each day. On May 7 he hit a sacrifice fly; on May 10 he was walked twice, once with the bases loaded; and on May 11 a run scored on his infield out. After driving in two runs with two hits on May 13, he had another hitless day on May 14 but drove in a run with an infield out. He knocked in four runs with a homer and a single on May 15 and then had two more hitless games in which he moved one runner home with a sacrifice fly and another with a force out. He made up for the hitless days with four hits on May 18, producing four runs. After two more run-producing games, the thirteen-game streak came to a close in Philadelphia on May 21.

Wright's achievement is made more remarkable by the fact that in six games he knocked in runs without any hits. In that way he edged out the great AL sluggers like Ruth, Gehrig, Foxx, Simmons, and Ted Williams of an important run production record. Wright ended the 1941 season with 97 RBIs, the most on the White Sox team, and the best of his nine-year career.

The NL record was established by Ray Grimes, who made it to the majors with the Red Sox in 1920. That was also the year of the debut of his twin brother, Roy. Roy lasted only one year, but Ray went on to the Cubs, where he played first base and had a very good season in 1922, hitting .354. That was the year of his streak, which started in the second game of a twin bill with Pittsburgh on June 27. The next day he had lumbago and did not play. He returned to the lineup on June 30 and had at least one RBI through the July 8 twin bill. Ironically, he played only one inning of the second game but connected for an RBI single before leaving the game with a wrenched back.

The injury was serious, and he did not return to first base until July 18, when he celebrated with a homer, a double, and two singles to lead the Cubs to a 6–3 victory over the Phils. On July 21 he doubled in the only run of the game to give Grover Alexander a 1–0 thriller over Dutch Ruether of the Dodgers. Grimes continued to hit well, driving out extra-base hits in six straight games. Finally, on July 25, in a game against Boston he failed to produce a run. His big chance came in the fourth inning with two teammates on base, but Grimes was walked to load the bases.

His spectacular seventeen game RBI streak was not noted at the time, probably because he was absent from the lineup on two occasions, once for nine days. However, the RBI streak, like a consecutive-game hitting streak, is based on the games the individual plays, not necessarily those that the team plays.

Taft Wright, White Sox, 1941

Date	AB	R	H	RBI	Comment
May 4	4	1	1	1	First start of 1941
May 5	5	0	2	1	Double
May 7	4	0	0	1	Sacrifice fly
May 10	2	0	0	1	Walk with bases full
May 11	3	0	0	1	Infield out
May 13	4	0	2	2	
May 14	5	0	0	1	Infield out
May 15	5	2	2	4	Homer
May 16	4	0	0	1	Sacrifice fly
May 17	5	1	0	1	Force out
May 18	5	2	4	4	Double
May 19	4	2	2	2	Triple
May 20	2	1	1	1	Double

Ray Grimes, Cubs, 1922

Date	AB	R	H	RBI	Comment
June 27 (2)	5	1	1	1	
June 30	4	1	2	1	Missed June 28 game
July 1	4	0	2	3	Double
July 2	4	0	1	1	Double
July 3	4	0	1	1	
July 4 (1)	4	0	1	1	
July 4 (2)	3	2	2	1	
July 5	4	2	1	1	Double
July 7	4	2	2	2	Double, triple
July 8 (1)	3	2	2	1	
July 8 (2)	1	0	1	1	Played one inning
July 18	4	1	4	2	Homer, double
July 19	5	0	1	1	Double
July 20	5	2	2	3	Homer
July 21	4	0	1	1	Double for 1–0 win
July 22	5	1	3	4	Double, triple
July 23	3	1	1	2	Homer

Triples, the Pirates, and Forbes Field
Richard L. Field Burtt

The three-base hit made a tremendous comeback in 1979, with outstanding leadership totals in both leagues. George Brett led the American League with an even 20, the most since Dale Mitchell of Cleveland hit 23 in 1949. The Kansas City Royals hit 79 in 1979, the most for any team in the majors since the Pittsburgh Pirates hit 80 in 1944. Even the KC catcher, Darrell Porter, got into double figures with 10. In the National League, Garry Templeton hit 19, the most since Willie Mays hit 20 in 1957. It marked the third straight year that the switch-hitting Cardinal shortstop led the NL in triples, a new senior circuit record.

The resurgence in triples comes after almost a generation of the lowest figures in the game's history. In 1969, for an extreme example, Del Unser led the American League with only eight. In three other seasons in that era the AL leader had only nine. The National League has fared somewhat better, with the low figure at ten in 1962, when four players were tied.

The ratio of triples to total hits has not been constant during this century, having started out in the early years much higher and having significantly declined in favor of the home run. From 1900 to 1920, three-base hits represented 5.5 percent of all hits and home runs less than 2 percent. In the period from 1921 through 1946, triples dropped to 4.3 percent of all hits and home runs moved up to 4.9 percent. But the great change occurred during the post–World War II years (1947–79), when triples became just 3 percent of all hits and home runs went up to 9.2 percent.

Over the past 80-odd seasons the frequency of triples has fallen from 1 in 18 hits to 1 in 33 hits. At the same time, the home run, which occurred but once in about 55 hits in the first two decades of the century, is now seen once in each 11 hits. The home run has not only replaced many triples but has also cut into the singles and doubles totals. These basic hits represented 93 percent of all hits in the earlier period but now are less than 88 percent of the total. In regard to the relationship between triples and home runs, a strange thing happened with the Houston club in 1979, and it also seems to support the resurgence of the three-base hit. The Astros hit 52 triples compared to only 49 home runs. The last time a club hit more triples than homers was in 1949, when the Chicago White Sox hit 66 triples and 42 homers.

As of the end of the 1979 season, there had been nearly 76,000 triples hit in the majors since 1900. The National League had the edge with 38,274 over the AL with 37,653. These totals include the 1900 season in the senior circuit, which is balanced out by the four seasons when the AL had two more teams than the NL. The NL leads in triples because of one club that has completely dominated the three-base hit category in this century. While the New York Yankees have dominated in home runs for part of this period, the Pittsburgh Pirates have done even better in triples—and for essentially the entire period since 1900.

Since 1900 the Pirates have led the league in triples 40 times and have finished second 23 times. In comparison, their chief NL rival has been the Cardinals, with 13 firsts and 23 seconds in 80 years. In the American League there has been no such dominant club. The Washington/Minnesota franchise ranked first or second on 33 occasions, and the Yankees 30 times. Actually, the Pittsburgh dominance started prior to 1900. The club also led the NL in 1893, 1897, and 1899.

In the 1900–20 period, 1 of every 14 Pirate hits was a triple, compared to 1 of about 18 for all of major league baseball. In the 1921–46 period, the Pirate ratio slipped to 1 in 18, but the major league average also dropped, to 1 in 23. In the period 1947–79, the Pirates hit 1 triple in every 27 hits, while the overall average was 1 in 33. So while the Pirate triple ratio has continued to drop, the club has maintained its edge over other teams.

Why has there been such a domination by the Pittsburgh club in three-base hits? The obvious answer would appear to be Forbes

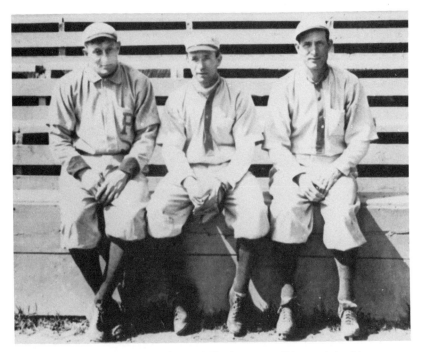

Honus Wagner, Tommy Leach, Fred Clarke—great Pirate triples hitters

Field. For 62 years, spacious Forbes was the home of major league baseball in Pittsburgh. The size and configuration of this park were conducive to batted balls rolling a long way and to outfielders running no end while chasing the ball and then throwing to very deep cutoff men. The fences, except near the right field foul pole, were at such great distances that many potential home runs became very long outs; or if they were line drives, they frequently went for three bases or sometimes for four (ten Pirates hit inside-the-park homers at Forbes in 1925).

Before we accept the easy answer of the field dimensions, however, let's consider the 18 seasons between 1900 and 1979 that the Pirates did not call Forbes Field their home. In the first nine seasons (1900–08), the Pirates played in Exposition Park, a typically expansive ball ground of that era, and in those nine years the Pirates hit more triples by a good margin than any other team in either league. During the first nine full seasons of play (1971–79), at Three Rivers Stadium, Forbes's successor, the Pirates hit more triples than any other NL team—although they fell slightly behind Kansas City in the AL, which had come on very strong in triples in the preceding five years.

Therefore, without discounting the influence of Forbes Field, let's concede that the Pittsburgh team has had more than its share of good, fast-running line-drive hitters.

Who were the Pittsburgh players who hit all of these three-baggers? On a career basis, there are no fewer than a dozen Pirates who hit 100 or more triples for the club. Included are some of the big names in three-cushion manufacture, dating back to the 1890s: Jake Beckley, Fred Clarke, Tommy Leach, Honus Wagner, Max Carey, Pie Traynor, Paul and Lloyd Waner, Arky Vaughan, and Roberto Clemente. Wagner, the all-time NL leader, hit 231 as a Pirate.

On a season basis, Pittsburgh players have led in triples 24 times. Some of these players have had very high totals. In fact, the four top season totals in the NL since 1895 were by Pittsburgh players. Of course, Owen Wilson had that incredible season of 1912 when he hit 36 (24 at home), which is not only a major league record but one for organized baseball as well. Kiki Cuyler hit 26 in 1925, which has gone unchallenged for more than five decades. Going back to 1897, Harry Davis hit 28, and Jimmy Williams, in his rookie season of 1899, hit 27. A Pirate hit 20 or more triples in a season on 16 occasions, which is twice as many as for any other club. And this doesn't count the 1890 season in the Players' League when two Pittsburgh players—Jake Beckley and Joe Visner—tied for the lead with 22 triples.

The strength of the Pittsburgh club in triples was not concentrated in one or two players at a time but ran through most of the regular lineup. While Mel Ott was leading the New York Giants in home runs for eighteen consecutive years, the Pirates were rotating their leaders in triples almost on a seasonal basis. Take, for example, the twelve-year period from 1922 to 1933, when the club leaders were as follows:

1922 Bigbee and Maranville, 15	1928 Paul Waner, 19
1923 Carey and Traynor, 19*	1929 Lloyd Waner, 20*
1924 Rabbit Maranville, 20	1930 Adam Comorosky, 23*
1925 Hazen Cuyler, 26*	1931 Pie Traynor, 15
1926 Paul Waner, 22*	1932 Gus Suhr, 16
1927 Paul Waner, 18*	1933 Arky Vaughan, 19*

* Asterisk indicates league leaders

In 1929 and 1930 the Pirates had a record six players in double figures in triples, a feat no other twentieth-century club has attained.

1929	1930
Lloyd Waner, 20*	Adam Comorosky, 23*
Paul Waner, 15	Paul Waner, 18
Dick Bartell, 13	George Grantham, 14
Pie Traynor, 12	Gus Suhr, 14
Adam Comorosky, 11	Dick Bartell, 13
George Grantham, 10	Pie Traynor, 11

* Asterisk indicates league leaders

The team hit a total of 116 triples in 1929 and 119 in 1930, figures unapproached in either league since then. The Pirates had established the major league team record with 129 in 1912. That was the season Wilson had 36 triples and Wagner was the runner-up with 20. Although the Pirates still occasionally lead the league in triples, their players have not had any high individual totals in many years. Omar Moreno in 1979 was runner-up to Templeton with 12, and Dave Parker in 1978 also was the runner-up to Templeton with 12. In 1965 Clemente and Don Clendenon tied for second with 14 apiece. The individual totals have been down since World War II or since Johnny Barrett hit 19 in 1944. Part of this reduction could be attributed to the temporary installation of what was called Greenberg Gardens in left field from 1947 through 1953. Placing the bullpen in front of the fence cut the distance down about 20 feet and was aimed at helping the home run exploits of Hank Greenberg and Ralph Kiner.

Now that Forbes Field is gone, maybe the triple domination of the Pirates should be viewed as a thing of the past. It has certainly been reduced in recent years, with the Kansas City Royals taking up the slack. That should not diminish the important historical significance of the great three-way association of the Pirates, the three-base hit, and Forbes Field. The following statistical tabulations should confirm that status.

100 or More Triples, Career, for Pittsburgh

Player	Triples	Years	Player	Triples	Years
Honus Wagner	231	18	Tommy Leach	137	14
Paul Waner	187	15	Arky Vaughan	116	11
Roberto Clemente	166	18	Jake Beckley	114	8
Pie Traynor	164	16	Lloyd Waner	112	16
Fred Clarke	155	15	Gus Suhr	112	10
Max Carey	148	17	Elmer Smith	100	7

20 or More Triples, Season, for Pittsburgh

Player	Triples	Season	Player	Triples	Season
Owen Wilson	36	1912	Jake Beckley	20	1891
Harry Davis	28	1897	Jake Stenzel	20	1894
James Williams	27	1899	Jake Beckley	20	1895
Hazen Cuyler	26	1925	Tommy Leach	20	1902
Elmer Smith	23	1893	Honus Wagner	20	1912
Adam Comorosky	23	1930	James Miller	20	1913
Honus Wagner	22	1900	Rabbit Maranville	20	1924
Paul Waner	22	1926	Lloyd Waner	20	1929

Inside-the-Park Home Runs: An Interim Report

Mil Chipp

In 1976 SABR launched a research project to gather information about what is now a rather rare baseball occurrence—the inside-the-park home run (IPH). Some of the questions raised at the outset of this project were rather basic: How many inside-the-park homers are being hit at the present time, and how does this compare with earlier eras? Who hits them—power hitters or fast runners, or a combination of both? How important a factor is the size and configuration of the ball park?

Not all of these questions have been answered in detail, but enough research results have been obtained to present an interim report. Fortunately this report can be made at a time when additional attention has been focused on inside-the-park homers because of the exploits of Willie Wilson of the Kansas City Royals. Wilson hit five homers within the grounds in 1979, the top season total in the past forty years, and by the end of 1982 he had accumulated a career total of ten, which appears to be the best in the past thirty years. Many of his IPHs have been hit in the vast interior of Kansas City's Municipal Stadium, and the club has taken pleasure recording the relatively large number hit there.

Some of the other major league clubs still do not tabulate IPHs

Willie Wilson

hit in their own parks, although cooperation with SABR in that regard is improving. Baltimore, for example, has records of all those hit by Oriole players or against Oriole pitchers since the club came (back) into the American League in 1954. The same holds true for the Minnesota Twins since 1961, and the Montreal Expos and San Diego Padres since 1969. The Detroit Tigers also have been keeping tabs on their IPHs for the past twenty years. Most other clubs have scattered information on this subject. These records, plus the research of SABR members, have given us a ball park estimate of how many IPHs have been hit in recent years.

To put the matter in proper perspective, we also did research on selected seasons back to 1900. We have no intention of going back further than that, because some parks in the nineteenth century had open areas in the outfield, making the IPH the typical home run rather than the home run hit out of the park. On the other hand, there were some balls hit over the fence in at least one park that were ground rule doubles. Ironically, by today's standards, home runs hit within the confines even as recently as 1910–15 were called by some reporters "real" or "bona fide" home runs. The implication was that those hit over the fence, particularly if it was a short-distance fence, were a little tainted in that the outfielder was robbed of a chance to play the ball.

This might be a good place to define an inside-the-park home run. Basically it is a drive that stays within the fences and is playable. It would include, for example, the rare instance where a fair ball might roll under the tarpaulin. It does not include cases where the ball might roll under an exit gate, bounce through a hole in the fence, or bounce over the outfield fence. Those were legitimate home runs—at least the bounce home run was until 1930—but we do not include those hits as IPHs because they ultimately become unplayable.

The number and percentage of IPHs have gradually declined since 1901, when about 35 percent were inside jobs. Of course, the home run totals were not very great in those days, with the combined figure for both leagues being 454 in 1901 and only 357 in 1902. Several new parks were built in the next fifteen years, and by 1915 the IPH percentage was reduced to less than 25 percent. With the advent of the lively ball in 1920, the number of four-baggers increased considerably, but the percentage and even the real numbers of IPHs continued to drop off. The percentage declined from 7–8 percent in 1930 to 3–4 percent in 1950.

With the near standardization of field dimensions as a result of the construction of new parks in the 1960s and 1970s, the percentage of IPHs went down to about 1 percent of the total. For example, in 1966, one of the recent seasons for which we have solid IPH data, there were 2,743 homers hit, of which 30 were inside jobs. In 1979 there were 3,433 round-trippers hit, including 31 IPHs.

To get a feel for how many IPHs were hit and where, we conducted surveys of certain seasons and parks. A big boost was received early in the project by the discovery of material left by the late Lee Allen at the Hall of Fame which included all the 360 IPHs hit by Cincinnati players from 1900 to 1955. Those were the years when the Reds played in League Park, Redland Field, and Crosley Field. This was essentially the same ball park, but it was altered considerably over the years. It was a haven for IPHs in the early years of this century, particularly in 1901, when 50 IPHs were hit there by the Reds and visiting clubs. That was a very high figure, and it has not been duplicated at any other park in one season. Sam Crawford, the great triple hitter, extended himself and hit 12 IPHs (out of a total of 16 homers) that season, which is a record.

Cincinnati IPHs went down considerably the next season as total NL home runs shrank to 98, the lowest figure in this century; team IPH figures ranged from 20 in 1909 to 7 in 1921. In 1931 no Cincinnati player hit a four-base blow within the grounds, and the numbers thereafter were very small. The fact that the Reds were one of the leading home run teams in the mid-1950s made no difference. In 1955 they hit a total of 181, but nary a one inside the park.

Some of the other parks and seasons checked were those of the Boston Red Sox, 1912; Boston Braves, 1915–27; Brooklyn Dodgers and New York Giants, 1907; New York Yankees, 1907 and 1923;

Pittsburgh Pirates, 1911, 1922–27, and 1945; and Washington Senators 1921–23 and 1936–37.

Braves Field in Boston was ideal for the IPH from the time of its opening in August 1915 to the start of the 1928 season, when it was altered drastically to aid the club's long-ball hitters. In those dozen years, the Braves easily had the largest playing field in the majors. Balls hit sharply to right center could roll 550 feet to the flagpole. In those twelve years, according to research conducted by Paul Doherty, only seven balls were hit out of the park. Another seven bounced into the stands or rolled under the gate, etc. All 209 of the others were IPHs. On April 29, 1922, the New York Giants hit four IPHs in one wind-swept game at Braves Field, two by George Kelly. As a visiting player, Rogers Hornsby hit eight IPHs there from 1916 to 1927. In 1928 the outfield fence was moved in considerably, and balls started to fly out of Braves Field. Unfortunately, the majority of them seemed to be hit by opposition players.

Pittsburgh's Forbes Field (1909–70) was a large park where relatively few homers were hit until after World War II. Many of the great triples hitters on that club, such as Tommy Leach, Honus Wagner, Owen Wilson, Max Carey, Pie Traynor, Kiki Cuyler, Paul Waner, and Arky Vaughan, also hit a fair number of IPHs in their respective eras. In 1925, the year that Cuyler hit 26 triples, he also hit eight IPHs, the best season total in at least the past sixty years. When Cuyler was traded to the Chicago Cubs after the 1927 season, his chances for a high career total of IPHs were sharply reduced. Wrigley Field was (and still is) one of those parks where it was extremely difficult to achieve four bases without hitting the ball into the stands.

Griffith Stadium in Washington was in many ways the Forbes Field of the American League. In 1945, for an extreme example, the Senators hit only one home run there, and it was an IPH by Joe Kuhel. It was a discouraging place for power hitters, except for the big muscle men like Ruth, Gehrig, Foxx, Greenberg, and Joe DiMaggio, all of whom could hit them out of almost any park. Sam Rice, who was 5'9" and weighed about 150 pounds, played nineteen seasons in Washington and never hit the ball into the stands at Griffith Stadium. His nine homers there were all within the grounds. That is not a record for that park, however, as teammate Buddy Myer hit all but one of his 14 IPHs in Griffith Stadium.

Rice also hit IPHs in other parks, including the first in Yankee Stadium on April 25, 1923. The "house that Ruth built" didn't have the squared-off, fairly even dimensions of spacious Griffith Stadium; it had an uneven configuration with a short right field that tapered to extremely deep in center. More that twenty IPHs were hit in the new park in its initial season, probably because the outfielders were a little uncertain how to play the garden. Babe Ruth, who had ten IPHs in his career, hit four at Yankee Stadium in 1923. On a career basis, Earle Combs hit the most as a Yankee, 23, and the most at Yankee Stadium, 18.

The Polo Grounds in New York was another park where plenty of home runs were hit into the stands, but a fair number were also hit inside the grounds. The right- and left-field foul lines were the shortest in the majors, and even a little guy like Rabbit Maranville could pull one in there; yet if a player could hit the ball past the center fielder, he had a good chance of making four bases before the ball could be retrieved. When parks like this were closed down, the number of IPHs was reduced.

The only other big playing field of the old days which is still in use is Comiskey Park in Chicago. Ironically, it has not been a favorite place for hitting IPHs, in spite of its size, because of its well-balanced configuration. On the other hand, the lines of Baker Bowl in Philadelphia, usually referred to as a bandbox, were not symmetrical, and a batter occasionally could connect for a homer there inside the grounds. In fact, Kiki Cuyler hit two in one game at Baker Bowl on August 28, 1925, in the first and eighth innings.

Now that we've described the types of parks where IPHs can be hit most frequently, we should identify what type of player hits them most frequently, the slugger or the fast runner. We probably gave away the answer at the beginning when we noted that Willie Wilson hit five IPHs in 1979. With 83 stolen bases to his credit that season, Wilson, it is safe to say (in spite of his sturdy build), gets his extra-base hits primarily because of his legs rather than his bat. Wilson hit only one ball into the stands in 1979 and only three out of 13 for his career.

We found that IPHs are essentially an extension of the three-base hit. If a player hits a sizable number of triples, is a fast runner, and plays his home games in a large park, there is a good chance that he has hit a number of home runs inside the lot. Another factor that could be added to the list is the size of the player. If he is small in addition to being fast and a sharp hitter, that enhances the possibility that many of his home runs, even if he hit just a small number, were IPHs.

Three historical examples are Tommy Leach, Rabbit Maranville, and Sam Rice. Leach, the diminutive outfielder-third baseman for the Pirates in the first decade of this century, led the NL in home runs in 1902 with only six and was a contender the next year with seven. In

1903 he hit all seven inside the park, including two in one game. Leach hit 62 homers in his career, and 48 were IPHs, including four grand slams. When Leach hit the last home run of his career, for the Cubs against the Cards in St. Louis on October 4, 1914, the St. Louis reporter covering the game marveled at the tremendous speed and spirit of the aging star, as he scored standing up just ahead of the relay throw.

Maranville, who was just getting established at short for the Braves as Leach was fading out, was 5'5" and 155 pounds, an inch or so shorter than Leach but five pounds heavier. He was probably not as fast as Leach, but he was a colorful, aggressive little player. He was not much of a hitter—he connected for only 28 homers—but 22 of them were IPHs, including two in one game. Rice, discussed earlier, hit a total of 34 home runs, and a check of each one has revealed that 21 were IPHs. Another little guy, Miller Huggins, hit all nine of his lifetime homers inside the grounds.

The total number of four-baggers a player hits has no bearing whatsoever on how many he hits inside the park. To use two extreme examples, Tommy Thevenow, NL infielder between 1924 and 1938, hit two homers in his career of 1,229 games, and both were IPHs. (He also hit one IPH in the 1928 World Series, when his drive got by Babe Ruth.) Ted Williams hit 521 home runs in his career and only one was IPH. That one was on Friday, the 13th of September, 1946, when Ted took advantage of the Boudreau shift in the pennant-clinching 1–0 victory over Cleveland. He hit the ball to left field, which was practically deserted.

In the tabulation of more than 1,800 inside-the-park homers since 1900, we have noted many strange happenings involving the crazy caroms, outfield collisions, and even a ball that rolled up the sleeve of a warm-up jacket. Obviously, Williams's IPH was not the most unusual. In fact, in a game 35 years before, Stuffy McInnis of the A's caught the Red Sox outfielders even more out of position than Williams did the Indians. At the beginning of the seventh inning on June 27, 1911, McInnis swung at a warm-up pitch from Boston hurler Ed Karger. It went sailing into the outfield, but Tris Speaker and his fellow gardeners were not even out there yet. McInnis ran around the bases and was credited with a home run by Umpire Ben Egan, who upheld American League President Ban Johnson's new rule that there would be no warm-up pitches before the start of an inning.

Who has hit the most IPHs on a career and season basis? This answer really should be broken down by decades or at least by eras, because the number decreases in each period since 1900. In the deadball era of 1900–19, Sam Crawford hit 50 for his career, including 12 for

Cincinnati in 1901. Tommy Leach had a career total of 48, counting 3 he hit in 1899. Ty Cobb, in his long career from 1905 to 1928, hit 47 IPHs, but only six after 1918. By contrast, he hit 9 in the one season of 1909.

Edd Roush hit 29 IPHs, including 4 in the Federal League in 1914–15, over a career that ran to 1931. Kiki Cuyler had the best season mark for a player in that period, with 8 in 1925. Rogers Hornsby hit at least 28 in a long career that finally wound up in 1937. However, the great majority were hit in his early years. In a review not yet complete, not one IPH was found for him in Sportsman's Park, where he hit most of his round-trippers. Ben Chapman closed out his playing days in 1945 with 15 IPHs for his career. No significant season totals were achieved in that period, or at least research has not uncovered anything better than the four IPHs hit by Chapman, the aggressive speedster with the Yankees, in 1935. The career totals also were insignificant in the 1940s, 1950s, and 1960s. All of Richie Ashburn's 29 homers were checked, and eight were IPHs. Incomplete reviews revealed eight for Willie Mays and Roberto Clemente and nine for Lou Brock. Hence, Willie Wilson appears to be the modern career leader with ten. Among active players, teammate Amos Otis is next, with six.

Complete IPH data are available on only a couple dozen outstanding players. Some of these are of the recent period, including active stars, and the results are available primarily because certain clubs or individuals have been compiling this information. On old-time players such as Sam Crawford, Edd Roush, and Babe Ruth, curiosity became so great after noting encouraging preliminary information that each home run was checked. This wasn't as big a job with Ruth as might be expected, because SABR member Al Kermisch had already gone through most of his home runs for other purposes.

In the case of Crawford, he had done so well with Cincinnati with 21 IPHs in only three years, 1900–02, that the question of how he did with Detroit was begging to be answered. A very strong line drive hitter who also ran the bases well, Crawford racked up an additional 29 IPHs while playing for the Tigers in spacious Bennett Field (later Navin Field) in the deadball era of 1903–17.

If Crawford could hit that many with Detroit (we reasoned), what about teammate Ty Cobb, who was a more aggressive base runner and an excellent place hitter (with hands a couple of inches apart on the bat)? This theory was well founded and research of every one of his home runs revealed that he hit 47 IPHs for the Tigers, best in the AL. Research revealed also that on several occasions the Tiger Terror swelled his total by making a mad dash for home when the opposition outfielders assumed he was going to stop at third.

If Babe Ruth hit ten of his 714 homers within the grounds, how many IPHs did Henry Aaron hit? An incomplete review failed to turn up any for Hammerin' Hank. The question was put to him on an impromptu basis at the baseball meetings in Florida in December 1981, and he said he did not recall hitting any inside-the-park home runs. He then laughed and said he didn't enjoy running that hard.

There are several great long-ball hitters, in addition to Aaron, for whom we currently have no IPH. They include Frank Robinson, Frank Howard, Rocky Colavito, Ralph Kiner, Johnny Mize, Yogi Berra, Tony Perez, Lee May, and Roy Sievers.

There follows a list of the better-known players for whom we have complete IPH data, followed by a list of players with incomplete numbers. Finally this interim report concludes with a list of those players who have hit two IPHs in one game since 1900.

Complete Career IPHs (regular season)		Incomplete IPHs	
Richie Ashburn	8	Joe Adcock	5
Ernie Banks	2	Richie Allen	7
Johnny Bench	1	Luis Aparicio	5
George Brett	3	Lou Brock	9
Max Carey	26	Roberto Clemente	8
Rod Carew	1	Eddie Collins	6
Ben Chapman	15	Joe Cronin	2
Ty Cobb	47	Kiki Cuyler	16
Earle Combs	23	Willie Davis	6
Sam Crawford	50	Joe DiMaggio	2
Lou Gehrig	6	Jimmie Foxx	2
Gil Hodges	2	Frank Frisch	7
Harmon Killebrew	1	Hank Greenberg	2
Dave Kingman	1	Goose Goslin	7
Tommy Leach	48	Babe Herman	4
Mickey Mantle	6	Rogers Hornsby	28
Rabbit Maranville	22	Reggie Jackson	4
Willie McCovey	1	Al Kaline	1
Tony Oliva	3	Roger Maris	3
Amos Otis	6	Pepper Martin	1
Boog Powell	1	Eddie Mathews	1
Sam Rice	21	Willie Mays	8

Complete Career IPHs
(regular season)

Brooks Robinson	0
Pete Rose	2
Edd Roush	29
Babe Ruth	10
Duke Snider	2
Honus Wagner	45
Ted Williams	1
Owen Wilson	31
Willie Wilson	10
Carl Yastrzemski	3

Incomplete IPHs

Bob Meusel	11
Stan Musial	3
Melvin Ott	1
Jackie Robinson	1
Mike Schmidt	2
Al Simmons	1
George Sisler	5
Tris Speaker	16
Willie Stargell	3
Bill Terry	8
Pie Traynor	15
Paul Waner	5
Lloyd Waner	9
Billy Williams	4
Hack Wilson	1

Two IPHs in Same Game (post-1900)

Date	Player, Teams, Parks	Innings
July 8, 1900	Jesse Burkett, Cardinals (vs. Pirates) at St. Louis	3, 7
July 8, 1901	George Davis, Giants (vs. Reds) at Cincinnati	1, 9
Aug. 5, 1901	Topsy Hartsel, Cubs (vs. Reds) at Cincinnati	1, 5
Apr. 25, 1902	Homer Smoot, Cardinals (vs. Reds) at Cincinnati	1, 5
Apr. 28, 1902	Monte Cross, Athletics (vs. Senators) at Washington	2, 9
May 30, 1902 (1)*	Roger Bresnahan, Orioles (vs. Indians) at Baltimore	6, 7
May 4, 1903	Hobe Ferris, Red Sox (vs. Senators) at Boston	3, 6
May 21, 1903	Tommy Leach, Pirates (vs. Dodgers) at Brooklyn	5, 7
May 12, 1904	Danny Hoffman, Athletics (vs. White Sox) at Philadelphia	1, 7
June 6, 1904	Roger Bresnahan, Giants (vs. Pirates) at New York	1, 3
Aug. 24, 1904	Willie Keeler, Yankees (vs. Browns) at New York	3, 8
May 8, 1906	Chief Bender, Athletics (vs. Red Sox) at Boston	7, 9
Aug. 22, 1907	Heinie Wagner, Red Sox (vs. Tigers) at Detroit	2, 7
July 15, 1909 (2)	Ty Cobb, Tigers (vs. Senators) at Detroit	1, 5
Sept. 2, 1911 (2)	Bill McKechnie, Pirates (vs. Cardinals) at Pittsburgh	3, 7
July 2, 1912	Larry Gardner, Red Sox (vs. Yankees) at Boston	2, 8
Aug. 14, 1912	Stuffy McInnis, Athletics (vs. Indians) at Philadelphia	1, 7
May 1, 1913	Casey Stengel, Dodgers (vs. Braves) at Brooklyn	1, 2
Aug. 4, 1913	George Cutshaw, Dodgers (vs. Cubs) at Chicago	1, 7
Aug. 16, 1913 (2)	Bob Fisher, Dodgers (vs. Cardinals) at Brooklyn	3, 8

(Continued)

Two IPHs in Same Game (post-1900)

Date	Player, Teams, Parks	Innings
Oct. 4, 1913	Hal Janvrin, Red Sox (vs. Senators) at Washington	2, 9
Aug. 31, 1914	Jack Fournier, White Sox (vs. Senators) at Washington	8, 10
July 1, 1919	Rabbit Maranville, Braves (vs. Phillies) at Boston	2, 4
Sept. 20, 1920	Maurice Rath, Reds (vs. Giants) at New York	6, 7
Apr. 29, 1922	George Kelly, Giants (vs. Braves) at Boston	4, 9
Aug. 28, 1925	Kiki Cuyler, Pirates (vs. Phillies) at Philadelphia	1, 8
Sept. 22, 1925 (1)	Ben Paschal, Yankees (vs. White Sox) at New York	4, 8
July 2, 1930 (2)	Carl Reynolds, White Sox (vs. Yankees) at New York	1, 3
July 9, 1932 (2)	Ben Chapman, Yankees (vs. Tigers) at New York	2, 6
Aug. 16, 1939 (1)	Terry Moore, Cardinals (vs. Pirates) at Pittsburgh	7, 9
Aug. 16, 1950	Henry Thompson, Giants (vs. Dodgers) at New York	1, 7
July 31, 1972	Richie Allen, White Sox (vs. Twins) at Minnesota	1, 5

* Numbers in parentheses indicate first or second game of a doubleheader

In a historic game played in rural Iowa in the 1890s the batter hit a long drive which rolled almost to the fence in deep center field. There a pig was rooting in the grass, and before the center fielder could recover the ball, the pig had eaten it. In the meantime the batter rounded the bases with baseball's first inside-the-pork home run.

They Never Played in the Minors

Ted DiTullio

With the nation's colleges playing a greater role in the training of players for the major leagues, it is possible that we may see an increase in the number of stars who bypass the minor leagues on the way up. And since the days have passed when big leaguers go down to the minors toward the close of their careers, we may have some new members of the rather small group of ten-year players who never participated in a minor league game.

Since Jim "Catfish" Hunter retired after the 1979 season, Dave Winfield of the Yankees is the only ten-year player in the majors who has been able to avoid the bush league experience. Hunter was originally assigned by Kansas City to the Daytona Beach club in 1965, but he was placed on the disabled list because of a hunting accident and never got into a game. Winfield came right up to the Padres from the University of Minnesota. Another Collegian, Bob Horner, came up directly from Arizona State to the Atlanta Braves in 1978. Early in the 1980 season he was ordered down to the Richmond club to get in shape; however, he successfully resisted that demotion.

Research has revealed that there have been 21 players who spent at least ten years in the majors without ever playing a game in the minors. We have not gone back before 1900, because the few minor leagues then in existence reduce the significance of this survey. More than half the "pure" major leaguers were pitchers, starting with Eddie Plank in 1901. He got his baseball experience at Gettysburg College before Connie Mack brought him to the Athletics. Jack Coombs, another of Mack's hurlers, came up from Colby College in 1906.

An even more famous pitcher is not on the list because of a handful of token appearances. This is Walter Johnson who hurled 21 years for the Washington Senators before retiring after the 1927 season. He managed Newark in the International League in 1928, and on Walter Johnson Day in that city on June 23 he went to the mound to face the first Buffalo batter, Maurice Archdeacon. The Big Train walked him and then returned to the dugout. That was a token appearance on the mound, but Johnson also appeared in six games as a pinch hitter that season.

Another player whose published record would seem to make him eligible for the major-league-only list is Frank Chance, who played from 1898 to 1914 with the Chicago Cubs and, briefly, with the New York Yankees. However, while managing the Los Angeles club in the Pacific Coast League in 1916 he made several brief appearances in the lineup. This wasn't noted until his centennial in 1977, when the SABR Minor League Committee called attention to it.

On the other hand, Ernie Banks is included in the list even though he played, not in the minors, but with the Kansas City Monarchs of the Negro American League in the period 1950–53.

The two who played longest in the majors without a minor league game to mar their records are Mel Ott, with the New York Giants, 1926–47, and Al Kaline, with the Detroit Tigers, 1953–74, each playing 22 years with one club. Next in the seniority line are Eppa Rixey and Ted Lyons, both with 21 years in the majors. Rixey came up from the University of Virginia and Lyons from Baylor University.

Only about one-half of the players on the accompanying list had college backgrounds. A number of others were signed while very young, some as "bonus babies" after World War II. Mel Ott, Bob Feller, and Eddie Yost started in the majors when they were seventeen; Johnny Antonelli and Al Kaline were eighteen.

Ten-Year Men Who Never Played in the Minors

Years	Player, Position(s)	Period
22	Melvin Ott, OF	1926–47
22	Al Kaline, OF	1953–74
21	Eppa Rixey, P	1912–33
21	Ted Lyons, P	1923–46
19	Tom Zachary, P	1918–36
19	Frank Frisch, 2B-3B	1919–37
19	Ernie Banks, SS-1B	1953–71
18	Bob Feller, P	1936–56
18	Eddie Yost, 3B	1944–62
17	Eddie Plank, P	1901–17
17	Danny MacFayden, P	1926–43
15	Jack Coombs, P	1906–20
15	Catfish Hunter, P	1965–79
14	Dick Groat, SS	1952–67
13	Ethan Allen, OF	1926–38
13	Billy O'Dell, P	1954–67
12	John Antonelli, P	1948–61
12	Sandy Koufax, P	1955–66
11	Jack Barry, SS	1908–19
11	Milt Gaston, P	1924–34
10	Dave Winfield, OF	1973–

When Joe Bauman
Hit 72 Home Runs
Bart Ripp

Some places where only baseball is played are called fields, like Wrigley. Others are parks, as in Fenway. In Roswell, New Mexico, it's a hybrid: Park Field.

Hank Aaron and Babe Ruth never played at Park Field. Roger Maris and Mickey Mantle never were cheered there. George Foster and Jim Rice have never hit home runs at Park Field. Joe Bauman did.

Where the box seats sat and the clubhouses stood at Park Field, there are now just slabs of concrete, with rabbit brush and blazing star sprouting through the cracks. The left field scoreboard is no more. There used to be a wooden fence around the outfield, but it's gone, too, replaced by chicken wire.

Joe Bauman was a 6′ 5″, 235-pound left-handed hitter, with an uppercut swing that propelled baseballs over the right-field wall, just 329 feet from home plate at Park Field. A quarter century ago, Joe Bauman accomplished something that had never been done in professional baseball, something that has not been equaled since.

Joe Bauman hit 72 home runs in one season.

Zooming into the record books for the Roswell Rockets in the old Class C Longhorn League in 1954, Bauman, then thirty-two, not only hit a home run once every 6.9 at bats, he led the league with a .400 batting average, 225 runs batted in, 456 total bases, and 150 walks and played first base in all 138 of his club's games. Bauman's .916 slugging percentage was 69 points better than Ruth's best.

Bauman is now the "Sultan of Schlitz" in Roswell, managing a beer distributorship for Albuquerque's Pete Matteucci. In the spring of 1980, Joe, who was then fifty-eight, took time to rock in his office chair, left hand behind his head, smoke L&M cigarettes, and remember a nine-year pro career in which he hit 337 home runs.

Bauman grew up in Oklahoma City, signed his first professional contract with Little Rock in 1941, served in the Navy as a landlocked ballplayer at Norman, Oklahoma, then played three more years professionally. Except for one game with Milwaukee in Triple A, he never played at a higher classification than Class A ball. The property of the Boston Braves in 1948, Bauman quit the Hartford club after that season to run a Texaco gas station in Elk City, Oklahoma. For the next three years, he changed oil and hit homers for the Elk City Elks semipro team.

"Boston had called me that winter of '52 and wanted me to go play for the Atlanta Crackers in double-A," Bauman said. "But this doctor, I can't recall his name now, he wanted me to play for Artesia in the Longhorn League.

"Hell, I didn't know they had baseball out there. Anyhow, this doctor wanted to buy my contract from Boston, and he did. I don't know what he got, maybe a dollar bill or a jock strap. But he came back and we made the deal on the driveway of my service station. So, I came out to Artesia and played two years for the Drillers."

Bauman drilled 50 homers in 1952, a league-record 53 in 1953. He then bought his own release from Artesia and moved up Route 285 to Roswell.

"I was ready to move on," Bauman said. "I always did like Roswell. Liked this part of the country after I got acquainted."

Joe liked western skies, he liked seeing rabbits race tumbleweeds across the plains, and most of all he liked the ten-foot-high whitewashed wooden fence 329 feet from the batter's box at Park Field. He bought a gas station and renamed it Joe Bauman's Texaco Service.

When the Rockets were home, Bauman pumped gas during the day, then pumped home runs out of Park Field at night.

By September 1, 1954, Bauman had hit 64 home runs in 131 games. The pro record was 69, set by Joe Hauser for Minneapolis in 1933 and tied by Bob Crues for Amarillo in 1948.

On the night of September 1, there were 524 fans at Park Field to see Roswell beat Sweetwater 15–9. Joe hit four home runs. He also doubled, and his box score line for the evening read:

7—5—5—10

In the *Roswell Daily Record,* Buck Lanier's column, "Riding Herd on Sports," stated, "The eyes of the United States are on Roswell at present. It isn't too often that the activities of a Class C league are pegged on the national Associated Press trunk wires as prime material. . . . If Joe does break it, pictures of him will be on the sports pages of every paper in the U.S." Below Buck's column was a Worley Auto Sales ad—you could buy a new Ford Mainliner, two-door, six-cylinder, for $1,645.

"I had to have something like that," Bauman says, sitting in the deserted grandstand at Park Field. "I wasn't really trying for home runs, but after I hit those four, I really got conscious of the durned record. It went from an impossibility to a possibility in one night."

The next night, Bauman went from No. 4 in Rocket manager Pat Stasey's lineup to the leadoff spot, to get more times at bat. Bauman had two doubles, a single, and a sacrifice fly. But Stasey, also Roswell's third baseman, inserted himself into the seemingly magic cleanup slot and belted three home runs.

The evening of September 3 was Bauman's last home game, with four more left on the road. "The pressure really mounted then," said Bauman, watching the wind blow old newspapers against the mesh fence at Park Field. "There were four or five photographers shooting every time I went up to the plate. There were guys there from *Life* and *Sports Illustrated,* plus the local boys. They'd be snapping while I was hitting. It's bound to affect you, and it did me."

Lanier's game story the next day led with: "It couldn't have happened to a nicer guy," ending "altogether, it was a great night." In between, Buck managed to mention Bauman's three-run homer that sailed over the right-field wall in the eighth inning, which, incidentally, beat Midland 7–4. It was Bauman's sixty-ninth home run, tying the pro record. On the *Roswell Daily Record* sports page was a State TV ad for a "Precision Special Scintillator . . . it detects uranium deposits 100 times easier!" It cost $299.50.

The Rockets bused to Big Spring, Texas, and Bauman didn't hit a home run in either of the next two games.

"They pitched around me in Big Spring," Bauman says. "The fans in their own damn ball park even got riled. So, we go down to Artesia, and their manager, Jim Adair, told me before the game that he's heard what happened in Big Spring. 'We're not gonna walk you,' he told me."

It was Sunday, September 5, a doubleheader between Roswell and the Artesia NuMexers on the final day of the regular season. In the first inning of the first game, Bauman hit No. 70 to set the record. The home run was smote off Jose Galardo, who thus joined the gopher genre that includes Tom Zachary, Tracy Stallard, and Al Downing.

Bauman hit two more home runs in the second game, one off John Goodell and No. 72 off Frank Galardo, uncle of Jose. There was no score mentioned in the *Daily Record* of that first game, but Roswell numbed the NuMexers, 17–0 in the nightcap.

"It was the ultimate thrill as far as I was concerned," Bauman says of home run No. 70. "Artesia had a big ball park—350 or 60 feet down the right-field line, and the wind blew in against you."

Joe's quote in the next afternoon's *Daily Record* was: "No. 70 was getting the piano stool off my back. No. 69 was the piano." At the bottom of that page, the Big T Service Station, perhaps sensing the free publicity its competitor Bauman was reaping, took out an ad for gasoline costing 25.5 cents a gallon. The ad's clever copy proclaimed: "No tricky pills added, no horse-feathers, just plain, high grade gasoline."

On the following Sunday, September 12, the *Daily Record* reported that Carlsbad's Potashers had eliminated Roswell from the league play-offs. Joe took out a three-column ad on the sports page and thanked local merchants and fans for their support. A photo showed Joe signing autographs for three boys wearing baseball caps. One boy studied the ball Joe had just signed, another looked up in awe at the slugger, while the third gazed at the right-field wall, maybe imagining all those home runs sailing over it.

There was, and still is, a rodeo grounds beyond the right-field wall. Joe's home runs occasionally would splat into the ring; one might say he was swinging for bull's-eyes.

"It was easy to hit balls out here, in a sense," Bauman says, glancing at the right-field wall. "The ball carries so good here. Plus we got a free ham for every home run. We had the best-fed ballclub in the country."

Bauman didn't even get a salary raise the next season. He slumped to a mere 46 home runs and 132 RBIs in 1955. Slowed by injuries in 1956, he called it a career in midseason after hitting 17 round-trippers in 52 games.

Hillerich & Bradsby, the people who make Louisville Sluggers, took the bat Bauman bombed No. 70 with and used it in a travel-ing bat show. He received a black bat, with gold engraving, in return.

"I just look at that year as what it was. Nothing earthshattering,"

Bauman says. "I didn't get any real money out of it. Just a wonderful feeling. I sit around some nights, have a beer, and get to thinking about the funny little things that happened. The home runs. The people. It seems like a long time ago. It reminds me how slow the world runs."

Just How Fast Was Cool Papa Bell?

Just how fast was Cool Papa Bell? Well, listen to the master storyteller, Satchel Paige. "One day, when I was pitching to Cool, he drilled one right through my legs and was hit in the back by his own ground ball when he slid into second."

Or how about this? Satchel again. "Bell was so fast that he could turn out the light and jump in bed before it got dark." Paige amused people with this claim for nearly 40 years, but of course nobody really believed him.

Finally, at the 1981 Negro Baseball Reunion in Ashland, Kentucky, Cool Papa assured everyone that his friend was telling the truth. "During the 1937 winter season, Satchel and I roomed together in California. One night, before he got back, I turned out the light, but it didn't go off right away. There was a delay of about three seconds between the time I flipped the switch and the time the light went out. Must of been a short or something.

"I thought to myself, here's a chance to turn the tables on ol' Satch. He was always playing tricks on everybody else, you know. Anyway, when he came back to the room, I said, 'Hey, Satch, I'm pretty fast, right?' 'You're the fastest,' he said.

"Well, you ain't seen nothin' yet,' I told him. 'Why, I'm so fast, I can turn out the light and be in bed before the room gets dark.' 'Sure, Cool. Sure you can,' he said.

"I told him to just sit down and watch. I turned off the light, jumped in bed, and pulled the covers up to my chin. Then the light went out.

"It was the only time I ever saw Satchel speechless. Anyway, he was telling the truth all these years."

Jim Bankes

Baseball Brothers
Larry Amman

The start of the 1979 season served as a good reminder of the interesting and significant role brothers have played in major league baseball. First there was Jesus Alou, back for his 15th season in the big time. This gave the three Alou brothers (Felipe, 17 years, and Matty, 15 years) a record 47 man-years in the majors.

Then there was Gaylord Perry, forty years old at the time, a Cy Young Award winner like his brother Jim, who was adding to the pitching laurels of baseball's best family pitching duo. Another forty-year-old starting the 1979 season was Phil Niekro, who was pitching as hard as ever but was being upstaged a little by his kid brother Joe, who was finally carrying his share of the family load.

Moreover, on April 7, 1979, Ken Forsch of Houston pitched a no-hit, no-run game against Atlanta to duplicate the no-hitter hurled by his brother Bob of the Cardinals against the Phils on April 16, 1978. Although there have been several cases of one brother achieving this milestone—such as Frank Pfeffer, Jesse Barnes, Paul Dean, Phil Niekro, and Gaylord Perry—it marked the first time that two brothers had hurled no-hitters.

And on May 31, Pat Underwood made his major league debut pitching for Detroit against Toronto. On the mound for the Blue Jays

Jesus, Matty, and Felipe Alou, who played briefly together in the San Francisco Giants' outfield on September 15, 1963

was his older brother, Tom. They both hurled zeros for seven innings, but Pat won out 1–0 with relief help in the ninth. This was one of the relatively few cases where pitching brothers faced each other in a regulation game. Less unusual was the case of brothers Mickey and Dick Mahler pitching in the same game for the Atlanta Braves on April 20 and again on May 7, 1979.

With this introduction, let us go back all the way to the Wright Brothers—in this case George, Harry, and Sam—to review specific aspects of brother combinations. Since 1876 there have been more than 275 brother combinations as players. There has been one family group of five players (the Delahantys), one of four (the O'Neills), thirteen of three members, and the remainder of two. The latter group includes six sets of twins who made it to the big time.

In a list of 275-plus combinations, it is easy to see that in many cases neither brother made much of a contribution. In other cases, the contribution was very one-sided. Most baseball fans can quickly pick out the stars among such brothers as Christy and Henry Mathewson, Joe and Johnny Evers, Al and Honus Wagner, Mack and Zack Wheat, and Bill and George Dickey.

Our primary concern here is on brothers where more than one made a significant contribution and more specifically where brothers compiled impressive combined statistics. One way to get a handle on this subject is to treat separately the pitcher–catcher combinations, the brothers who were both pitchers, and the brothers who were non-pitchers.

This may tend to downgrade somewhat those combinations where one brother was a pitcher and the other an infielder or outfielder. Examples include Jesse and Lee Tannehill and Ken and George Brett; but Lee, with a .220 lifetime batting average, and Ken, with a 78–81 lifetime won–lost record, really have not contributed that much. Now, if Wild Bill Donovan and Patsy Donovan had been brothers, the combined credentials would be pretty impressive. However, the SABR Biographical Research Committee has reaffirmed that Bill and Patsy were *not* brothers. While we are on that subject, we should note that the committee also has come up with enough demographic data to show that Chick Stahl and Jake Stahl were *not* brothers.

Brother Batteries

There have been fifteen brother batteries on the same major league team since 1876. A number of these made little more than token appearances, but we will cite the full list for the record. The pitcher is listed first.

Will and Deacon Jim White, Boston (NL), 1877; Cincinnati (NL), 1878–79
Ed and Bill Dugan, Richmond (AA), 1884
Pete and Fred Wood, Buffalo (NL), 1885
Dick and Bill Conway, Baltimore (AA), 1886
John and Buck Ewing, New York (PL), 1890; New York (NL), 1891
Mike and John O'Neill, St. Louis (NL), 1902–03
Tom and Homer Thompson, New York (AL), 1912
George and Fred Tyler, Boston (NL), 1914
Milt and Alex Gaston, Boston (AL), 1929
Wes and Rick Ferrell, Boston (AL), 1934–37; Washington (AL), 1937–38
Mort and Walker Cooper, St. Louis (NL), 1940–45; New York (NL), 1947
Elmer and Johnny Riddle, Cincinnati (NL), 1941, 1944–45; Pittsburgh (NL), 1948
Bobby and Billy Shantz, Philadelphia (AL), 1954; Kansas City (AL), 1955; New York (AL), 1960
Jim and Ed Bailey, Cincinnati (NL), 1959
Larry and Norm Sherry, Los Angeles (NL), 1959–62

Not on the list, surprisingly, are the twins Claude and Clarence Jonnard, pitcher and catcher, respectively, who each spent six years in the majors in the 1920s but who never played on the same team. Nor did the three Sadowski brothers—pitchers Ted and Bob and catcher Eddie—ever get together in the 1960s.

The Ferrells and Coopers were easily the top brother batteries in major league history. This is not meant to downgrade the Whites. Will White was almost a one-man mound staff for the Red Stockings in 1879 when he started a record 75 games and completed all of them. Actually, Deacon Jim caught only 59 of those games because he also played in the outfield and at first base. In fact, Jim caught no games in 1880 and after that spent much of his time at third base. Consequently, they were not a battery very long. The Ewings also might have developed into a good battery, but pitcher John hurt his arm in 1891 while leading the NL with a 21–8 won–lost record. He never pitched again.

Wes Ferrell six times won 20 or more games in a season, and his brother Rick caught more games, 1,806, than any other backstop in the AL. They were together five years, first with the Red Sox and then with the Senators, to whom they were traded midway in the 1937 season They had a couple of interesting experiences while they were playing for different teams. On April 29, 1931, Wes pitched a no-hitter for the Indians over the Browns. Rick was the St. Louis catcher, and he smacked a ball off his brother which some thought was a hit. However, it was officially ruled an error, and Wes had his no-hitter.

Ironically, Wes the pitcher hit more lifetime home runs (38) than Rick the catcher did in his long career (28). However, on July 19, 1933, when Rick was with the Red Sox, he hit a four-bagger off Wes, who was pitching for the Indians. This was one of the rare instances when one brother connected off another. It also happened to be one of those unusual games where each brother connected, as Wes belted one off Henry Johnson.

Mort and Walker Cooper of the St. Louis Cardinals had three exceptional years together as pitcher and catcher—1942–43–44. They were World Series batteries on all three teams. They were NL All-Star Game batteries in 1942 and 1943, and in 1943 and 1944 Walker was the catcher and Mort one of three pitchers on the *Sporting News* Annual All-Star Major League Teams. It is hard to imagine a higher level of attainment for two brothers than that.

Pitching Brothers

There have been more than sixty pitching brothers in the majors since 1876. We have to generalize on the exact number because some of those who pitched, such as the twins Eddie and Johnny O'Brien, also played at other positions. A remarkable number pitched on the same teams, if for ever so brief a period. They are listed below:

Larry and Mike Corcoran, Chicago (NL), 1884
Matt and Mike Kilroy, Baltimore (AA), 1888
John and Arthur Clarkson, Boston (NL), 1892
Frank and John Foreman, Cincinnati (NL), 1896
Christy and Henry Mathewson, New York (NL), 1906–07
Harry and Howard Camnitz, Pittsburgh (NL), 1909
Grover and Louis Lowdermilk, St. Louis (NL), 1911
Vean and Dave Gregg, Cleveland (AL), 1913
Jesse and Virgil Barnes, New York (NL), 1919–23
Johnny and Phil Morrison, Pittsburgh (NL), 1921
Ted and Homer Blankenship, Chicago (AL), 1922–23
Dizzy and Paul Dean, St. Louis (NL), 1934–37
Alex and Walter Kellner, Philadelphia (AL), 1952–53
Eddie and Johnny O'Brien, Pittsburgh (NL), 1957
Lindy and Von McDaniel, St. Louis (NL), 1957–58
Dennis and Dave Bennett, Philadelphia (NL), 1964
Phil and Joe Niekro, Atlanta (NL), 1973–74
Jim and Gaylord Perry, Cleveland (AL), 1974–75
Paul and Rick Reuschel, Chicago (NL), 1975–78
Mickey and Dick Mahler, Atlanta (NL), 1979

Many of these brothers actually worked in the same game, one as a starter and the other in relief. This includes the Mathewsons, Barneses, Deans, O'Briens, McDanielses, Reuschels, Niekros, and Mahlers. Jesse and Virgil Barnes did this on several occasions, with Virgil usually in relief. Rogers Hornsby did not discriminate between them, at least on one occasion. In a game between the Cards and Giants on September 24, 1922, Hornsby completed a record NL home run year by hitting his 41st off Jesse and his 42nd off Virgil.

Rick Reuschel, as the starter, and Paul Reuschel, as the reliever, pitched in the same game for the Cubs on many different occasions from 1975 to 1978. The starter and the relief man strongly resembled each other in build, and the casual fan had to be reminded which one of the huge hurlers was on the mound. Their most impressive joint effort came on August 21, 1975, when they beat the Dodgers 7–0. Rick went six and one-third, and Paul finished out the shutout, the first ever by two brothers.

For two brothers pitching on the same club, primary recognition must go to Dizzy and Paul (Daffy) Dean for their efforts in 1934–35. Paul won 19 each season, while Diz was overpowering with 30 and 28 victories. On September 21, 1934, with the Cardinals shutting out the Dodgers twice, Diz took the opener 13–0, giving up only three hits. In the nightcap, Paul pitched a no-hitter, winning 3–0. That fall in the World Series, they each won two games over the Tigers.

The list of brothers pitching against each other is much shorter. Over the years there has been a natural reluctance to go head to head as starting hurlers. Actually that didn't happen until major league baseball was nearly fifty years old.

As noted in the list above, the Foreman brothers were together on the Cincinnati team in 1896. However, at the start of the season, John (Brownie) Foreman pitched briefly for Pittsburgh. In fact, on April 18, 1896, he pitched against Cincinnati and was leading 8–6 when he was knocked out in the seventh inning. Frank Foreman came in to pitch the ninth for the Reds, who pulled out the victory. Actually, they were not in the game at the same time.

On September 4, 1916, in the first game of a Labor Day doubleheader, Stan Coveleski started for Cleveland but was bombed out in two-thirds of an inning by Detroit. In the seventh the Tigers brought in Harry Coveleski, who also pitched two-thirds of an inning and gave up no runs. The Coveleski boys never wanted to face each other, and that was the closest they came to a confrontation.

The above list shows that the Barnes brothers pitched together on the Giants in 1919–23. In 1923 Jesse was traded to Boston and two years later to Brooklyn. From 1923 to 1927 Jesse and Virgil met ten times in NL games, five times as starters and five in relief. There were no spectacular contests; in fact, they never pitched complete games against each other. The closest was on June 25, 1926, when Jesse of the Dodgers beat Virgil of the Giants 7–4, with the latter leaving for a pinch hitter after seven. In these games, Jesse won five and lost three. Virgil was three and four.

The Niekro brothers have faced each other nine times, and these have been more interesting games. Phil, with Atlanta, won the opener 8–3 on July 4, 1967, when Joe was a rookie with the Cubs. On April 23, 1968, Joe came out on top, 10–4. After being traded to San Diego, Joe beat his older brother 1–0 in a great mound duel on July 13, 1969. Phil came back to win 10–4 on September 26, 1969. Joe then moved to the AL for three years before joining Phil in Atlanta in 1973–74. In

1975 Joe moved to Houston, where he next met Phil on May 29, 1976. Joe won this one 4–3 and had the distinction of hitting his first major league home run off his brother. Phil, laboring hard to win his 20th game in 1978, came up against Joe on September 26. It was a bitter disappointment to Atlanta fans as Joe beat him 2–0 with ninth-inning relief help from Ken Forsch. On September 13, 1982, Joe beat Phil 5–3. In the head-to-head confrontations, Joe has five victories to four for Phil.

The Perry brothers faced each other only once, on July 3, 1973, when Jim was with the Tigers and Gaylord with the Indians. The Tigers won 5–4 after Jim had left the game. Gaylord didn't finish either, but he took the loss.

The Forsch brothers have never faced each other as starting hurlers. However, on July 21, 1974, Bob, of the Cardinals, won a complete-game victory over the Astros, who had relief in the last two frames from Ken. The latter gave up three runs but did not lose. As noted earlier, Pat and Tom Underwood faced each other as starters on May 31, 1979.

In the summary on pitching brothers, the Perrys are still the best family pitching combination in major league history. Jim closed out with 215 victories, and Gaylord had 307 at the end of the 1982 season. Their superiority is challenged only in number of 20-win seasons. They have seven (five for Gaylord and two for Jim). Stan Coveleski had six, and Harry in his brief career had three. The only category that the Perrys have not been able to dominate is complete games, because pitching has changed considerably since 1900. Jim Galvin pitched 639 complete games, and his brother Lou, up briefly with St. Paul in the Union Association in 1884, had 3, for a combined total of 642. Here are the records for the most noteworthy and balanced of the brother pitching combos, with statistics on active hurlers through the 1982 season.

Brothers	Years	G	IP	W	L	SO	ShO	CG
Barnes								
Jesse	13	422	2570	153*	149*	653	26*	180
Virgil	9	205	1094	61	59	275	7	58
	22	627	3664	214	208	928	33	238
Clarkson								
John	12	531*	4536*	327*	177	1978*	37*	485*
Arthur	6	96	705	39	39	133	2	63
Walter	5	78	375	20	18	178	4	23
	23	705	5616	386	234	2289	43	571

(Continued)

* Indicates that within career span player led league in category at least one season

Brothers	Years	G	IP	W	L	SO	ShO	CG
Coveleski								
Stan	14	450	3093	217	141	981	38*	226
Harry	9	198*	1248	81	57	511	13	83
	23	648	4341	298	198	1492	51	309
Dean								
Dizzy	12	317*	1966*	150*	83	1155*	26*	154*
Paul	9	159	787	50	34	387	8	44
	21	476	2753	200	117	1542	34	198
Forsch								
Ken	13	477	1873	102	99	943	17*	58
Bob	9	274	1766	108	83	721	14	51
	22	751	3639	210	182	1664	31	109
Niekro								
Phil	19	705	4417*	257*	220*	2784*	43	224*
Joe	16	534	2563	162*	141	1197	26*	87
	35	1239	6980	419	361	3981	69	311
Perry								
Jim	17	630	3286	215*	174	1576	32*	109
Gaylord	21	747	5165*	307*	251	3452	52*	300*
	38	1377	8451	522	425	5028	84	409

* Indicates that within career span player led league in category at least one season

Nonpitching Brothers

The majors are currently a little weak in nonpitching brother combinations. However, as late as 1979 the presence of Jesus Alou, at that time limited to pinch hitting, was a reminder that it was not always that way. In fact, there are two examples of long service on the same team, the Sewells and Waners. Joe and Luke Sewell were both with the Indians from 1921 to 1930. Luke was a good catcher but was weak at bat, hitting only .259 in a period when batting averages were quite high. In the meantime, Joe, with wonderful bat control, was compiling a lifetime average of .312 while playing short and third.

Paul and Lloyd Waner were both immediate successes at the plate for the Pirates. Paul led the NL with a .380 bat mark in his second year in 1927. As a rookie, Lloyd finished third that year (after Rogers Hornsby) with a .355 mark. He had 223 hits to 237 for Paul. The NL has not had two players with that many hits in the last forty years, to say nothing about teammates or brothers.

Although outmanned by the three DiMaggio brothers and the three Alous, the Waners still had the most career hits for one family, as well as the most triples. Although neither was a long-ball hitter—

and this was particularly true of Lloyd, who once hit 198 singles in a season—they did accomplish some unusual home run feats. Three times they hit home runs in the same game—twice in the same inning. The last time, on September 15, 1938, they clipped Cliff Melton of the Giants for back-to-back homers in the fifth inning at the Polo Grounds. This is the only time brothers have hit successive home runs.

Other brothers who homered for one team in the same game include Henry and Tommy Aaron, three times for the Milwaukee Braves in 1962; Tony and Billy Conigliaro, twice for the Red Sox in 1970; Felipe and Matty Alou, once for the San Francisco Giants in 1961; and Jesus and Matty Alou, once for the Giants in 1965.

The three Alou brothers achieved a unique milestone on September 15, 1963, exactly 25 years after the Waner achievement, when all three played briefly together in the San Francisco outfield. This necessitated the "benching" of Willie Mays.

In 1966, Matty and Felipe finished first and second in the NL batting race, a feat even the Waners were unable to achieve. Matty, with the Pirates, hit .342, and Felipe, who led the league in hits, runs scored, and total bases, hit .327 for Atlanta.

The only two brothers to win batting titles were Dixie Walker, who hit .357 with the Dodgers in 1944, and Harry, who hit .363 with the Cards and Phils in 1947. Similarly, the only brothers to win RBI titles were Emil Meusel with the New York Giants in 1923, and Bob with the New York Yankees in 1925. No two brothers ever won home run titles.

Other than the Coopers, who were on the *Sporting News* Major League All-Star Teams in 1943 and 1944, the only other brothers to make the team were Joe (who made it eight times on his own) and Dom DiMaggio in 1946. The only brothers to win Gold Glove awards, instituted by the *Sporting News* for fielding excellence in 1957, were the Boyers. Ken won five titles at third base for the NL, and Clete won at the same position for the NL in 1969. All three DiMaggios probably would have been cited had this award been in force in the 1930s and 1940s.

Most of the combined career records for brothers are now shared by the three Alous, the three DiMaggios, and the two Waners. The five Delahantys, who formerly held the mark for the most years, now qualify only for the most entries. In spite of the long career of Steve O'Neill, that family of four players never accumulated significant statistics. The home run record for brothers is held by Henry (755) and Tommy (13) Aaron. The stolen base mark is held by Honus (722) and Al (4) Wagner. The records of some of the more durable brother combinations are carried on the next page.

Brothers	Years	G	H	R	2B	3B	HR	RBI	SB	BA
Alou										
Felipe	17	2082	2101*	985*	359	49	206	852	107	.286
Matty	15	1667	1777*	780*	236*	50	31	427	155	.307*
Jesus	15	1380	1216	448	170	27	32	377	31	.280
	47	5129	5094	2213	765	126	269	1656	293	.292
Boyer										
Cloyd	5	113	20	12	5	1	0	8	0	.167
Ken	15	2034	2143	1104	318	68	282	1141*	105	.287
Clete	16	1725	1396	645	200	33	162	654	41	.242
	36	3872	3559	1761	523	102	444	1803	146	.266
Delahanty										
Ed	16	1835	2597*	1599	522*	185*	100*	1464*	455*	.346*
Tom	3	19	16	13	5	0	0	6	4	.239
Jim	13	1186	1159	520	191	60	18	489	151	.283
Frank	6	287	223	109	22	22	5	94	50	.226
Joe	3	269	222	68	30	15	4	100	24	.238
	41	3596	4217	2319	770	282	127	2153	684	.311
DiMaggio										
Joe	13	1736	2214	1390*	389	131*	361*	1537*	30	.325*
Vince	10	1110	959	491	209	24	125	584	79	.249
Dom	11	1399	1680	1046*	308	57*	87	618	100*	.298
	34	4245	4853	2927	906	212	573	2739	209	.291
Johnson										
Roy	10	1153	1292	717	275*	83*	58	556	135	.296
Bob	13	1863	2051	1239	396	95	288	1283	96	.296
	23	3016	3343	1956	671	178	346	1839	231	.296
May										
Lee	18	2071	2031	959	340	31	354	1244*	39	.267
Carlos	10	1165	1127	545	172	23	90	536	85	.274
	28	3236	3158	1504	512	54	444	1780	124	.269
Meusel										
Emil	11	1294	1521	702	250	92	107	820*	113	.310
Bob	11	1407	1693	826	368	95	156*	1067*	140	.309
	22	2701	3214	1528	618	187	263	1887	253	.309
Sewell†										
Joe	14	1902	2226	1141	436*	68	49	1051	74	.312
Luke	20	1630	1393	653	273	56	20	696	65	.259
	34	3532	3619	1794	709	124	69	1747	139	.292
Walker										
Dixie	18	1905	2064	1037	376	96*	105	1023*	59	.306*
Harry	11	807	786	385	126	37*	10	214	42	.296*
	29	2712	2850	1422	502	133	115	1237	101	.303
Waner										
Paul	20	2549	3152*	1626*	603*	190*	112	1309*	104	.333*
Lloyd	18	1992	2459*	1201*	281	118*	28	598	67	.316
	38	4541	5611	2827	884	308	140	1907	171	.325

* Indicates season leader
† A third brother, Tommy, had one at bat in majors

Relative
Batting Averages
David Shoebotham

Who has the highest single-season batting average in major league history? The modern fan would probably say that it was Rogers Hornsby, with his .424 in 1924. Old-timers would point out that Hugh Duffy hit .438 in 1894. But the correct answer is Ty Cobb, with his .385 in 1910.

How can .385 be higher than .438? The answer is that .385 is higher when it is compared to the average of the entire league for the year in question. In other words, it is a hitter's *relative* batting average that is the true measure of his ability to hit safely. The only way performances from different seasons and different leagues can accurately be compared is by means of relative batting averages.

The relative batting average (RBA) is computed as follows:

$$\text{RBA} = \frac{\text{player's BA}}{\text{league BA}} = \left(\frac{\text{player's hits}}{\text{player's ABs}}\right) \bigg/ \left(\frac{\text{league hits}}{\text{league ABs}}\right)$$

As a further refinement (since it is unfair to compare a player with himself), the player's own hits and ABs can be subtracted from the league totals, thus giving an average relative to the remainder of the league.

As an example, compare Bill Terry's National League–leading .401

121

in 1930 with Carl Yastrzemski's American League–leading .301 in 1968. At first glance the 100-point difference would make it appear that Yastrzemski's average should not be mentioned in the same breath as Terry's. But look at the calculations of their RBAs:

Terry

$$\left(\frac{254}{633}\right) \bigg/ \left(\frac{13,260 - 254}{43,693 - 633}\right) = 1.328$$

Yastrzemski

$$\left(\frac{162}{539}\right) \bigg/ \left(\frac{12,359 - 162}{53,709 - 539}\right) = 1.310$$

The two relative averages are almost identical, meaning that had the two performances occurred in the same season, the batting averages would have been within a few points of each other. The big difference, of course, is that in 1930 the NL had a combined average of .303, the highest of any major league season in this century (and two points higher than Yastrzemski's 1968 average), whereas in 1968 the AL had a combined average of .230, the lowest ever for a major league season. (A relative average of 1.30 indicates that a player's batting average is 30 percent higher than the remainder of the league.)

The following two graphs show league averages since 1900. It can be seen that the 1920s and 1930s, following the introduction of the lively ball, were fat times for hitters. Both leagues reached their recent lows in 1968, the "year of the pitcher." Note that starting in 1973 the AL's designated hitter rule has artificially raised that league's average and thus has lowered individual RBAs.

The table on page 123 shows the highest single-season RBAs since 1900. The list is clearly dominated by Ty Cobb, who has ten of the top nineteen averages, including the highest of all: 1.594 in 1910. Interestingly, the second highest RBA is Nap Lajoie's 1.592, also in 1910. That epic batting race, enlivened by the offer of a new car to the winner, resulted in a major scandal, the awarding of two automobiles, and incidentally the two highest relative averages of all time.* Rogers Hornsby's batting average of .424 produced the highest NL mark, 1.51,

---

* The 1910 AL batting race generates controversy even now, more than seventy years later. Recent research by SABR members and Paul MacFarlane of the *Sporting News* indicates that several errors were made in reporting Cobb's and Lajoie's statistics for that season and that when these are corrected, Lajoie had an average of .383 that beats Cobb's .382. While the evidence supporting Mac-Farlane seems excellent, baseball's Official Records Committee has rejected these findings. I have decided to stick with the "official" records. Either way these are still the two highest RBAs.

NATIONAL LEAGUE SEASON AVERAGES

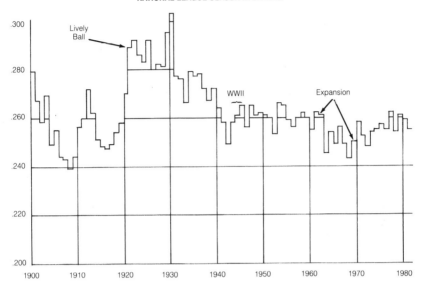

AMERICAN LEAGUE SEASON AVERAGES

but this ranks only fourteenth on the list. (Duffy's .438 reduces to a relative average of 1.42.) Note that five of this century's .400 averages do not qualify for this list.

Single-Season RBAs of 1.45 or Greater

Rank	Player	Year	League	AB	H	BA	Lea. BA	RBA
1	Ty Cobb	1910	AL	509	196	.385	.242	1.594
2	Nap Lajoie	1910	AL	591	227	.384	.241	1.592
3	Nap Lajoie	1904	AL	554	211	.381	.243	1.57
4	Tris Speaker	1916	AL	546	211	.386	.247	1.57
5	Ty Cobb	1912	AL	553	227	.410	.263	1.56
6	Ty Cobb	1909	AL	573	216	.377	.242	1.56
7	Ty Cobb	1917	AL	588	225	.383	.246	1.56
8	Ty Cobb	1911	AL	591	248	.420	.271	1.55
9	Nap Lajoie	1901	AL	543	229	.422	.275	1.53
10	Ty Cobb	1913	AL	428	167	.390	.254	1.53
11	Ted Williams	1941	AL	456	185	.406	.265	1.53
12	Ted Williams	1957	AL	420	163	.388	.254	1.53
13	Ty Cobb	1918	AL	421	161	.382	.252	1.52
14	Rogers Hornsby	1924	NL	536	227	.424	.281	1.51
15	Joe Jackson	1911	AL	571	233	.408	.271	1.51
16	Joe Jackson	1912	AL	572	226	.395	.263	1.50
17	Ty Cobb	1916	AL	542	201	.371	.247	1.50
18	Ty Cobb	1915	AL	563	208	.369	.247	1.50
19	Ty Cobb	1914	AL	345	127	.368	.246	1.49
20	Honus Wagner	1908	NL	568	201	.354	.237	1.49
21	Cy Seymour	1905	NL	581	219	.377	.253	1.49
22	George Sisler	1922	AL	586	246	.420	.283	1.49
23	Joe Jackson	1913	AL	528	197	.373	.254	1.47
24	Rod Carew	1977	AL	616	239	.388	.265*	1.46
25	Tris Speaker	1912	AL	580	222	.383	.263	1.45
26	Stan Musial	1948	NL	611	230	.376	.259	1.45
27	George Brett	1980	AL	449	175	.390	.268*	1.45
28	George Stone	1906	AL	581	208	.358	.247	1.45
29	Joe Torre	1971	NL	634	230	.363	.251	1.45
30	George Sisler	1920	AL	631	257	.407	.282	1.45
31	Honus Wagner	1907	NL	515	180	.350	.242	1.45

* Designated hitter rule in effect

With the modern preoccupation with home runs, RBAs, not to mention high absolute averages, have become rare. In recent years only three players have had relative averages over 1.45: George Brett in 1980, Rod Carew in 1977, and Joe Torre in 1971. For a look at other recent high marks, the next table shows the highest RBAs of the last twenty-five years. It is interesting to note that without the designated hitter rule in the American League, Carew in 1977 and Brett in 1980 would have been around 1.50, and Carew in 1974 and 1975 would have been over 1.45.

Highest Single-Season RBAs (1957–81)

Rank	Player	Year	League	AB	H	BA	Lea. BA	RBA
1	Ted Williams	1957	AL	420	163	.388	.254	1.53
2	Rod Carew	1977	AL	616	239	.388	.265*	1.46
3	George Brett	1980	AL	449	175	.390	.268*	1.45
4	Joe Torre	1971	NL	634	230	.363	.251	1.45
5	Roberto Clemente	1967	NL	585	209	.357	.248	1.44
6	Mickey Mantle	1957	AL	474	173	.365	.254	1.44
7	Rico Carty	1970	NL	478	175	.366	.257	1.42
8	Norm Cash	1961	AL	535	193	.361	.255	1.42
9	Rod Carew	1974	AL	599	218	.364	.257*	1.41
10	Harvey Kuenn	1959	AL	561	198	.353	.252	1.40
11	Rod Carew	1975	AL	535	192	.359	.257*	1.40
12	Pete Rose	1969	NL	627	218	.348	.249	1.39
13	Carl Yastrzemski	1967	AL	579	189	.326	.235	1.39
14	Ralph Garr	1974	NL	606	214	.353	.254	1.39
15	Pete Rose	1968	NL	626	210	.335	.242	1.39
16	Roberto Clemente	1969	NL	507	175	.345	.250	1.38
17	Bill Madlock	1975	NL	514	182	.354	.256	1.38
18	Hank Aaron	1959	NL	629	223	.355	.259	1.37
19	Matty Alou	1968	NL	558	185	.332	.242	1.37
20	Tony Oliva	1971	AL	487	164	.337	.246	1.37

* Designated hitter rule in effect

The final table shows the all-time leaders in career RBAs. Not surprisingly, Ty Cobb tops the list with an average that is just a few hits short of 1.40. Close behind Cobb is Shoeless Joe Jackson, though the closeness of their averages is deceptive. Jackson's career was abruptly terminated while he was still a star performer, and therefore he did not have the usual declining years at the end of his career that would have lowered his average. During the years that Jackson averaged 1.38, Cobb averaged 1.50.

It can be seen that despite the preponderance of pre-1920 hitters in the single-season leaders, the career list has players from all periods since 1900, including four who are active and four whose careers ended in the 1970s. Rod Carew is currently in fifth place after being in third place for most of the 1970s. Whether all four active players will finish their careers among the leaders is an open question, but at least they show that hitting for high average is not altogether a lost art.

Career RBAs of 1.20 or Greater
(Over 4,000 ABs; through 1981)

Rank	Player	Years	AB	H	BA	Lea. BA	RBA
1	Ty Cobb	1905–28	11429	4191	.367	.263	1.39
2	Joe Jackson	1908–20	4981	1774	.356	.258	1.38
3	Ted Williams	1939–60	7706	2654	.344	.261	1.32
4	Nap Lajoie	1896–1916	9589	3251	.339	.258	1.31
5	Rod Carew	1967–81*	7548	2505	.332	.253	1.31
6	Rogers Hornsby	1915–37	8173	2930	.358	.275	1.30
7	Tris Speaker	1907–28	10208	3515	.344	.266	1.29
8	Stan Musial	1941–63	10972	3630	.331	.258	1.28
9	Honus Wagner	1897–1917	10427	3430	.329	.258	1.28
10	Eddie Collins	1906–30	9949	3311	.333	.265	1.26
11	Roberto Clemente	1955–72	9454	3000	.317	.254	1.25
12	Tony Oliva	1962–76	6301	1917	.304	.246	1.24
13	Harry Heilmann	1914–32	7787	2660	.342	.278	1.23
14	Sam Crawford	1899–1917	9579	2964	.309	.252	1.23
15	Pete Rose	1963–81*	11910	3697	.310	.253	1.23
16	George Sisler	1915–30	8267	2812	.340	.278	1.23
17	Babe Ruth	1914–35	8399	2873	.342	.279	1.23
18	Elmer Flick	1898–1910	5597	1764	.315	.259	1.22
19	Matty Alou	1960–74	5789	1777	.307	.252	1.22
20	George Brett	1973–81*	4291	1366	.318	.261	1.22
21	Joe Medwick	1932–48	7635	2471	.324	.266	1.21
22	Paul Waner	1926–44	9459	3152	.333	.275	1.21
23	Lou Gehrig	1923–39	8001	2721	.340	.281	1.21
24	Bill Terry	1923–36	6428	2193	.341	.282	1.21
25	Ginger Beaumont	1899–1910	5660	1759	.311	.257	1.21
26	Dave Parker	1973–81*	4052	1259	.311	.257	1.21
27	Joe DiMaggio	1936–51	6821	2214	.325	.269	1.21
28	Hank Aaron	1954–76	12364	3771	.305	.254	1.20
29	Jackie Robinson	1947–56	4877	1518	.311	.260	1.20

* Active player

The War of 1912:
The Wood-
Johnson Duel
Emil H. Rothe

Baseball history is replete with games in which great pitchers have been called upon to face each other in mound duels. Christy Mathewson vs. Three-Finger Brown; Carl Hubbell against Dizzy Dean; those two lefties, Gomez and Grove; Juan Marichal facing Sandy Koufax—each era has had its exciting match-ups. But no single such confrontation was ever played in a more dramatic and emotional atmosphere than the game of September 6, 1912, in Boston's Fenway Park, with Walter Johnson taking the hill for the visiting Washington Senators, opposing the Red Sox pitching ace, Smoky Joe Wood.

Earlier that season Walter Johnson had fashioned a personal win streak that had reached 16, a new American League record, breaking by two the record that had been held by Jack Chesbro of the New York Highlanders since 1904. Johnson's record-breaking fifteenth successive win came on August 20, and he added No. 16 as he beat Detroit 8–1 on August 23.

A heartbreaking loss in relief on August 26 ended his string. Walter had taken over from starter Tom Hughes in the seventh of the second game of a doubleheader with the score tied and two St. Louis Browns on base. One of them scored the winning run before Johnson could retire the side. Under today's scoring rules Hughes would have been charged with that winning run, but Ban Johnson, president of the

Smoky Joe Wood and Walter Johnson before the crucial 1912 game

AL, decreed the loss be charged to Walter Johnson. His decision was bitterly denounced, especially in Washington. On August 28, however, that edict and the storm that it created became academic when Walter started against the Browns, went the distance, and lost 3–2. While he only gave up four hits that day, he also walked four and hit his pitching opponent, Jack Powell.

In that same year, 1912, Rube Marquard opened the season for the New York Giants with an 18–3 win over Brooklyn. The game was played before an overflow crowd and had to be called after six innings because of "congestion"; the fans had encroached on the foul lines to the extent that they hampered further play. Rube went on without a loss for nineteen consecutive victories.

Again, by today's standards, Rube's record would have been twenty, and he would not now be sharing the major league record with Tim Keefe of New York. (Keefe also ran up nineteen in 1888, under different pitching rules than those extant since the turn of the century.)

Early in the 1912 season, Marquard was sent in to relieve Jeff Tesreau with the score 3–2 against the Giants in the ninth. In the bottom of that inning New York rallied to win 4–3, but the victory was credited to Tesreau.

As Johnson's streak between July 3 and August 23, 1912, grew and began to pose a threat to Marquard's major league mark achieved earlier in the season, Joe Wood started a consecutive string of wins of his own. His began on July 8, and as the series between Washington and Boston approached, he was threatening Johnson's newly acquired AL record.

Recognizing the drama of a head-to-head meeting between these two great pitchers, baseball fans and writers everywhere clamored for the opportunity for Johnson himself to put an end to Wood's threat to his record sixteen consecutive wins, acquired less than two weeks before. Walter's regular turn was to be Friday, September 6, but Wood was not scheduled to take the mound again until Saturday.

Jake Stahl, Boston manager, aware of the sporting nature of the proposal, agreed to start Wood a day earlier. The fans responded— over 30,000 strong—far more than Fenway Park could accommodate in those days. On the day of the game, fans who could not be seated overflowed onto the playing field. Standing room was established behind ropes in front of the outfield walls and bleachers. Other spectators crowded along the foul lines. The teams were not even able to use their own dugouts, but were obliged to use chairs set up in front of the multitudes ranged along the foul lines.

In the second game of a twin bill against the New York Highlanders on September 2, Joe Wood had won his thirteenth game without a loss. And so, on September 6, he was seeking his fourteenth straight. Johnson, meanwhile, was hoping to end Smoky Joe's threat to his record, which he had scarcely had time to get used to owning.

As expected, the game developed into a bona-fide pitching battle. Boston put together two singles in the second, but Walter escaped that threat as Heinie Wagner raced into the outfield to grab a pop fly in spectacular fashion for the third out. Washington filled the bases in the third, two on walks, but Smoky Joe fanned Danny Moeller for the third out.

The lone tally of this memorable game came in the sixth after Walter had disposed of the first two batters of the inning. Tris Speaker hit into the crowd in left for a ground-rule double. Duffy Lewis, next up, drove a hard liner along the right-field foul line which Moeller, the Senator right fielder, almost caught; the ball just ticked his glove as Speaker scored and Lewis reached second.

The Senators had men in scoring position, at second, in the sixth, eighth, and ninth, but Wood was tough when he had to be. In two of those innings he got the final out via a strikeout. In all, he fanned nine Senators, and the shutout was one of ten he registered in 1912.

Having registered win No. 14 in his heart-stopping 1–0 conquest of Walter Johnson and the Senators, Wood next faced Doc White in Chicago on September 10. Going into the ninth of this game with a 5–3 lead, Joe was touched for a lead-off double by Wally Mattick and a single by Harry Lord, running the hit total for the home club to a round dozen. Manager Stahl realized that Joe was not at his best and called in Charles "Sea Lion" Hall to save the game. A sacrifice fly by Shano Collins brought the White Sox to within one run of a tie, but Hall disposed of the next two to preserve No. 15 for Joe Wood.

Wood's next turn occurred in St. Louis on September 15, in the second game of a doubleheader. He beat the Browns 2–1 in an eight-inning game for No. 16 and a tie with Johnson for the AL consecutive-game record. The game had to be called after eight innings because of darkness, and it was Wood himself who scored the winning run in the top of that last inning.

Joe's bid to better the AL pitcher's win streak and threaten the major league mark came to an end in Detroit on September 20, when the Tigers scored two unearned runs to win 6–4. While Wood went the distance, he was not effective, surrendering seven hits and being wild. In the third inning, for example, he walked his pitching opponent, Bill Covington, and then, in succession, Donie Bush, Red Corriden, and Wahoo Sam Crawford.

While Johnson won a spectacular 32 games in 1912, Wood closed out the season with an even more impressive mark. He won 34 and lost only 5, one of the all-time great season records.

In the "strange but true" category, it should be noted that the modern records (since 1900) for consecutive wins by a pitcher in a single season were established in that one year; Marquard's 19 (the NL and major league record) and Johnson's and Wood's 16 (the AL record). The AL record has since been tied, by Lefty Grove of Phila-delphia in 1931 and by Schoolboy Rowe of Detroit in 1934. The most remarkable display of avoiding a pitching defeat, however, belongs to Carl Hubbell of the New York Giants. King Carl, the Meal Ticket, ended 1936 with a run of 16 straight wins and then started the 1937 season with 8 more, to make it 24 games without tasting defeat.

Baseball games are remembered by players and fans for a multi-tude of reasons: maybe it was the first game a player ever played, or the day he could do no wrong on the field, the first time a child's father took him or her to a game, or a game of historical import. Whatever the reason, almost every game will live in someone's memory as long as that someone lives. Some games, though, deserve to be remembered by the entire baseball community for all time. The Walter Johnson–Joe Wood contest played on September 6, 1912, should be one of those. Here is the box score.

Washington	AB	R	H	Boston	AB	R	H
Milan, cf	3	0	1	Hooper, rf	4	0	0
Foster, 3b	3	0	1	Yerkes, 2b	4	0	1
Moeller, rf	4	0	0	Speaker, cf	2	1	1
Gandil, 1b	4	0	0	Lewis, lf	2	0	1
Laporte, 2b	4	0	2	Gardner, 3b	3	0	1
Moran, lf	3	0	0	Engle, 1b	3	0	1
McBride, ss	4	0	1	Wagner, ss	3	0	0
Ainsmith, c	2	0	0	Cady, c	3	0	0
Johnson, p	3	0	1	Wood, p	3	0	0

```
Washington  . . . . . . . . . .  000 000 000 — 0
Boston  . . . . . . . . . . . . .  000 001 00x — 1
```

2-base hits—McBride, Laporte, Speaker, Lewis
Sacrifice hits—Ainsmith, Lewis, Moran
Runs batted in—Lewis
Stolen base—Foster
Left on bases—Boston 4, Washington 8
Double play—Wood to Wagner to Engle
Bases on Balls—Johnson 1, Wood 3
Struck out—Wood 9, Johnson 5
Time—1:46
Umpires—Connolly and Hart

Do Walks Always Hurt a Pitcher?

Evelyn Begley

In 1974, Nolan Ryan led the majors for the third consecutive year in giving up bases on balls. His total was a near record, 202, and one might think that with the other young throwers on the Angels' staff there might be a new team record for issuing passes. But no, Andy Hassler gave up 79 walks, Frank Tanana 77, Dick Lange 47, and Bill Singer 43. The team total was 649, nowhere near a new record, and less than the Padres (715) and Phils (682) in 1974.

The major league team record for giving up walks was set by the 1915 Philadelphia Athletics, one of Connie Mack's worst teams. Led by Weldon Wyckoff with 165 and Rube Bressler with 118, the staff, such as it was, gave up 827 free passes. Mack tried more than 25 different throwers that year, but it seems that none of them could get the ball over the plate. One recruit, Bruno Haas, gave up a record 16 walks in his first game.

The 1915 A's finished deep in the cellar, but this should not be taken as a direct effect of all the bases on balls. A contrasting situation occurred in 1949, when Yankee hurlers gave up 812 bases on balls; yet that aggregation won the pennant that season, and the World Series. The bases-on-balls brigade was led by Tommy Byrne with 179, Vic Raschi with 138, and Allie Reynolds with 123. No team ever had three hurlers with such high totals. Even the great Joe Page walked 75 batters in 135 innings, a very high total for a relief hurler.

Baseball fans are probably aware of the legendary control problems of Wild Bill Hallahan, Rex Barney, Bob Turley, Sam McDowell, and even Nolan Ryan, but when it comes down to walks per inning, there was no one as generous as Tommy Byrne. In a couple of seasons he gave up more walks than hits. In 1951, for example, when St. Louis Brown hurlers gave up 801 bases on balls, Byrne walked 150 in 144 innings (more than 9 walks per 9-inning game), while giving up only 120 hits. Over his career, he issued 1,037 walks in 1,362 innings, the highest rate for any 10-year hurler.

The pitching staff with the best control was the quintet that pitched the Red Sox to the 1904 pennant. Yes, the BoSox used only five pitchers all season, quite a contrast to the crowd that assembled for the 1915 A's. With Cy Young leading the way with only 29 walks, and Jesse Tannehill following with only 33, the club gave up only 233 in 157 games. Tannehill apparently had picked up some control pointers while with the Pirates, for they had given up only 250 walks in 142 games in 1902. Substitute hurler Honus Wagner contributed to that total with 2 walks himself; however, the real leaders were Tannehill with 25, Deacon Phillippe of the Pirates with 26, and Sam Leever with 31. This was the lowest level of walks issued by any team trio of regular hurlers, and it contrasts sharply with the totals of the Yankee trio of Byrne, Raschi, and Reynolds in 1949. The contrast is put into sharper focus by the realization that while Byrne issued bases on balls at the most frequent rate—nearly 7 per 9-inning game for his career—Deacon Phillippe was statistically the best control pitcher. He issued only 363 passes in 2,607 career innings, or about 1.25 per 9-inning game.

The Pirates of 1902 and the Red Sox of 1904 were pennant winners. A team of more recent vintage, the Reds of 1933, with Red Lucas leading the way with only 18 bases on balls, gave up only 257 free passes. This proved to be the best record in three-quarters of a century, but the Reds finished last in the NL.

The lesson that can be learned from this brief analysis is that bases on balls are bad, but they can be canceled out to a large degree if the same pitcher doesn't give up many hits. This is particularly true if the man is a good strikeout pitcher. Prime examples are Bob Feller, Sam "Toothpick" Jones, Bob Turley, Sam McDowell, and, again, Nolan Ryan. It is remarkable that Ryan could walk 202 batters in 1974 and still have a 2.89 ERA. The key is that he gave up only 221 hits in 333 innings—and those 367 strikeouts didn't hurt him either.

Farce Game Hurt Johnson Record

Walter Johnson held the major league ERA record for pitchers with over 300 innings in a season from 1913, the first year the American League compiled earned run averages, until 1968, when Bob Gibson broke it. But did you know that Johnson would still own that record if it weren't for a farcical game played by the Senators and Red Sox in the final contest of the 1913 season? The game was played at Washington on October 4, and with nothing at stake, the two teams put on a good comedy show for a gathering of 8,000, including 3,000 servicemen.

The Senators used a total of 18 players, with 8 of them taking a turn on the mound. This included manager Clark Griffith and nonpitchers Germany Schaefer, Eddie Ainsmith, and Joe Gedeon. Although Boston used only 11 players, outfielder Duffy Lewis played third base and pitcher Charley Hall started at second base, while rookie Fred Anderson pitched all the way. Manager Griffith, forty-three years old, pitched the eighth inning, and his catcher was coach Jack Ryan, who was forty-four. Schaefer was supposed to be the right fielder but spent most of his time roving between second base and first. Many times the fielders had their backs to the batter. Several times four men were retired before the teams changed positions. The veteran umpires—Tom Connolly and Bill Dinneen—were too busy laughing at the antics to pay too much attention to details.

In the sixth inning, with the Senators holding a 10–3 lead, comedian Schaefer brought the frolicking to a high pitch. He started the last inning as a pitcher, but after Lewis bunted safely, Griffith called in Johnson, who had played all the way in center field. Walter joined in the festivities by grooving a few pitches—giving up a single to Steve Yerkes and a double to Clyde Engle. Over Griffith's objection, Schaefer ordered Johnson back to the outfield and assumed the pitching duties himself once again.

Before the inning was finished, Ainsmith, a catcher, and Gedeon, an outfielder, had also toed the rubber for the Nats. When it was all over, the Senators had survived Schaefer's shenanigans and eked out a 10–9 victory. The final out was made by Lewis, who had started the inning with a hit. It wasn't his turn at bat, but Harry Hooper, who had made the last out in the eighth inning, hadn't thought much of the Red Sox' chances and had gone to the clubhouse for his shower. Lewis just moved up a notch without anyone noticing the difference.

When the league records were issued in 1913, the American League statistician paid no attention to Johnson's pitching stint in the joke game. He credited Johnson with a 1.09 ERA, and that's the way it went into the official records. It wasn't until many years after Johnson had retired that a game-by-game check of his career revealed that the two men he had put on base in that jocular ninth inning had scored and had to be charged as earned runs, thereby increasing his ERA to 1.14. That's how the final game of 1913, which the *Boston Globe* called "the most farcical exposition of the national game that was ever staged," cost Johnson the ERA title fifty-five years later when Gibson turned in a 1.12 earned run average for the Cardinals.

Al Kermisch

Bleacher Bums of Yesteryear
William G. Nicholson

The baseball fans of the 1930s and 1940s were a special breed, far removed from their counterparts of today. The colorful fans of recent years—the sign carriers, the inane and loud-mouthed drunks, the affluent junketeers who follow their teams on a road trip a year—are pale copies of their hardier predecessors. Vocal in the extreme, the bleacher bums of yesteryear were knowledgeable and ardent, and they were found in every major league ball park. Virtually every city had at least one who stood out from the herd, from the gentle "Megaphone Lolly" Hopkins in Boston to the raucous "Horse Lady of St. Louis," Mrs. Mary Ott, who tormented all National Leaguers who had the temerity to take the field against her beloved Cardinals.

Blessed with a scream that was piercing and bloodcurdling, Mrs. Ott was the scourge of umpires and opposing ballplayers in Sportsman's Park. For more than twenty-five years she put subtle nuances in her neigh which forcefully, often dramatically, communicated triumph or tragedy, exultation or excoriation.

The Horse Lady once confided to a sportswriter, "I like scientific rooting, something that helps the home boys win and makes the other guys sore. I figure if I really work on 'em, I can knock a lot of them pitchers out of the box in three innings." Her vocal chords lubricated with countless bottles of beer, she particularly enjoyed making afternoons hideous for the Dodgers.

But Dodger fans, many of whom the Mets inherited, justifiably earned the reputation of being collectively the most knowledgeable and frenetic in the league. Encouraged by a bedraggled group of musicians who passed through the stands, Brooklyn fans turned the cozy bandbox that was Ebbets Field into something that resembled a huge, outdoor psychopathic ward.

The Dodgers had two outstanding fans, one extremely vocal, the other relatively quiet, actually quite benign. Miss Hilda Chester, known to her numerous admirers as Howling Hilda, was a calm, middle-aged woman who sold newspapers in downtown Brooklyn. But when she arrived at the ball park with a cowbell, a remarkable transformation would occur. By constantly ringing her bell and bellowing, Miss Chester became Howling Hilda.

For years Jack Pierce showed his devotion to the Dodgers in a less prosaic, more ritualistic manner than Howling Hilda. Pierce firmly believed that Cookie Lavagetto, the journeyman third baseman the Dodgers had acquired from the Pirates in 1937, was the greatest ballplayer who had ever appeared on a diamond. The performance of Pierce was an incredible one, and it even continued when the redoubtable Cookie had enlisted in the Air Force after the 1941 season.

Pierce, a prosperous Brooklyn restaurateur, would arrive almost daily at Ebbets with two large boxes of balloons, a hydrogen tank, a banner, a bottle or two of Scotch, and tickets for ten box seats just behind the visitors' dugout. His expense for an afternoon of rooting—between $40 and $50—was not an insignificant sum during the years of the depression and World War II. After bracing himself with a few drinks, Pierce would get down to business. First he would spread a large blue and gray banner with the word "Cookie" on top of the dugout. Then he would furiously inflate his "Cookie" balloons, screaming out his hero's name continually and capping his tribute by bursting the balloon. For a change of pace, especially after his idol had departed for the wars, Jack Pierce would let out an occasional bleat and pop a "Ducky" balloon for Joe Medwick, the veteran outfielder who had come to Brooklyn from the Cardinals in 1940.

Somewhat to the northeast of Flatbush during the same period, Mrs. Lolly Hopkins made regular trips from her Providence home to Boston, where she supported the local teams at Braves Field and Fenway Park. Infinitely more genteel than her Brooklyn and St. Louis counterparts, Mrs. Hopkins had earned her nickname of Megaphone Lolly by using a megaphone to disseminate her vast knowledge of the game to fans, players, umpires, and official scorers.

Mrs. Hopkins cheered good plays on both sides and did not like booing—"I am a *positive* fan," she once boasted. In one 1945 game when the Tigers' Hal Newhouser came to the plate during a pitchers' duel with Jim Wilson of the Red Sox, spontaneous applause from a youthful Sox supporter earned him a "Good for you, young man." Megaphone Lolly enjoyed carrying on conversations with individual players, and the Braves and Red Sox managements rewarded her support with season passes.

Cincinnati had its own elderly supporter in Harry Thobe, a bricklayer from Oxford, Ohio. Seventy-one years old in 1942, Thobe would dance a solemn jig in the ball park for hours without interruption. He wore a white suit with red stripes down the trousers, one red and one white shoe, and a straw hat with a red band, and he delicately carried a red and white parasol.

Old Harry earned national fame in 1939 when his beloved Reds won their first pennant in twenty years. He jigged, walked an imaginary tightrope, circled the bases at a trot, and managed a slide into home plate. Mugging unmercifully, the old fellow danced his jig and flashed his twelve gold teeth for the photographers two hours before each World Series game that fall.

Philadelphia has long been noted for fans who indiscriminately heap calumny on their own and visiting players, more often than not on the former. But the abusive artistry of the Kessler brothers, Bull and Eddie, in old Shibe Park has never been equaled. They had awe-inspiring voices and did not hesitate to use them while sitting on opposite sides of the diamond and conducting a private conversation.

Unpredictably, the Kessler boys had an aversion to Jimmy Dykes, the Athletics' third baseman, that defied all reason. They would rattle the usually unflappable Dykes to such a point that old Connie Mack tried to bribe them with season passes. When that failed, he took them to court in an attempt to silence them. Finally, Mack sold Jimmy to the White Sox, who found the denizens of Comiskey Park somewhat more accommodating than the Kesslers.

Patsy O'Toole's technique in Detroit was not spectacular, but it was steady and earned him the dubious honor of annoying an American president at an athletic event. His rallying cry, usually delivered from the roof of the Tigers' dugout was "Boy, oh boy, oh boy, oh boy! Keep cool wit' O'Toole!" The incredible repetition, coupled with one standard insult and compliment, did not endear him to his fellow spectators. Patsy would bellow, "Jimmie Foxx, you're a bum! Babe Ruth, you're a bum!" or "Charlie Gehringer, you're a great guy! Doc Cramer, you're a great guy! Boy, oh boy, oh boy, oh boy! Keep cool wit' O'Toole!"

During the third game of the 1933 World Series between the

Giants and Senators, Patsy somehow found himself in Washington, seated a few rows behind President Franklin Roosevelt. After two or three O'Toole blasts, Roosevelt, obviously shaken, turned to a Secret Service man. Within minutes the agent was at Patsy's side. "I'm sure you'd like to do the President a favor," he said. "He'd like you to move to the other side of the field, and Mr. Griffith has already made the arrangements."

Not long after his encounter with the President, O'Toole's twenty-five years of bellowing for the Tigers necessitated a throat operation. His incredible roar became just a memory. But when he had his voice, Patsy O'Toole was the champion of all of baseball's leather-lunged fans who deserve a niche in any history of the colorful national pastime.

Three Men on Third

What about the old story that the Brooklyn Dodgers once had three base runners on one base? Well, it might get embellished with the telling, but it is basically true. The date was August 15, 1926, first game of two, Boston Braves at Brooklyn. It is the seventh inning, with the bases full of Bums. Babe Herman hits the ball off the right field wall. Catcher Hank DeBerry scores from third, but pitcher Dazzy Vance, on second, holds up, thinking the ball will be caught. Finally he takes off, rounds third, and heads for home. But the ball is thrown home, and Vance heads back to third. He is met there by Chick Fewster, the runner who had been on first, and Herman, the hitter, who was right on his heels. They decide to let Vance have possession of third and head back toward second, but both are tagged out. The fielding play on Boston's part went from right fielder Jimmy Welsh to second baseman Doc Gautreau to catcher Oscar Siemer to third baseman Eddie Taylor to Gautreau, who came over from second. What it came down to for Herman was doubling into a double play.

Grounding into Double Plays

Stanley Kuminski

Joe Torre's frustrating 1975 season was epitomized by the July 21 game against the Astros in which he grounded into four consecutive double plays. Batting ahead of him was Felix Millan, who had four singles but was wiped out each time Torre hit the ball. For Torre it was a National League record for grounding into twin killings in one game. He is one of the all-time leaders in that department, having been victimized 265 times in his career.

The double play is an important part of game strategy, for nothing ruins a rally like a twin killing. Yet little statistical research has been done in this area. The NL started compiling such records in 1933, and the AL has kept them only since 1939. Consequently, no one knows how many times Ty Cobb was doubled up or Honus Wagner or even Zeke Bonura in his early years. However, it is safe to say that the all-time record for grounding into double plays was not established by Cobb or Wagner. This is not just because they were fast runners but also because there were fewer double plays made in their eras.

Who, then, holds the career record? Apparently it is Henry Aaron, with 328 futile efforts. He is followed by two other long-service stars: Carl Yastrzemski with 310 through 1982, and Brooks Robinson, who closed out his career with 297 GDP. Ernie Lombardi hit into double plays the most frequently, once every 20 times at bat. This is based on his career record since 1933 of 261 wipeouts in only 5,260 at bats. He had 30 GDPs in 1938, the NL season record.

If Lombardi was the easiest player to double up, who was the toughest? Logic would indicate that he would have to be a left-handed hitter (so he wouldn't have to take that extra step or two). Well, it is necessary to settle for a compromise candidate, Don Buford, who was a switch-hitter. Before he left for Japan in 1973, Buford had grounded into only 33 double plays in 4,553 at bats, or once every 138 times at the plate. He tops all left-handed batting speedsters like Lou Brock, Richie Ashburn, and Joe Morgan. And don't forget another Don who went to Japan—Don Blasingame—who was almost as tough to double up as Buford.

The right-handed batters most difficult to catch in double plays were George Case, based on less than his full career, and Bert Campaneris. Research on the available records has turned up some surprises. For example, Bill "Swish" Nicholson of the Cubs was harder to double up than Willie Davis, one of the fastest runners in the game, who also batted from the left side. In Nicholson's case, he was known to uppercut the ball a little to get it out of the park. And Johnny Mize, hardly a gazelle on the basepaths, was an infrequent victim of the double play. The same applies to big Willie Stargell. Of course, both batted from the left side and went for the fences.

Here are some career totals and frequency rates.

High Career Totals for GDP

Player	Bat	AB	GDP	/AB
Henry Aaron	R	12364	328	38
Carl Yastrzemski	L	11608	310	37
Brooks Robinson	R	10654	297	36
Rusty Staub	L	9488	291	33
Joe Torre	R	7874	284	28
George Scott	R	7433	277	27
Roberto Clemente	R	9454	275	34
Al Kaline	R	10116	271	37
Frank Robinson	R	10006	269	37
Ernie Lombardi	R	5260*	261*	20
Ron Santo	R	8143	256	32
Willie Mays	R	10881	251	43
Stan Musial	L	10972	243	45
Harmon Killebrew	R	8147	243	34
Tony Perez	R	9005	243	37

* Incomplete career records

Low Frequency Rates for GDP

Player	Bat	AB	GDP	/AB
Don Buford	S	4553	33	138
Don Blasingame	L	5296	43	123
Mickey Rivers	L	5007	42	119
Richie Ashburn	L	8365	83	101
Joe Morgan	L	8508	86	99
George Case	R	4494*	48*	94
Vic Davalillo	L	4017	43	93
Stanley Hack	L	7100*	78*	91
Bill Nicholson	L	5546	61	91
Lou Brock	L	10332	114	91
Bud Harrelson	S	4744	53	90
Arky Vaughan	L	6125*	70*	88
Rick Monday	L	5911	68	87
Del Unser	L	5215	62	84
Bert Campaneris	R	8541	102	84

* Incomplete career records

It is obvious that on a career basis the right-handed batters will usually have the higher GDP totals and the left-handed hitters usually dominate the low frequency rates. There are exceptions, however, when it comes to season leaders. In fact, in 1975 the tables got turned when Don Money of Milwaukee, a right-handed batter, was nabbed only 1 time, while Willie Montanez, batting left, was doubled up 26 times to lead the National League.

Rusty Staub, batting left, twice led the AL in most GDPs. So did Yastrzemski, once with a surprisingly high total of 30. In fact, the Red Sox have traditionally had some rather high totals, whether they batted left or right. Jackie Jensen, one of the best base stealers of the 1950s, nevertheless led the league three times in GDPs. In 1954 he set a major league record with 32. Bobby Doerr and Vern Stephens each led twice, and six other Boston players led once each. Maybe the infielders at Fenway Park play in closer because of the nearness of the left field wall.

Only six players have gone essentially a complete season without hitting into a double play. This is based on a minimum of 350 at bats over a 154-game schedule and 400 for 162 games. Augie Galan holds the all-time mark by hitting into no GDPs in 646 at bats in 1935. In 1968, both Dick McAuliffe and Roger Repoz in the AL had unblemished records. Tony Bartirome of the Pirates had the distinction of never having grounded into a double play in the majors. He topped the NL in 1952, and that was the only season he played.

Numbers on Players' Backs

Numbers appeared on the backs of players' uniforms in the majors for the first time more than fifty years ago. While the New York Yankees were the first big league club to wear numbers on their backs on a permanent basis, home and away, they were not the first team to appear in a major league game so attired. That honor belongs to the Cleveland Indians, who wore numbers on the backs of their home uniforms in 1929. Cleveland, it may be remembered, was also the first major league club to have players wear numbers on their sleeves, for a brief time in 1916.

Both the Yankees and Indians were scheduled to open at home on April 6, 1929, but the Yanks were rained out at New York for two straight days, while the Indians opened as scheduled. Cleveland defeated Detroit 5–4 in 11 innings, spoiling Bucky Harris's debut as Tiger manager. Earl Averill, wearing No. 5, celebrated his first time at bat with a number on his back, which was also his initial trip to the plate in the majors, by blasting an Earl Whitehill two-strike pitch over the right field screen in the first inning. Charlie Gehringer hit a home run for Detroit off Joe Shaute in the third inning.

The Yankees finally got started at home on April 18, defeating the Boston Red Sox 7–3. Babe Ruth, wearing No. 3, also celebrated his first time at bat with a number on his back by hitting a home run off Red Ruffing in the first inning, a drive into the lower left field stands. Lou Gehrig, No. 4, also homered, with his coming in the sixth inning off Milt Gaston. It is interesting to note that the first Yankees to wear 5 and 7, eventually retired by Joe DiMaggio and Mickey Mantle, were Bob Meusel and Leo Durocher, respectively.

When the Yankees played at Boston on April 23, it was the first time a visiting major league club appeared with numbers on the players' backs. The Red Sox spoiled that one for the Yanks by winning 4–2. The first time that both clubs appeared with numbers in the big leagues was at Cleveland on May 13, with the Indians defeating the Yankees 4–3. Mark Koenig, No. 2, hit a home run for the Yanks off Willis Hudlin in the sixth inning.

Al Kermisch

The First Player-Broadcaster

Ted Patterson

John Gladstone "Jack" Graney was born in St. Thomas, Ontario, on June 10, 1886, and died in 1978 at the age of 91. In St. Thomas he is still referred to as the finest baseball player in the city's history. There he was known as Glad Graney, and during his days in the big leagues, whenever he heard a fan shout, "Hey, Glad," he knew someone from his hometown was in the crowd.

But after his playing career as the left fielder of the Cleveland Naps, later the Indians, Jack Graney was *the* voice of the Cleveland Indians from 1932 until age and the demanding schedule of major league baseball forced his exit from radio. He was there during the time of Earl Averill, Joe Vosmik, Hal Trosky, Willis Hudlin, Mel Harder, and Johnny Allen; witnessed the heady years of Bob Feller, Lou Boudreau, and Ken Keltner; and bowed out when Bob Lemon, Early Wynn, Larry Doby, and Al Rosen were at their peaks. He would tell you it was hard to forget the days he spent in baseball.

Possessing a crisp, stirring delivery, Graney was a master at setting a scene, and his enthusiasm packed a sense of built-in drama. His ability to re-create a game from just a telegraphic report was unparalleled. "My association with Jack Graney was one of the finest I have ever known," affirms his last broadcasting partner, Jimmy Dudley.

"He was a tremendous announcer and taught me many tricks of

the trade. Jack had an exceedingly high-pitched voice which generated more excitement than anybody else's I have ever heard. Had he a voice like Ted Husing's, he might be considered today with the four or five greatest sports broadcasters of all time."

Baseball broadcasting has undergone immense changes in the past forty years. Until Graney's last few years as an announcer, traveling with the team to broadcast the *away* contests was unheard of. Only the home games were broadcast from the scene; the away games were re-created by telegraphic report.

It took a special talent to broadcast an entire ball game from several brief slips of paper, at the same time maintaining a semblance of realism and authenticity. Sitting at a table, describing an event occurring hundreds of miles away, truly tested the mettle of a good baseball announcer. With a unique talent that combined accuracy and an electric enthusiasm, Jack Graney made re-creations into a high art form, which won him legions of admirers. He said he had an advantage over the broadcasters from other cities because he had played in and was quite familiar with every American League park. When the telegrapher handed him a note saying a ball had just been hit off the scoreboard in right center field in Boston, Jack knew exactly where the spot was, because he had bounced them off the same wall numerous times during his playing days.

"Actually, I disliked re-creations," he recalled. "It was a dizzy job, and more than once I'd wake up in the middle of the night in nervous fright over what had transpired in the enclosed studio the night before. So much had to be remembered. If I mistakenly positioned a base runner on third instead of second, or had two runners inadvertently switched around in the order they had scored, I'd get hundreds of letters saying 'Why did you have Trosky scoring in front of Averill when it was the other way around?' "

Many Clevelanders can still recall the time Jack was re-creating a game between the Indians and the Senators with his partner Pinky Hunter. Washington was in a jam and elected to change pitchers. They brought in a lad by the name of Joe Krakauskas, who was not listed on the scoreboard. The two announcers tossed the pronunciation around all evening, neither one landing on the right combination. In spite of minor embarrassments like this, Jack was a resourceful man at the mike. A trophy from the *Sporting News* supports that contention.

The baseball announcers of a generation ago were held in greater esteem than the broadcasters of today. It was such a novel treat to listen to a game direct from the field, which was the next best thing to being there, that the fans developed a strong personal regard for the radio reporter. In fact, most of the early voices from the field reached legendary heights during and after their broadcasting careers. There was Ty Tyson in Detroit, Fred Hoey in Boston, Rosey Rowswell of Pittsburgh, Arch McDonald from Washington, France Laux in St. Louis, Hal Totten and Pat Flanagan in Chicago, and of course, Jack in Cleveland. These were magic names.

Graney's AL career spanned fourteen seasons, 1908 to 1922. He was never a star, playing in the shadows of the spectacular Napoleon Lajoie, after whom the team was named, Tris Speaker, Addie Joss, Jim Bagby, Steve O'Neill, and others. A left-handed batter, Graney had a lifetime average of .250 for 1,402 games, but he tied for the league lead in doubles once and led the league in bases on balls twice. Being the leadoff batter, he was ordered to take two strikes for the ball club and "one for Graney," which didn't make hitting any easier. One year, though, he did manage to bat .299. One particularly satisfying moment occurred at the time that Philadelphia was dominating the league. "In this game in Philadelphia, Eddie Plank was pitching and the score was tied," Graney remembered. "We had runners on second and third and Lajoie was walked intentionally so they could pitch to me. But their game plan backfired when I tripled home three runs to win the game."

However inconspicuous he might have been as a player, Graney managed to carve out several firsts. Back in 1914 he had the distinction of being the first to hit against a raw left-hander for the Boston Red Sox named George Herman Ruth. As the leadoff man, Jack was also the first big leaguer ever to appear at the plate with a number sewn on his uniform.

Graney used to refer to baseball as "my whole life," and like so many oldtimers, he gave the game more than he received from it. It was a NL umpire named Bob Emslie, a resident of St. Thomas, who first took notice of young Graney, who was then a pitcher on the local team. Emslie convinced the Chicago Cubs to take a chance on the Canadian, and after stop-offs in Rochester, New York, and Erie and Wilkes-Barre, Pennsylvania, he was sold to the Naps and went to spring training with them at Macon, Georgia. It turned out to be one of the worst mistakes of his life.

> I threw batting practice one morning and was so wild, each batter stood up to the plate over five minutes before I served up anything in the neighborhood of a strike. When Lajoie came up to the plate I wanted to give it everything I had because he was the manager of the team and one of baseball's greatest hitters. That's all I could think about, the boys back in St. Thomas sitting around the coal stove talking about how Jack Graney struck out the great Lajoie. I reared

back and threw the fastest ball I had ever pitched and instead of striking him out I *knocked* him out. The ball glanced off the side of his head and bounded up into the stands. The next day I was handed a ticket to Portland, Oregon, by Mr. Lajoie, who insisted that all wildmen belong in the West.

In 1910 Jack returned to the big leagues for good, this time as an outfielder—Lajoie didn't want to take any chances. In this year, the Naps had George Stovall on first base, Lajoie on second, Bill Bradley on third, and Terry Turner at short. Cy Young and Addie Joss were two of the pitchers, but their big years were behind them. Jack remembers that he was so thrilled about making the big leagues that he slept for days with his uniform on. Nobody could take it off him, but then nobody tried.

They talk about the domination of the pitcher in modern baseball and the wide assortment of pitches, but it was no different years ago. According to Graney, "They threw everything." The spitter was prominent then. So was the emery ball, and the shine ball, "which was outlawed when big Dave Danforth of the White Sox hit Tris Speaker on the head and almost ended his career."

He remembers his roomie, Ray Chapman, and the day at the Polo Grounds in August 1920 that he was fatally struck by a pitched ball thrown by submariner Carl Mays. Sitting on the bench, Jack watched the ball hit Chapman's head and then bounce back to Mays on the fly. With fractures on both sides of his skull and a neck that was broken, Chapman did not have a chance. After they rushed the ill-fated shortstop to the clubhouse, Jack, in his haste to revive his dying comrade, tried to get him to write something, but in a state of unconsciousness and moaning incoherently, Chapman dazedly dropped the pencil to the floor. It was a tragic episode in baseball history, and several of the Cleveland players took leaves of absence to try to forget what had happened. Joey Sewell was quickly summoned from New Orleans to play short, and the youngster helped spark the Indians to the 1920 pennant and World Championship.

In 1922 at the antiquated baseball age of thirty-six, Graney drifted away from the game he loved after managing the last-place Des Moines outfit of the Western League for a half season to help his friend Jim Dunn, the owner of the Cleveland club. He turned to selling automobiles, and until 1927, when Ford changed its model types from T to A and shut down its plants for over a year, he operated a successful Ford agency in Cleveland. Jack invested his savings and lived contentedly for two years until the great crash of 1929.

By 1932 radio had become a powerful asset to baseball. The

Indians' games had been broadcast since 1927 on the team's flagship station, WTAM, but after the 1931 campaign the radio contract shifted to WHK and a search began for a new announcer. Unable to find a polished sportscaster, Billy Evans, the Indians' general manager, quickly summoned Graney, also having his troubles, and within a few hours the problems of both parties were solved.

Baseball broadcasting provided a new lease on life for Jack Graney, and he always said that broadcasting was the next best thing to playing. His biggest thrill in radio occurred in 1935 when he was asked by the Columbia Broadcasting System to cover the World Series between the Tigers and Cubs. He had been asked to do the 1934 classic but was forbidden by Commissioner Kenesaw Mountain Landis because he might show partiality, since he had played in the junior circuit. Graney was the first of what has become a long line of major leaguers to broadcast baseball. Perturbed and angered that the Judge would hold this against him, Jack wrote the commissioner a letter declaring that "my playing days are over. I am now a sportscaster and should be regarded as such." In 1935, he received no static from Landis.

Graney broadcast thousands of games and went through six partners (Bud Richmond, Gil Gibbons, Lou Henry, Pinky Hunter, Van Patrick, and Jimmy Dudley) before he retired. One of the occasions he remembers best was when the Indians pulled into Boston's South Station amid the jeers of partisan Red Sox fans in 1948, the day before the two teams played off for the AL pennant. The site was determined by the flip of a coin, and Boston won, sending nightmarish thoughts of Fenway Park's left field wall up the spine of every Indian. "Gene Bearden was elected to pitch because he had the best chance of keeping the ball low and preventing any ball from sailing over the wall. The game was scoreless around the second or third inning, when third baseman Kenny Keltner, with runners on first and second and no outs, strode to the plate in an obvious bunt situation. After failing in his first attempt to lay one down, Keltner drove the next pitch over the left-field wall to make it 3–0. It was the straw that broke the camel's back." The Sox crumpled, and the Tribe went on to take the World Series from the Boston Braves, four games to two, in what was Cleveland's finest baseball hour.

"I always tried to give the fans an honest account," Graney stated. "It was a tremendous responsibility, and at all times I kept in mind the fact that I was the eyes of the radio audience. I was like an artist trying to paint a picture. I never tried to predict or second guess, even though I had played the game. I just tried to do my best, and I hope my best was good enough."

Ty Cobb Steals Home!
Warren W. Mouch

Tyrus R. Cobb, the Georgia Peach, who ravaged American League diamonds and pitchers for twenty-four years, is rated by many as the greatest all-around player, having more records in more phases of the game than any other performer. In addition, Cobb possessed a competitive spirit and will and a keen brain unequaled by any other player. Cobb was a human dynamo whose fiery spirit generated the currents of baseball with a higher voltage than any other player. As a hitter and as a base runner, the Georgia Tornado was tall enough to look over the top of the trees in the forest, and even if his lifetime batting average were reduced from .367 to .267, he would still be outstanding because of his base running and competitive spirit.

As we ramble down the base lines to review Cobb's many records, we come across numerous amazing feats that confounded his opponents. Probably the most unusual feat of Cobb's is his record of stealing home 35 times in regular-season play (plus one time in a World Series). Only one other player—George J. Burns, National League outfielder from 1911 to 1925—came anywhere near the fast-moving Tiger, with 27 steals of home. Behind him is Frank "Wildfire" Schulte of the Cubs, who had 22.

In looking over the list of Cobb's steals of home, one of the first things to be noted is that they are well distributed over his career, with

Ty Cobb

a high of six coming in 1915, the year he set what was for a long time the AL record of 96 stolen bases. On June 18 of that year, Cobb stole home twice in one game against the Nats, once in the first inning and again in the fifth. The Detroit victory, by a 5–3 margin, indicated the importance of those two runs. Washington had two catchers in this game because Dutch Henry left with a spike wound after Cobb slid home in the first inning. Joe Boehling was on the hill during both steals and thus became one of only two hurlers to suffer through two thefts of home by Cobb. The other was Ray Caldwell of the Yankees. The second time it happened to Caldwell, on June 4, 1915, he was so angry at the call of safe by Umpire O'Loughlin that he threw his glove in the air. He was quickly ejected from the game. Cobb's favorite catchers were Agnew, Ainsmith, Carrigan, Crouse, Hartley, Lapp, Nunamaker, Picinich, Sewell, and Sweeney, each of whom had double embarrassment at the hands (and feet) of the elusive base thief.

Cobb had three spectacular days in which he stole second, third, and home in the same inning. The first time was July 22, 1909, against the Red Sox; the second was July 12, 1911, against the A's; and the third was July 4, 1912, against the Browns. In the 1911 game, he stole the three bases on consecutive pitches in a 9–0 Tiger romp.

Three times Cobb stole home as the lead man of a triple steal. In 1915 he did it with Veach and Crawford, in 1919 with Heilmann and Shorten, and in 1927 with Simmons and Branom. Cobb had four steals of home with the Athletics in 1927–28. Of these, his biggest day was April 26, 1927. He collected three hits, including a double that knocked in the winning run; he also walked and stole home in the seventh inning as the relief pitcher was about to deliver his first pitch. This was considered quite a feat, considering that a left-handed batter, Jim Poole, was at the plate, which gave the catcher full access to the forty-year-old base runner. In this same game, in the ninth inning, Cobb made a shoe-string catch in shallow right and trapped the runner off first in an unassisted double play that ended the game. No wonder he was called the greatest all-round player.

Cobb mastered all of the tools of the trade, which made him one of the greatest base runners in the game. By his own statement, Cobb was not the fastest runner. However, he was the smartest and most aggressive. He constantly studied pitchers' deliveries and developed the fall-away slide and some six other sliding maneuvers to foil the baseman. He also led the opposition into traps and feigned injuries to mislead the defense.

All of this was buttressed by his ability to apply psychology to any given situation that gave him an edge on the opposition. As an example of this, we cite his steal of home in the 1909 World Series against the Pirates. Victor Willis, a veteran hurler of considerable stature, came in as a reliever in the October 9 game. Cobb, on third, noted that Willis was concentrating on the batter. This created the lull that Cobb needed, and he dashed for home before Willis could gather his senses and throw to catcher George Gibson.

Anyone who took his mind off Cobb when he was on the bases was inviting trouble. On June 23, 1915, in a game against the Browns, Cobb was at second with Crawford at bat. Sam tapped to the pitcher, the lanky Grover Lowdermilk, who took a somersault going for the ball. Cobb went to third on the play and, seeing the befuddled Lowdermilk sitting on the ground with the ball in his hand, romped home for a clean steal.

Over the course of his career Cobb stole home in each month from April to October. He sneaked home at least once in each inning except the second. In eight games the run he scored stealing home proved to be the margin of victory. That was really the way he played—to win—and all it took was one run. The full list of his thefts of home follows.

Date	Teams and Score				Opposing Battery	Inning
July 22, 1909	Bos.	0,	Det.	6	Wolter & Donohue	7
Aug. 16, 1910	Det.	8,	Wash.	3	Groom & Ainsmith	4
May 12, 1911	N.Y.	5,	Det.	6	Caldwell & Sweeney	7
July 12, 1911	Phil.	0,	Det.	9	Krause & Thomas	1
Aug. 18, 1911	Det.	9,	N.Y.	4	Killalay & Carrigan	1
Apr. 20, 1912	Det.	6,	Clev.	5	Gregg & Easterly	1
May 1, 1912	Det.	2,	Chi.	5	Benz & Block	1
May 13, 1912	N.Y.	15,	Det.	4	Vaughn & Street	1
June 21, 1912	Det.	2,	Clev.	6	Blanding & O'Neill	6
July 4, 1912 (1)*	StL.	3,	Det.	9	Baumgardner & Krichell	5
May 18, 1913	Det.	1,	Wash.	2	Johnson & Ainsmith	7
May 20, 1913	Det.	8,	Phil.	7	Houck & Lapp	3
Aug. 25, 1913	Det.	6,	Wash.	5	Bedient & Nunamaker	5
Sept. 15, 1913	N.Y.	5,	Det.	7	Warhop & Sweeney	5
June 9, 1914	Phil.	7,	Det.	1	Shawkey & Lapp	4
Apr. 28, 1915	StL.	3,	Det.	12	James & Agnew	3
June 4, 1915	Det.	3,	N.Y.	0	Caldwell & Nunamaker	9
June 9, 1915	Det.	15,	Bos.	0	Collins & Carrigan	3
June 18, 1915	Det.	5,	Wash.	3	Boehling & Henry	1
June 18, 1915	Det.	5,	Wash.	3	Boehling & Williams	5
June 23, 1915	StL.	2,	Det.	4	Lowdermilk & Agnew	8
Aug. 23, 1916	Det.	10,	Phil.	3	Sheehan & Picinich	8
July 9, 1918 (2)	Det.	5,	Phil.	4	Perry & Perkins	5
Aug. 23, 1919	Bos.	4,	Det.	8	Hoyt & Walters	3
May 18, 1920	Phil.	2,	Det.	8	Martin & Myatt	8
Sept. 19, 1920 (1)	Wash.	7,	Det.	9	Bono & Gharrity	4
Oct. 2, 1923	Det.	7,	Chi.	5	Castner & Crouse	7
Apr. 22, 1924	Chi.	3,	Det.	4	Bayne & Collins	3
Apr. 27, 1924	Chi.	3,	Det.	4	Lyons & Crouse	5
Aug. 10, 1924	Det.	13,	Bos.	7	Ross & Picinich	7

* Numbers in parentheses indicate first or second game of a doubleheader

Date	Teams and Score	Opposing Battery	Inning
July 3, 1927	Det. 5, Clev. 7	Uhle & Sewell	1
Apr. 19, 1927	Phil. 3, Wash. 1	Crowder & Ruel	6
Apr. 26, 1927	Phil. 9, Bos. 8	Welzer & Hartley	7
July 6, 1927	Bos. 1, Phil. 5	Lundgren & Hartley	1
June 15, 1928	Phil. 12, Clev. 5	Grant & Sewell	8
World Series			
Oct. 9, 1909	Det. 7, Pitt. 2	Willis & Gibson	3

* Numbers in parentheses indicate first or second game of a doubleheader

The Grove–
Cochrane Debut
Bill Loughman

April 14, 1925, was a typical opening day of the baseball season. At least it seemed that way at the time. A quarter of a million fans watched the opening games. This included the 45,000 who watched the Yankees, led by Babe Ruth's stand-in, Ben Paschal, beat the Senators 5–1. Babe was in the hospital suffering from the aftereffects of his famous spring training tummyache.

The National League celebrated its fiftieth season with opening ceremonies marked by the appearance of NL president Heydler at Boston and Commissioner Landis at Chicago. Judge Landis and forty thousand others, the second largest crowd in Chicago history, saw Grover Cleveland Alexander hit a home run and two singles to lead the Cubs to an 8–2 win over the eventual league champions, the Pittsburgh Pirates.

Thirty-five runs and thirty-nine hits highlighted the Browns' opener at St. Louis as Cleveland won 21–14. Tris Speaker hit a home run for the Indians while the usually sure-fingered George Sisler made four errors for the Browns at first base. Several future Hall of Famers appeared in Boston as the Braves beat the Giants 5–4. Two of them appeared at first base for the Giants in that game, George Kelly and Bill Terry.

Six players made their first big league appearance at Philadelphia

Lefty Grove and Mickey Cochrane with the Athletics in 1925

as the A's faced the Red Sox. For Boston, Ewell Gross hit a triple in his first game while his teammate, Billy Rogell (the only player to have an expressway named after him) handled ten chances errorlessly at second base in his initial contest. Philadelphia rookie Marvin Smith batted unsuccessfully for Stan Baumgartner, a future member of the Baseball Writers of America, and Jim Poole, Connie Mack's new first baseman from Portland, Oregon, helped his team win with a home run.

The twenty-two thousand spectators at Shibe Park also had the rare treat of watching two future Hall of Famers appear in their first major league game. In the eighth inning, Mickey Cochrane substituted for catcher Cy Perkins, who had started the game. Cochrane contributed a single in his two at bats. The starting pitcher was Lefty Grove (known as Groves in those days), who pitched rather inauspiciously, walking four batters and hitting one. The victim was Ewell Gross, in his first big league time at bat ("Welcome to the big leagues, Mr. Gross"). Grove didn't strike out a batter and was knocked out of the box in the fourth. In his first time at bat, Lefty struck out. As a matter of fact, he fanned ten times in his first thirteen times at bat in the majors. (Connie Mack didn't worry much about Lefty's hitting prowess. A couple of weeks later, on May 1, another future Hall of Famer hit a pinch-hit single in his big league debut and went on to hit 534 home runs in a twenty-year career. He was seventeen years old during the 1925 season, and his name was Jimmie Foxx.)

So the double debut of Cochrane and Grove was not a planned event. The two players had a certain renown in the minor leagues, particularly Grove. However, the hard-throwing southpaw was known to have control problems, with both his fast ball and his temper. He might have had trouble in the majors with a manager less patient than Connie Mack. As for Cochrane, he was regarded as having good potential, but according to one newspaper report he was expected to be sent back to Portland for another year of seasoning. It didn't turn out that way. Grove and Cochrane became baseball's greatest battery as well as top-rank individual stars. They were the only players of Hall of Fame caliber to make their major league debuts in the same game.

Boston	AB	R	H	Philadelphia	AB	R	H
Flagstead CF	5	1	4	Bishop 2B	4	2	2
Prothro 3B	5	1	1	Dykes 3B	3	0	0
Boone RF	5	0	2	Lamar LF	5	1	2
Veach LF	5	0	1	Simmons CF	5	0	0
Harris 1B	5	2	1	Miller RF	5	1	1
Gross SS	3	2	1	Poole 1B	4	2	3
Rogell 2B	3	0	0	Galloway SS	3	0	0
Picinich C	4	1	2	Perkins C	3	0	0
Ferguson P	3	1	0	Groves P	1	0	0
Ross P	0	0	0	Harriss P	0	0	0
Wingfield P	1	0	0	1-French	1	0	1
Kallio P	0	0	0	Walberg P	0	0	0
				2-Hale 3B	3	2	2
				3-Welch	1	1	1
				4-Cochrane C	2	0	1
				Baumgartner P	0	0	0
				5-Smith	0	0	0
				Rommel P	0	0	0
	39	8	12		40	9	13

One out when winning run scored   1 Batted for Harriss in 6th
2 Batted for Walberg in 8th   3 Batted for Dykes in 8th
4 Batted for Perkins in 8th   5 Batted for Baumgartner in 9th

Boston .... 0 2 0 3 1 0 0 1 1 0   —8
Philadelphia .... 0 0 0 0 0 0 2 4 1 1   —9

Errors—Gross, Bishop 2, Poole. Two-base hits—Picinich 2, Boone, Lamar. Three-base hits—Gross. Home runs—Miller, Poole, Flagstead, Welch, Harris. Struck out—Ferguson 1, Harriss 2, Walberg 2, Rommel 2. Bases on Balls—Groves 4, Ferguson 1, Harriss 1, Ross 1. Sacrifice hits—Rogell, Flagstead, Smith, Galloway. Hit by pitcher—Groves, Gross.

Dean Was Ruthless with Aging Babe

Babe Ruth and Dizzy Dean, two of baseball's most colorful performers, faced each other in only two games, May 5 and 19, 1935. Dean was then in his prime with the Cardinals, whereas Ruth was forty and was closing out his career with the Boston Braves. Diz clearly had the upper hand, holding the Babe hitless in six trips in the two games, both of which he won.

The May 5 game, before 30,000 anxious fans in Boston, was the more exciting. Dean walked Ruth in the first, and in the fourth worked the count on the Bambino to one ball and two strikes. Diz, with a wide grin on his face, then waved his outfielders back to the fences. He reared back and steamed a fast one down the middle. The huge crowd was stunned into silence as Ruth swung mightily and missed. This was frosting on the cake for Dean, because, in his first time at bat, he had hit a screaming line drive over Ruth's head and into the left field stands for a home run. It was a big day for Dean as he blanked the Braves 7–0.

Under the Lights
Oscar Eddleton

More than one hundred years ago, on Thursday, September 2, 1880, teams representing two of Boston's prominent department stores, Jordan Marsh and Company and R. H. White and Company, played a game of baseball at Nantasket Bay on the ocean side of Hull, Massachusetts.

This game would have held no historic value and would long since have been forgotten had it not been for one unique feature. It was the first baseball game ever played at night under the lights.

The debut of night baseball a century ago was an ambiguous one in the sense that the game itself was not the main attraction. Rather, the primary event was an elaborate lighting display staged by the Northern Electric Light Company of Boston to demonstrate the feasibility of illuminating large areas, including cities. Thomas Edison had invented the incandescent lamp the previous year, so this baseball game under the lights was a means of proving a point.

The contest was played on the lawn at the rear of Nantasket's Sea Foam House. Three wooden towers were erected some 100 feet apart; at their summits were placed 12 electric lamps having a combined strength of 30,000 candlepower. Two engines with three electric generators, one for each tower, were located in a small shed.

The *Boston Post* of September 3, 1880, reported, "When the

lamps were lighted after dark the effect was fine. A clear, pure, bright light was produced, very strong and yet very pleasant to the sight."

Although the *Post* stated that this first nocturnal baseball game was played "with scarcely the precision as by daylight," Jordan Marsh and R. H. White did play nine innings to a 16–16 tie, at which time the game was called to allow the two teams to take the last boat back to Boston. Some three hundred spectators attended the historic encounter.

It would make a good story to be able to state that night baseball became an instant success following its debut at Nantasket Bay and that the professional leagues began to consider its possibilities with interest and enthusiasm. Of course, such was not the case. Actually, another fifty years passed before the moguls of organized baseball finally decided to give the arc lights a serious try.

The next night game on record was played on June 2, 1883, at Fort Wayne, Indiana, between Quincy, Illinois, and a team called the M. E. Church Nine. Quincy won 19–11 in a seven-inning game played before some two thousand fans.

There is evidence of other night games played during the nineteenth century, but they were strictly exhibitions and were considered by organized baseball as merely "a craving for novelty."

The long hiatus following the birth of night baseball in 1880 did, however, produce some interesting experiments that perhaps enhanced the development of the concept of playing under the lights.

In 1909 there appeared on the scene one George F. Cahill, an inventor from Holyoke, Massachusetts. In addition to a pitching machine, he had devised a portable lighting system and obviously possessed a vision of what night baseball could become. He journeyed about the country trying to interest ball clubs in his invention.

With the permission of Garry Herrmann, president of the Cincinnati Reds, Cahill staged a night game on June 19, 1909, in the Reds' park between the Elk lodges of Cincinnati and Newport, Kentucky. Surprisingly, the game was played without difficulty, and the 3,000 spectators, including the Cincinnati and Philadelphia teams, who had played that afternoon, had little trouble following the ball. President Herrmann appeared impressed, as were others, but nothing of consequence came of it.

A month later, on July 7, 1909, there was a breakthrough of sorts. On that date Grand Rapids and Zanesville of the Class B Central League played a night game at the Ramona Athletic Park, Grand Rapids, Michigan. The mayor of Grand Rapids, George Ellis, officiated as umpire.

The *Grand Rapids Herald* of July 8, 1909, reported that Grand

Rapids won the seven-inning contest 11–10 over Zanesville before a crowd of 4,500 fans "drawn by the novelty of the play by artificial light." The *Herald* also stated, "outfielders had their troubles in judging the balls hit in their direction, but the light was perfect for the batters, and how they did land on the ball."

The question immediately arose as to whether the contest would count in the league standings. It did not. There was a rule of that period which prohibited league games from starting later than two hours before sunset.

Meanwhile, George F. Cahill was persistent in his efforts to convince the major leagues of the wisdom of attempting night baseball. This time he turned to the American League.

On August 27, 1910, using his patented lighting system, Cahill staged a night game at the new White Sox Park in Chicago with the approval of president Charles Comiskey. Over twenty thousand fans watched the Logan Square and the Rogers Park teams play nine innings under the glare of twenty 137,000-candlepower arc lights. Once again the experiment was successful, but there were meager results beyond the event itself.

George F. Cahill, a man ahead of his time, was doomed to disappointment and frustration. Despite his determined and apparently successful efforts, the magnates of baseball refused to take his vision of night baseball seriously. Fortunately, he did live long enough to attend the first major league night game, in Cincinnati on May 24, 1935. His dream was now a reality.

There was one final experiment with baseball under the lights before the advent of the real thing. It occurred on June 24, 1927, when Lynn and Salem of the Class B New England League played an exhibition game sponsored by the General Electric Employees' Athletic Association. The contest, a seven-inning affair, was played at General Electric Field, West Lynn, Massachusetts, with Lynn the victor, 7–2. The game itself was an artistic success with several spectacular catches, a double play by Lynn, and only two errors.

The crowd, estimated at more than five thousand, included Claude B. Johnson, president of the New England League, who predicted that within five years all leagues, including the majors, would have night baseball. Also on hand were delegations from the Boston Red Sox and Washington Senators, who were playing in Boston. Both managers, Bucky Harris of the Senators and Bill Carrigan of the Red Sox, were high in their praise, both foreseeing night exhibition games in the major leagues in the near future. The players were impressed as well, with Goose Goslin, Washington's star outfielder, expressing a personal desire to play in a night game. Adding to the pleasure of the occasion was the famed baseball comedian Al Schacht, who delighted the crowd with his pregame antics.

In retrospect, it is difficult to comprehend the aversion of organized baseball to the night game when so much interest and enthusiasm were expressed whenever and wherever it was played. Certainly some innovative and venturesome club owner or general manager would seize the initiative and become a pioneer on this new frontier. But it did not happen immediately. Finally, in late 1929, E. Lee Keyser, president of the Des Moines club of the Class A Western League, announced at the annual National Association convention that he intended to open the 1930 season at night in Des Moines. The race for the honor of the first regular season night game was on.

Keyser meant for his home opener against Witchita to be a gala occasion *and* the first night game played in regular league competition. The game was a festive event, as planned, but it was not a nocturnal first. Unfortunately for the Des Moines team, the Western League schedule called for it to open the season on the road. The home opener could not be played until May 2, 1930.

Meanwhile, the Producers of Independence, Kansas, of the Class C Western Association, were to open their season at home against Muskogee and they were intent upon the honor of playing the first league game under the lights. The lighting equipment had been installed at Riverside Park, and the historic game was scheduled for April 26, 1930. However, the honor was delayed, as the game was rained out. A Sunday afternoon game was played on April 27. The big game finally came off on Monday, April 28.

Around one thousand fans turned out for the nocturnal first, which was played on a soggy field and won by Muskogee, 13–3. One old Producer recalls the famous game. "I don't remember having much trouble with the lights," stated catcher Sherman Walker. "They were pretty good, although I do remember you'd get a shadow which gave you the impression it was only half a ball."

Very quickly minor league teams discovered that in spite of the financial difficulties caused by the Great Depression, baseball under the lights often doubled and tripled their attendance figures. The writer attended the first night game in Richmond, Virginia, in 1933, when that city had a team in the Class B Piedmont League, and recalls the positive impact it had. Indeed, it is fair to say that night baseball was the economic savior of many minor league teams during those dark days of the depression. By 1934, 15 of the 19 minor leagues had one or more parks equipped with lights. Still the major leagues declined to participate. Their 1934 schedules listed day games only.

In 1935, however, there was a capitulation. At the National

League meeting in December 1934 Leland Stanford "Larry" MacPhail, the dynamic general manager of the Cincinnati Reds, requested permission to introduce night baseball in Cincinnati. MacPhail had experienced considerable success with the innovation at Columbus of the American Association.

The idea of playing major league baseball under artificial lights was still repugnant to most of the NL executives, who regarded the night game as a risky experiment. This sentiment is clearly reflected in the report of the matter in the 1935 Spalding's *Baseball Guide*.

With great reluctance, however, MacPhail was granted permission to play seven night games at Cincinnati in 1935, one with each team, provided each consented. The NL's concession to Cincinnati was justified as an attempt to assist a franchise that was in perilous financial condition.

The first night game in major league history was played at Cincinnati's Crosley Field on May 24, 1935, with an attendance of 20,422. President Franklin D. Roosevelt, seated in the White House, pushed a button, and 1,090,000 watts of electric power from 632 lamps flooded the field, turning night into day. Ford Frick, president of the National League, threw out the first ball, after which the Reds defeated the visiting Philadelphia Phillies 2–1 behind the six-hit pitching of Paul Derringer. The initial reacton was mixed and enthusiasm was tempered, but overall there was no denying that the arc light debut had been a genuine success.

It was indeed appropriate that Cincinnati, the birthplace of professional baseball in 1869, should host the occasion marking the beginning of a bright new chapter in the game's colorful history.

Larry MacPhail continued to be the apostle of night baseball as he moved from Cincinnati to Brooklyn in 1938 and quickly installed lights at Ebbets Field. There the first game under the lights was played on June 15, and this time Cincinnati was the visiting team. It was an artistic success in every way as the Reds' Johnny Vander Meer pitched his second successive no-hit game in blanking the Dodgers 6–0 before 38,748 fans.

By now the American League was becoming interested in the night game. Ironically, the first convert was the league's oldest executive, Connie Mack, age seventy-six, president and manager of the Philadelphia Athletics. Connie had noted the surge in attendance and receipts at Cincinnati and Brooklyn for night contests. Lights were erected at Shibe Park in 1939, and on May 16 the Athletics and Cleveland played the inaugural night game with the Indians winning 8–3 in ten innings before 15,109. The NL Phillies, who had become tenants of Shibe Park, also played seven night games in 1939.

In 1940, 70 night games were scheduled in the majors, and for the first time more parks had lights than not. The only holdouts were Boston and Chicago in the National League and New York, Boston, Detroit, and Washington in the American. Lights were erected at Griffith Stadium in Washington in 1941, while the Yankees and the Boston Braves waited until 1946 to install lights. The Red Sox followed in 1947, and Detroit was the last AL team into the fold in 1948.

The first major league All-Star Game played under the lights, on July 6, 1942, at the Polo Grounds in New York, was not intended to be a nocturnal contest. However, an afternoon rain delayed the game's start until 7:22 P.M. The contest ended two minutes before a World War II blackout test at 9:30, with the AL winning 3–1.

As the decade of the 1950s began, Sportsman's Park in St. Louis was the scene of the first season-opening night game, on April 18, 1950, as the Cardinals defeated the Pittsburgh Pirates 4–2.

A year later, on April 17, 1951, the AL staged its opening night inaugural at Shibe Park, where the Philadelphia Athletics lost to the Washington Senators 6–1.

Twenty years passed before the first World Series night game was played. On October 13, 1971, at Three Rivers Stadium, Pittsburgh, the Pirates edged the Baltimore Orioles 4–3 before a record throng of 51,378 in game No. 4 of that series.

Today major league schedules include a preponderance of night games. Only the Chicago Cubs play all their home games in daylight. Picturesque Wrigley Field provides the young fan interested in baseball history with an opportunity to see the way it used to be.

In terms of the history of night baseball, 1980 marked the centennial of the first game played under the lights (September 2, 1880); the golden jubilee of the first regular season night game in the minor leagues (April 28, 1930); the 45th anniversary of the first major league night game (May 24, 1935); and the 30th anniversary of the first season opening night game (April 18, 1950). These anniversaries reflect to some extent the slow but determined progress of night baseball despite the barriers of apathy, skepticism, hostility, and fear of innovation.

The Gehrig Streak Reviewed

Raymond J. Gonzalez

On June 1, 1925, Lou Gehrig began his remarkable record of playing in 2,130 consecutive major league games. For the next fourteen years Yankee managers did not have to worry about who was playing first base for the New Yorkers. This does not mean that Gehrig always played first base or that he played every inning of every game. Only in 1931 did Lou play every inning, and one game he was in the outfield.

Actually, this is a story about those players who briefly replaced Gehrig when he was sick or injured or when he eased up in September after the Yankees had clinched another of their numerous pennants or when he was ejected from a game. Yes, he was ousted at least six times in his career. To modern Gehrig fans, this may come as a surprise because it seems inconsistent with his quiet demeanor off the field. While Gehrig did not have Babe Ruth's bombastic and tempestuous personality on the field (for which the latter was suspended several times), Lou nevertheless was a very forceful player and was on top of every play. He was very competitive and was not averse to confronting the umpires.

In 1925, when Gehrig was breaking in, there was no indication that he was going to be an everyday performer any more than Earle Combs, Bob Meusel, or any other Yankee. In fact, on the first day of what we now know as his streak, he was a pinch-hitter. Two days later

Aaron Ward pinch-hit for him in the ninth, and when the game went into extra innings, Wally Pipp, heretofore the regular first sacker, took Lou's place in the field. This happened several times that month. On July 5 the starting Yankee first baseman was Fred Merkle, renowned for a miscue with the Cubs two decades earlier. Lou got into the game only in the last inning when the aging Merkle fainted from the heat. On July 21, Gehrig was injured by an Earl Whitehill pitch, and Merkle relieved him.

Since all the variations in Gehrig's fourteen-year streak at first base are noted on the accompanying list, I will cite only a few cases of particular interest.

In a late-season stunt on September 28, 1930, Gehrig played the entire game in left field while Ruth pitched a complete-game victory over the Red Sox. Harry Rice played first base. This ended Lou's streak of 885 games at first, still a major league record.

Early the following season another switch was made, necessitated by Ruth's leg injuries. To keep the Bambino's big bat in the lineup, the Yanks played Ruth at first base against Washington on May 4, 1931, and Lou took the Babe's place in right field. The Iron Horse starred at bat but made one error.

In 1934, Gehrig had several threats to his streak, but each time he responded brilliantly. On May 10 he played only five innings because he was suffering from a severe cold. Of course, by that time he had already hit two homers and two doubles for seven runs batted in. On June 29 he was hit in the head by a pitched ball in an exhibition game in Norfolk. Surprisingly, he was able to start the next day in Washington, where he hit three triples in 4½ innings before the game was rained out.

The biggest threat to his string came on July 13, 1934, with the Yanks playing in Detroit. He had a severe case of lumbago. After singling off Tommy Bridges and rounding first base, he was immobilized with pain. He was helped from the field, and Jack Saltzgaver took over at first. It looked as though his streak was to end at 1,426 games. The next day Detroit fans were startled to see Gehrig's name listed in the starting lineup—and at shortstop and leading off. It was a managerial maneuver for the visiting team. Lou, hardly able to stand, banged out a single as the first man up. He quickly gave way to pinch runner Red Rolfe and retired to his hotel bed. Rolfe played the entire game at short, although Gehrig was officially credited with an appearance there. Saltzgaver played the entire contest at first.

Although still wobbly, Gehrig returned to the lineup at first base the next day, July 15, and collected four hits in four trips, including three doubles off Schoolboy Rowe. His consecutive-game streak nearly came to an end in that Detroit series, but his batting average did not suffer. He went 6 for 6 on the way to his only batting title and the triple crown.

Gehrig continued in the Yankee lineup for the next five years. Finally, on May 2, 1939, in another series with the Tigers in Detroit, the Iron Horse stayed in the dugout. For the first time in fourteen years, his name did not appear in the Yankee lineup—in any capacity.

In summary, during those 2,130 consecutive games, Lou was relieved by a pinch hitter 8 times, by a pinch runner 4 times, by a first baseman 66 times. Sometimes the first baseman was the pinch hitter or runner, and sometimes Gehrig was installed at another position. In case you wonder what Yankee substituted the most times for Gehrig at first base in the period 1925–39, it was Jack Saltzgaver, who played varying lengths of time in 17 games. Fortunately, Jack was able to play second and third, or he wouldn't have had much activity.

Here is the full replacement log for Gehrig from June 1, 1925, to May 2, 1939.

Date	Opposing Team	Comment
June 3, 1925	Washington	Ward PH; Pipp played 1B
June 4, 1925	Washington	Pipp played 1B in 9th
June 18, 1925	Detroit	Paschal PH; Pipp played 1B
June 19, 1925	Chicago	E. Johnson PH; Pipp played 1B
June 23, 1925	Washington	Paschal PH; Pipp played 1B
July 5, 1925	Washington	Merkle started at 1B; Gehrig in 9th
July 15, 1925*	Cleveland	Merkle PH and played 1B
July 17, 1925	Cleveland	Merkle replaced Gehrig at 1B
July 19, 1925	Detroit	Merkle started at 1B; Gehrig in 6th
July 21, 1925	Detroit	Hit by pitch; replaced by Merkle
Aug. 2, 1925	Cleveland	Paschal PH in 9th
May 25, 1926	Boston	Injured chasing fly; Ruth to 1B
June 29, 1926	Philadelphia	Ejected by umpire; Ruth to 1B
Sept. 26, 1926	St. Louis	Pennant clinched; Merkle to 1B in 7th
July 9, 1927	Detroit	Durst came in at 1B in 9th
Sept. 29, 1927	Washington	Pennant clinched; Durst to 1B
May 31, 1928	Washington	Ejected by umpire; Durst to 1B
July 9, 1928*	St. Louis	Ejected by umpire; Durst to 1B
Aug. 5, 1928	Chicago	Lame foot; Gazella PR in 9th
Aug. 6, 1928	Chicago	Durst PR and played 1B

* Second game

Date	Opposing Team	Comment
Sept. 29, 1928	Detroit	Pennant clinched; G. Burns to 1B
Sept. 30, 1928	Detroit	KOed by batted ball; Burns to 1B
July 21, 1929	Cleveland	Gehrig-Huggins ejected; Durst to 1B
May 7, 1930	Cleveland	Injured foot; Lazzeri to 1B
Sept. 5, 1930	Washington	Replaced by Rice in lost cause
Sept. 14, 1930	Detroit	Replaced by Rice in 9th
Sept. 16, 1930	St. Louis	Replaced by Rice in 9th
Sept. 21, 1930	Chicago	Replaced by Rice in 9th
Sept. 27, 1930	Philadelphia	Replaced by Rice in 9th
Sept. 28, 1930	Boston	Played LF; Ruth pitched; Rice 1B
May 4, 1931	Washington	Played RF; Ruth played 1B
Apr. 23, 1932	Philadelphia	Replaced by Ruth at 1B midgame
Sept. 15, 1932	Chicago	Combs PH; Hoag to 1B
Sept. 17, 1932	St. Louis	Pennant clinched; L. Lary to 1B
Sept. 18, 1932	St. Louis	Replaced by Lary and E. Farrell at 1B
Sept. 18, 1932*	St. Louis	Replaced by Lary and Farrell
Sept. 23, 1932	Boston	Pennant clinched; Lary to 1B
Sept. 24, 1932	Boston	Pennant clinched; Lary to 1B
Sept. 25, 1932	Boston	Pennant clinched; Lary to 1B
May 26, 1933	Chicago	Replaced by Lary at 1B in 9th
June 14, 1933	Boston	Gehrig-McCarthy ejected; Lary to 1B
July 26, 1933*	Boston	Ejected by umpire; Lary to 1B
Sept. 28, 1933	Washington	To get married; Ruth to 1B in 4th
May 10, 1934	Chicago	Had severe cold; Lary to 1B
July 13, 1934	Detroit	Lumbago; replaced by Saltzgaver in 2nd
July 14, 1934	Detroit	Rolfe PR in 1st; Saltzgaver to 1B
Sept. 20, 1934	Detroit	Spiked; Saltzgaver to 1B
Sept. 29, 1934	Washington	Saltzgaver PR in 1st and played 1B
June 8, 1935	Boston	Injured shoulder; Saltzgaver 1B
Aug. 5, 1935	Boston	Lumbago; Hoag PH in 4th; Saltzgaver 1B
Aug. 9, 1935	Philadelphia	Ill; replaced by Saltzgaver at 1B
Sept. 18, 1935*	St. Louis	Resting; replaced by Saltzgaver at 1B
Sept. 24, 1935	Washington	Resting; replaced by Saltzgaver at 1B
Sept. 26, 1935	Washington	Resting; Saltzgaver took over in 5th
May 24, 1936	Philadelphia	Replaced by Saltzgaver in 25–2 win

* Second game

(Continued)

Date	Opposing Team	Comment
Aug. 2, 1936	Cleveland	Replaced by Saltzgaver in 14th inning
Sept. 26, 1936	Washington	Pennant clinched; Saltzgaver to 1B
Sept. 27, 1936	Washington	Pennant clinched; Saltzgaver to 1B
Sept. 28, 1937*	Washington	Replaced by Saltzgaver and Heffner
Sept. 29, 1937*	Philadelphia	Pennant clinched; Saltzgaver to 1B
Sept. 30, 1937*	Philadelphia	Pennant clinched; Saltzgaver to 1B
Oct. 3, 1937	Boston	Pennant clinched; Saltzgaver to 1B
May 22, 1938	Cleveland	Lame back; replaced by Dahlgren
July 17, 1938	Detroit	Injured thumb in 4th; Dahlgren to 1B
Aug. 16, 1938	Washington	Yanks in lopsided win; Dahlgren to 1B
Sept. 19, 1938	St. Louis	Pennant clinched; Dahlgren to 1B
Sept. 29, 1938*	Philadelphia	Pennant clinched; Dahlgren to 1B
Oct. 2, 1938	Boston	Pennant clinched; Dahlgren to 1B
May 2, 1939	Detroit	Out; Dahlgren full game at 1B

* Second game

Dave Barnhill
James A. Riley

Dave Barnhill was small, weighing only 130 pounds "when it snowed on him." But on the mound he stood tall. Leon Day, a six-time All-Star pitcher for the Newark Eagles and a contemporary of Barnhill's, marvels, "That's what I couldn't understand about him. He was so small, but he could throw that ball like he did. Very few people could throw as hard as he did."

A strikeout artist, Barnhill threw so hard that he scared himself. "I was afraid I might hit somebody," he says. Fortunately his control was as good as his fastball. When he was right, he could throw as hard as the legendary Satchel Paige. Hall of Famer Buck Leonard of the Homestead Grays, who faced Barnhill year in and year out, concurs, "He was a humdinger. He was one of the best we had in our leagues. He threw just as hard as anybody. He was right up there with Slim Jones and Satchel Paige, right next to them."

Indeed, there were some who maintained that there really wasn't any difference between Satchel and Dave. This contention was illustrated one year when Barnhill was recruited to pitch behind Satchel Paige for the Kansas City Monarchs on a barnstorming trip. This particular day the Monarchs were playing the Toledo Mudhens, a AAA white ballclub. Satch shut out the Mudhens over the first four innings, yielding a single hit while striking out ten batters. The slightly embarrassed Toledo manager approached Frank Duncan, the Monarch's manager, and said, "Hey, how about putting somebody else in so we can kinda even things up. After all, we're a major league farm club." Duncan looked down to the bullpen, where Barnhill was warming up, and said, "How about that little guy down there?" The Toledo manager quickly agreed, "Okay, put him in." Dave walked out to the mound, wound up and threw the first pitch—and the batter just stood there with his bat on his shoulder, not believing a little man could throw so hard. And so it went for the rest of the ball game. Dave pitched the last five innings without allowing a hit while striking out eleven. After the game Toledo's manager came into the clubhouse and said to Duncan, "You think you're smart, that you pulled a fast one or something." Duncan said, "What do you mean?" Toledo's manager explained, "You said that you'd take Satchel out, but you didn't. You just took him over behind the dugout and cut his legs off and put him right back in." Dave chuckles when recounting the incident.

Satchel figured prominently in Barnhill's career. As the ace on the New York Cubans' pitching staff, Dave was matched up with Satch every time the Kansas City Monarchs came to town. Dave remembers, "Normally when Satchel pitched against other teams, he would pitch only three innings and if he got one score ahead, he would come out. But anytime he came to play the Cubans, I had to pitch against him so he had to pitch nine innings. He didn't let my team get nothing, and I didn't let his team get nothing. We didn't have any of that foolishness about pitching three innings and coming out."

It was the same way in the East–West game, which was the Negro Leagues' All-Star game. When Satchel pitched, Dave pitched; and when Satch started, Dave started. This classic match-up provided Dave with his biggest thrill in baseball, as he and Satchel were the opposing starting pitchers in the 1943 All-Star game at Comiskey Park in front of 52,000 fans.

Some might think that this would make anyone nervous. After all, facing a legend in front of 52,000 screaming fans is a far cry from playing stickball in the streets of Greenville, North Carolina, which is where Dave learned his baseball skills as a youngster. But Dave was always cool and collected on the mound. He recalls, "When I walked out of the clubhouse and saw all those people, then I wanted to put on my big show. That ain't no time to be nervous."

And the record backs up his claim. In his three All-Star appearances from 1941 through 1943, he pitched a total of nine innings, giving up only two runs while striking out six batters. This was accomplished against the best in the Negro American League, including such stalwart hitters as Cool Papa Bell, Newt Allen, Alex Radcliffe,

Dave Barnhill, left, and 1943 All-Star teammate Buck Leonard

Neil Robinson, Ted Strong, Buck O'Neill, Parnell Woods, Willard Brown, and Jimmy Crutchfield. The veteran Crutchfield, who was then playing with the Chicago American Giants, vouches for what the Toledo players had found out earlier. "There were days when he could throw as hard as Satchel." Johnny Davis, hard-hitting All-Star outfielder of the Newark Eagles (who had to face Barnhill all season long), picks Dave as the pitcher who gave him the most trouble. Hall of Famer Cool Papa Bell is more direct and to the point: "He threw smoke."

It was during these years that Barnhill received the first hope that he might get the opportunity to pitch in the major leagues. In a telegram dated July 24, 1942 (more than three years before Robinson signed with the Dodger organization and before any black player had a tryout with a major league team), he received the following message from sports editor Nat Low: Have just arranged with William Benswanger, president Pittsburgh Pirates, a tryout for you with team in Pittsburgh soon. Congratulations. Won't you please get in touch with me so that we can make full arrangements?

For whatever his reasons, Benswanger backed out of his commitment, denying Barnhill a chance to be the first black player in organized baseball in modern times. Regarding the incident, Dave remembers, "He [Benswanger] was scared to take a chance."

Dave wasn't discouraged. He knew from his barnstorming trips that he was good enough to play in the major leagues. He continued his winning ways in the Negro National League, coming back from a sore arm to team with Luis Tiant, Sr., and pitch the New York Cubans to a championship in 1947. Neither he nor Tiant lost a game during that season. He also picked up another victory in the Negro World Series that year, shutting out the Negro American League champion Cleveland Buckeyes 6–0, as the New York Cubans took the series four games to one. That winter Dave went to Cuba for the first of three winters that he spent with the Marianao team. He led the league in strikeouts while compiling a 2.26 ERA. One game, played on January 10, 1948, was especially noteworthy. In this game Barnhill locked up with Connie Marrero, who was to spend five major league seasons with the Washington Senators, in a 15-inning, 0–0 marathon. Dave struck out 15 batters while allowing only 2 walks and 5 hits before the game was called. In the opposing lineup were future major leaguers Monte Irvin, Sam Jethroe, and Dee Fondy as well as Negro All-Stars Gene Benson and Pee Wee Butts.

The next winter Dave did even better, leading the Cuban League in victories as well as complete games. The Giants' organization signed him and Ray Dandridge, veteran black third baseman, to contracts. Buck Leonard states, "Now you take Dandridge and Barnhill, they could have gone right on to the majors." Ray Dandridge himself agrees and says of Barnhill, "He was one of the best pitchers there was. During that time he was great." But the major league powers-that-be thought that black players needed time in the minors to adjust to playing with white players. And although both Barnhill and Dandridge had been playing with white players for years in the winter leagues, they were sent to the Giants' AAA farm team, the Minneapolis Millers. There they pitched and batted the team to the championship in 1950. Dandridge batted .311 and earned MVP honors while Dave compiled in 11–3 won–lost record. This earned him a second brush with the major leagues.

Dave remembers, "The year we won the championship, Leo Durocher was going to call me up because I had a pretty good year and he was going to call me up like they do a lot of ballplayers at the last part of the season. Let them play with the major leaguers. But we got into a play-off. I told Dandridge, 'My goodness, I could have gone up and got a cup of coffee and come on back.' "

But it was never to be. By then Dave was thirty-six years old and past his prime as a player. Instead of going to the major leagues he stayed at Minneapolis and helped launch a youngster named Willie Mays. Later the Giants sent him to Oakland in the Pacific Coast League.

From there he returned to Florida to be near his family and pitch for Pepper Martin's Miami Beach Flamingos. He closed out his career with Fort Lauderdale in 1953.

After ending his baseball career, he worked for the Miami Department of Recreation and Parks, retiring in 1981. A handsome plaque presented to him by the Miami City Commission upon his retirement reads as follows: To Dave Barnhill, in Grateful Appreciation for Your Outstanding Demonstration of Skills and Devotion to Duty While Employed by the City of Miami from September 1953 Through January 1981. Your Performance Has Been an Excellent Example to Those Who Worked with You. This vividly describes the qualities that made Dave the kind of ballplayer he was as well as the kind of man he is.

Ty Cobb's 4,000 Hit

Pete Rose, the Phils' superstar who hopes to play long enough to surpass Ty Cobb's major league record of 4,191 hits, or at least become the second player to reach the 4,000 mark, celebrated his forty-first birthday on April 14, 1982. Cobb was forty-one years and seven months old to the day when he registered his 4,000th hit at Detroit on July 18, 1927. Cobb, who was then with the Philadelphia Athletics after having spent twenty-two years with the Tigers, doubled in the first inning off Sam Gibson, but Detroit beat the A's and Lefty Grove 5–3. If Rose ever gets close to the 4,000 mark, television, radio, and newspaper coverage probably will be unprecedented. When Cobb made his 4,000th hit, many papers, except for those in Detroit and Philadelphia, didn't even bother to mention it.

Al Kermisch

Modern Base-Stealing Proficiency
L. Robert Davids

The new era of increased base stealing launched about twenty years ago by Luis Aparicio and Maury Wills has reached a level of activity and proficiency that compares very favorably with the era of base stealing that stretched from 1900 to about 1925. Some remarkable player, team, and league base-stealing records have been achieved in recent years that would have been thought impossible in the climate of the early 1950s. Much of the credit should go to the black and Hispanic players who have dominated the new running game.

In 1978, for example, National League players stole 1,533 bases and were caught only 725 times, a record success rate of 68 percent. Compare this with 1921, when the league had 803 steals and 771 caught stealing, a success rate of only 51 percent. In 1976 the Oakland A's stole a record 341 bases. They were thrown out 123 times, but this was not a major league mark for caught stealing. In 1924 the Cubs were thrown out 149 times while stealing only 137 bases. The theft record of the A's was very good in 1976, particularly in light of their great activity, but the Cincinnati Reds that same year did considerably better. Led by Joe Morgan, they stole 210 bases and were caught only 57 times. Their success rate was 79 percent compared to 48 percent for the 1924 Cubs.

Part of the reason for the higher stealing proficiency in recent years might be the use of artificial turf. Half the NL parks have this surfacing. Three parks have it in the AL, and a review of the success rate by both home and visiting teams for the years 1977–82 at Kansas City, Seattle, and Toronto reveal that there were 2,139 steals and 961 caught stealing (69.0) at home compared to 1,829—1,130 (61.8) for the same teams on the road.

There is not enough documentation to permit the comparison of the base-stealing proficiency of different eras. The NL, for example, has caught-stealing records only for the periods 1920–25 and 1951 to the present; the AL has caught-stealing data from 1920 to the present, with the exception of 1927. However, one great record from the old days that we know of that has not been surpassed is the 1922 season record of Max Carey of the Pirates. He stole 51 bases and was thrown out only two times. He did this in a season where NL players overall were successful in only about 54 percent of their attempts (755 SB to 634 CS). Carey's great success had to balance out the futile effort of players like Pat Duncan who stole 12 sacks in 40 attempts.

It is rare in modern times for a player with 30 or so theft attempts in a season to have less than a 50 percent success rate. However, in 1977, when the Pirates were having one of their big running years, Al Oliver had 13 steals and 16 caught stealing, and Dave Parker was 17 and 19. In 1974, Greg Gross of Houston was 12 and 20. In the old days these minus marks were much more common. In addition to Pat Duncan, who had 12 steals and 28 misses in 1922, Charles Hollocher was 19 and 29 that season. Barney Friberg was 19 and 27 in 1924, Babe Ruth 17 and 21 in 1923, Jack Fournier 20 and 22 in 1921, Billy Southworth 23 and 25 in 1920, and Miller Huggins 32 and 36 in 1914. The worst record was that of Larry Gardner of the Indians in 1920— only 3 steals in 23 attempts. Even Ty Cobb had some less-than-average years, stealing only 9 times in 22 attempts in 1922.

In the six years 1920–25 there were only two great theft percentage years by players—Max Carey's 51–2 mark in 1922 and Jack Smith's 20–2 combination for the Cardinals in 1925. In the six years 1975–80 there were more than a dozen outstanding theft records. Davey Lopes could qualify for three of them with marks of 77–12 in 1975, 45–4 in 1978, and 44–4 in 1979. Joe Morgan had marks of 67–10 in 1975 and 60–9 in 1976. Larry Bowa was 32–3 in 1977, Cesar Cedeno 23–2 in 1978, Bake McBride 28–3 in 1978, Willie Wilson 83–12 in 1978 and 79–10 in 1980, Jerry Mumphrey 52–5 in 1980, and Ken Griffey 23–1 in 1980.

Rickey Henderson's especially big season in 1982 is also cited, not so much because of the percentage (130–42) but because of the sheer magnitude of the effort. He made 172 attempts in 149 games, so

Davey Lopes has one of the highest stealing success rates of any player with at least 275 career steals in the past half century

there was little wonder that he set a new mark with 42 caught stealing. Ironically, the NL record is still held by Miller Huggins, who in 1914 was caught stealing 36 times while stealing only 32 bases.

Cobb held the AL record by being thrown out 38 times in 1915, the year he swiped 96 bases. Clyde Milan was 88–33 in 1913. Willie Wilson and Maury Wills show up very well in a comparison of the most active runners of this century. Wilson's percentage figures for both 1979 and 1980 and Wills's first big effort of 104–13 in 1962 were truly outstanding. The 1980 records of Rickey Henderson (100–26) and Ron LeFlore (97–19) also were remarkable considering how frequently they were running.

Both Willis in 1962 and Wilson in 1979 and 1980 led in theft percentage even though they had a very high number of attempts. Such an outstanding performance is unusual, as can be seen in the accompanying tabulation of those players since 1920 with the best annual steal percentage. The compilation is based on at least 20 attempts for a 154-game schedule and 21 for a 162-game slate. The second column shows the players caught stealing the most each season. To put their sometimes futile efforts in perspective, their number of thefts is also listed. Note that in the NL in 1962, Wills and Bill Virdon led in caught stealing with 13. Wills, however, had 104 steals to only 5 for Virdon. It also should be noted that in a few seasons the player with the most-caught-stealing record nevertheless had the highest stealing percentage. See, for example, Willie Mays in the NL in 1956 and Luis Aparicio in the AL in 1964.

American League

Year	Highest Proficiency	SB	CS	CS Leader	SB	CS
1920	George Sisler	42	17	Sam Rice	63*	30
1921	Joe Judge	21	6	Ken Williams	20	17
1922	George Sisler	51*	19	George Sisler	51*	19
				Ken Williams	37	19
1923	Sam Rice	20	8	Eddie Collins	49*	29
1924	Eddie Collins	42*	17	Eddie Collins	42*	17
				George Sisler	19	17
1925	Lu Blue	19	5	Johnny Mostil	43*	21
1926	Earl McNeely	18	6	Sam Rice	25	23
1927	(Caught stealing not available)					
1928	Joe Judge	16	4	Johnny Mostil	23	21
1929	Charlie Gehringer	27*	9	Bill Cissell	26	17
1930	Carl Reynolds	16	4	Charlie Gehringer	19	15
1931	Bill Cissell	18	6	Ben Chapman	61*	23
1932	Gerald Walker	30	6	Ben Chapman	38*	18
1933	Bill Werber	15	5	Ben Chapman	27*	18
1934	Jo-Jo White	28	6	Ben Chapman	26	16
1935	Lyn Lary	28	4	Odell Hale	15	13
1936	Lyn Lary	37*	9	Bill Werber	23	13
1937	Jesse Hill	18	4	Bill Werber	35*	13
1938	Lyn Lary	23	6	Bill Werber	19	15
1939	Barney McCosky	20	4	George Case	51*	17
1940	Gerald Walker	21	4	George Case	35*	10
				Buddy Lewis	15	10
				Jim Tabor	14	10
				Mike Tresh	3	10

* Asterisk indicates league leader   (Continued)

American League

Year	Highest Proficiency	SB	CS	CS Leader	SB	CS
1941	Joe Kuhel	20	5	Jeff Heath	18	12
1942	George Case	44*	6	Lou Boudreau	7	16
1943	George Case	61*	14	Oris Hockett	13	18
1944	George Stirnweiss	55*	11	George Case	49	18
1945	John Dickshot	18	3	George Stirnweiss	33	17
1946	George Stirnweiss	18	6	George Case	28*	11
1947	Bob Dillinger	34*	13	Dave Philley	21	16
1948	Bob Dillinger	28*	11	Dale Mitchell	13	18
	Gil Coan	23	9			
1949	Phil Rizzuto	18	6	Bob Dillinger	16	14
1950	Dom DiMaggio	15*	4	Hoot Evers	5	9
1951	Phil Rizzuto	18	3	Nelson Fox	9	12
1952	Jackie Jensen	18	6	Minnie Minoso	22*	16
1953	Jackie Jensen	18	8	Minnie Minoso	25*	16
1954	Forrest Jacobs	17	3	Minnie Minoso	18	11
1955	Minnie Minoso	19	8	Jim Rivera	25*	17
1956	Luis Aparicio	21*	4	Jim Rivera	20	9
1957	Jim Rivera	18	2	Minnie Minoso	18	15
1958	Jim Rivera	21	3	Luis Aparicio	56*	13
				Vic Power	9	13
1959	Mickey Mantle	21	3	Minnie Minoso	14	14
1960	Luis Aparicio	51*	8	Minnie Minoso	17	13
1961	Chuck Hinton	22	5	Luis Aparicio	53*	13
1962	Dick Howser	19	2	Luis Aparicio	31*	12
1963	Luis Aparicio	40*	6	Albie Pearson	17	10
1964	Luis Aparicio	57*	17	Luis Aparicio	57*	17
1965	Zoilo Versalles	27	5	Bert Campaneris	51*	19
1966	Bert Campaneris	52*	10	Don Buford	51	22
1967	Horace Clarke	21	4	Don Buford	34	21
1968	Tommy McCraw	20	5	Bert Campaneris	62*	22
1969	Bert Campaneris	62	8	Tommy Harper	73*	18
				Don Buford	19	18
1970	Amos Otis	33	2	Reggie Jackson	26	17
1971	Tommy Harper	25	3	Fred Patek	49	14
				Cesar Tovar	18	14

* Asterisk indicates league leader

American League

Year	Highest Proficiency	SB	CS	CS Leader	SB	CS
1972	Don Baylor	24	2	Dave Nelson	51	17
1973	Don Money	22	5	Bill North	53	20
	Cookie Rojas	18	4			
1974	Reggie Jackson	25	5	Bill North	54*	26
1975	Mickey Rivers	70*	14	Jerry Remy	34	21
1976	Mickey Rivers	43	7	Bill North	75*	29
1977	Mitchell Page	42	5	Bert Campaneris	27	20
1978	Bert Campaneris	22	4	Miguel Dilone	50	23
1979	Willie Wilson	83*	12	Bobby Bonds	34	23
1980	Willie Wilson	79	10	Rickey Henderson	100*	26
1981	Rick Manning	25	3	Rickey Henderson	56*	22
1982	Miguel Dilone	33	5	Rickey Henderson	130*	42

* Asterisk indicates league leader

National League

Year	Highest Proficiency	SB	CS	CS Leader	SB	CS
1920	Max Carey	52*	10	Billy Southworth	23	25
1921	Frank Frisch	49*	13	Jack Fournier	20	22
				Sammy Bohne	26	22
1922	Max Carey	51*	2	Charles Hollocher	19	29
1923	Max Carey	51*	8	George Grantham	43	28
1924	Max Carey	49*	13	Barney Friberg	19	27
1925	Jack Smith	20	2	Edd Roush	22	20
1926–50	(Caught stealing not available)					
1951	Sam Jethroe	35*	5	Pee Wee Reese	20	14
1952	Pee Wee Reese	30*	5	Billy Cox	10	12
1953	Jackie Robinson	17	4	Jim Gilliam	21	14
				Carlos Bernier	15	14
1954	Dee Fondy	20	5	Bill Bruton	34*	13
1955	Willie Mays	24	4	Ken Boyer	22	17

* Asterisk indicates league leader

National League

Year	Highest Proficiency	SB	CS	CS Leader	SB	CS
1956	Willie Mays	40*	10	Willie Mays	40*	10
1957	Johnny Temple	19	5	Willie Mays	38*	19
1958	Willie Mays	31*	6	Richie Ashburn	30	12
				Curt Flood	2	12
1959	Willie Mays	27*	4	Don Blasingame	15	15
1960	Julian Javier	19	4	Bill Bruton	22	13
1961	Frank Robinson	22	3	Maury Wills	35*	15
1962	Maury Wills	104*	13	Maury Wills	104*	13
				Bill Virdon	5	13
1963	Henry Aaron	31	5	Maury Wills	40*	19
1964	Tommy Harper	24	3	Lou Brock	43	18
1965	Jimmy Wynn	42	4	Maury Wills	94*	31
1966	Henry Aaron	21	3	Maury Wills	38	24
1967	Joe Morgan	29	5	Lou Brock	52*	18
1968	Henry Aaron	28	5	Maury Wills	52	21
1969	Bobby Bonds	45	4	Maury Wills	40	21
1970	Ken Henderson	20	3	Bobby Tolan	57	20
1971	Willie Mays	23	3	Lou Brock	64*	19
1972	Enzo Hernandez	24	3	Cesar Cedeno	55	21
1973	Dusty Baker	24	3	Lou Brock	70*	20
1974	Larry Lintz	50	7	Lou Brock	118*	33
1975	Joe Morgan	67	10	Cesar Cedeno	50	17
1976	Joe Morgan	60	9	Lou Brock	56	19
1977	Larry Bowa	32	3	Lou Brock	35	24
				Garry Templeton	28	24
1978	Cesar Cedeno	23	2			
	Davey Lopes	45	4	Bill North	58	24
1980	Ken Griffey	23	1	Omar Moreno	96	33
1981	Davey Lopes	20	2	Omar Moreno	39	14
1982	Bob Bailor	20	3	Omar Moreno	60	26
				Lonnie Smith	68	26

* Asterisk indicates league leader

The career records of those players of the past half century with more than 275 thefts are listed on the next page by successful stealing percentage. Figures for active players are through the 1982 season.

Base Stealer	SB	CS	Pct.
Willie Wilson	287	57	83.4
Davey Lopes	446	97	82.1
Joe Morgan	663	157	80.9
Luis Aparicio	506	136	78.8
Amos Otis	336	91	78.7
Tommy Harper	408	116	77.8
Bert Campaneris	643	192	77.0
Willie Mays	338	103	76.7
Ron LeFlore	455	142	76.2
George Case	349	109	76.2
Rickey Henderson	319	101	76.0
Cesar Cedeno	503	160	75.9
Lou Brock	938	307	75.3
Larry Bowa	296	97	75.3
Willie Davis	398	131	75.2
Omar Moreno	412	137	75.0
Fred Patek	385	131	74.6
Frank Taveras	300	106	73.9
Maury Wills	586	208	73.8
Bobby Bonds	461	169	73.2
Vada Pinson	305	122	71.4
Bill North	369	154	70.6
Jose Cardenal	329	139	70.3
Ben Chapman	287	136	67.8
Rod Carew	338	172	66.3

Here are the partial records of former stars for successful stealing, with years of available data.

Base Stealer	SB	CS	Pct.	Years
Max Carey	407	89	82.1	1916, 1918, 1920–25
Frank Frisch	186	74	71.6	1920–25
Ty Cobb	268	107	71.4	1915–16, 1920–26, 1928
Sam Rice	266	137	66.0	1920–26, 1928–34
Eddie Collins	214	111	65.8	1916, 1920–26, 1928–30
George Sisler	204	121	62.8	1916, 1920–26, 1928 AL

Unsung Heroes:
No-Hit Catchers
Stan Grosshandler

A pitcher who tosses a no-hitter receives instant acclaim and is assured of a lasting place in the record books. But what about the man behind the bat who skillfully calls the pitches that silence the opponents' bats?

One of the most famous of all sports photos shows Yogi Berra jumping on Don Larsen following the final out of the Yankee hurler's perfect game in the 1956 World Series. There is, however, no evidence of anyone congratulating Yogi for his part in calling the pitches in that memorable masterpiece. Yet all would agree that a catcher plays an important role in a pitcher's performance.

The all-time leader in catching no-hitters is Hall of Famer Ray Schalk. During his seventeen years with the White Sox he handled four of them. Curiously, his involvement in no-hitters came in bunches. The first occurred on May 14, 1914, when he was behind the plate as Jim Scott held Washington hitless for nine innings, only to lose in the tenth frame, 1–0. Seventeen days later Schalk caught Joe Benz when he stopped Cleveland without a hit 6–1.

In 1917, Schalk was involved in three no-hitters within a 23-day span, although in two instances he was on the wrong side. First he caught Ed Ciciotte in his 11–0 gem against the Browns in St. Louis on April 14. Three weeks later, on the White Sox' second trip to St. Louis, Cicotte and Schalk again formed the battery, in a game against

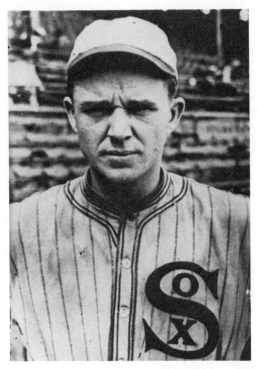

Ray Schalk, all-time leader in catching no-hitters

the Browns on May 5. This time they succumbed to the no-hit efforts of Ernie Koob, 1–0. The following day Benz and Schalk were on duty when Bob Groom of the Browns repeated Koob's hitless performance against the White Sox.

Following this flurry of no-hit activity, Schalk had to wait five years before being involved in another gem. And what a gem it was: Charley Robertson's 2–0 perfect game against Detroit on April 30, 1922.

Only two catchers—Jeff Torborg and Gus Triandos—have caught no-hitters in both leagues. Moreover, each has a perfect game to his credit.

While with the Dodgers, Torborg handled Sandy Koufax's 27 up, 27 down masterpiece in 1965 and then caught Bill Singer's 1970 hitless effort. As a member of the Angels, Jeff was the receiver in the second of Nolan Ryan's two 1973 no-hitters. Torborg thus holds the distinction of being the only man to be a working partner with the two no-hit record holders, Koufax and Ryan.

Triandos also enjoyed a special distinction. He wore the mask and pads when Hoyt Wilhelm, the great relief specialist, tossed a no-hitter against the Yankees in 1958 in one of his infrequent starts. This was the first no-hitter pitched for the modern Baltimore Orioles. Triandos also belted one out of the park that day for the game's only run. And then in 1964 when he was with the Phillies, Gus caught Jim Bunning during his perfect game vs. the Mets.

Val Picinich, an eighteen-year veteran of the mask-and-mitt trade, is the only man to catch no-hitters for three different teams. Val handled Joe Bush's effort for the Philadelphia Athletics in 1916, Walter Johnson's only no-hitter for Washington in 1920, and the masterpiece that Howard Ehmke delivered for the 1923 Red Sox.

Another catcher with an unusual claim to no-hit fame is Lou Criger. Three pitchers have tossed no-hitters in both leagues—Cy Young, Tom Hughes, and Bunning—and Criger was behind the bat in hitless efforts delivered by two of them.

He was Young's batterymate in his 1904 and 1908 masterpieces for the Red Sox, and he teamed with Hughes on the 1910 Yankees when Tom stopped Cleveland for nine innings, only to lose in the eleventh.

Several other practitioners of the tools of ignorance have been involved in three no-hitters. Bill Carrigan of the Red Sox caught the performances of Smoky Joe Wood in 1911 and George Foster and Hub Leonard in 1916.

Luke Sewell handled Wes Ferrell's efforts for the 1931 Indians against the Browns. Wes's brother Rick was the St. Louis catcher that day. Four years later Sewell caught Vern Kennedy's no-hitter for the White Sox, and in 1937 he was the receiver in Bill Dietrich's game.

Jim Hegan was the man behind the bat in three Cleveland Indian no-hitters. He caught Don Black and Bob Lemon and he was the catcher in Bob Feller's third no-hitter.

John Edwards worked in three hitless performances. In his first in 1965 he shared backstopping duties with Don Pavletich when Jim Maloney of the Reds tossed ten hitless innings before bowing to the Mets in eleven innings, 1–0. Two months later Edwards caught Maloney in his ten-inning, 1–0 conquest of the Cubs. And with the Cardinals in 1968 John was the partner in Ray Washburn's gem.

Besides Larsen's World Series perfect game, Berra caught two other no-hitters—the pair tossed by Allie Reynolds in 1951. The second clinched the pennant for the Yankees.

Another Hall of Fame receiver, Roy Campanella, worked three no-hitters for the Brooklyn Dodgers. He was behind the plate in both of Carl Erskine's and teamed for another with Sal Maglie.

Del Crandall handled a trio delivered by Jim Wilson, Lew Burdette, and Warren Spahn for the Milwaukee Braves. A sore arm deprived Crandall of a possible opportunity of catching a fourth no-hitter. Because of the ailment, Charlie Lau was back of the bat when Spahn tossed his second no-hitter in as many years in 1961. Wilson tells an interesting story about his 1954 gem against the Phillies:

> In the last inning with two out I had to face Puddin' Head Jones, a real dangerous hitter. My best pitch was a curve, so Del calls for it and Jones hits a screamer over third that both of us thought was fair, but it was called foul. Well, now what should Del call? He knows the curve is my best pitch, and so does Jones. Del calls for my fast ball, which really was not very fast. Jones hits a grounder to Danny O'Connell at second, and all I could think was that ball is going to hit a stone, bounce over his head and I lose my no-hitter. Fortunately, it did not, and I had a no-hit game.

Crandall also helped Wilson that day by hitting a home run. Other catchers besides Crandall and Triandos who contributed homers to their pitcher's no-hit efforts were Frank Hayes, whose blast in the top of the ninth inning was the lone run the day Bob Feller pitched his no-hitter against the Yankees; Ernie Lombardi, who connected in the first of Johnny Vander Meer's pair; Campanella, who helped both Erskine and Maglie with distance pokes, and Paul Casanova, who delivered one in Phil Niekro's game.

Eight receivers have teamed with the same pitcher twice in no-hit performances. As was previously mentioned, Criger handled a pair by Young, while the Edwards–Maloney, Berra–Reynolds and Campanella–Erskine duos delivered a pair. Lombardi worked both of Vander Meer's, Nig Clarke handled two by Addie Joss (the second a perfect game), John Roseboro worked two of Koufax's masterpieces, and Fran Healy was back of the bat in both of Steve Busby's efforts for Kansas City.

Several other catchers called the pitches in two no-hitters. Rollie Hemsley handled Bobo Newsom's for the Browns in 1934 and Feller's opening-day masterpiece for Cleveland in 1940. In the latter Rollie tripled in the lone run of the game.

Smoky Burgess, the premier pinch hitter, went all the way in Harvey Haddix's futile twelve-inning gem for Pittsburgh in 1959 and was back of the plate when Johnny Klippstein, Hershell Freeman, and Joe Black combined for a ten-inning no-hitter for Cincinnati against Milwaukee in 1956, only to lose in the eleventh frame.

Art Wilson caught Jeff Tesreau for the New York Giants in 1912 and then Hippo Vaughn of the Cubs in the famous double no-hitter of

1917. Jim Pagliaroni was back of the bat for Bill Monbouquette of the Red Sox in 1962 and also when Catfish Hunter threw his perfect game for the 1968 Oakland A's.

Others to catch two no-hitters for different teams were Jose Azcue, John Bateman, Walker Cooper, Ray Fosse, and Tim McCarver. Catchers with two no-hit games on the same club were Bill Bergen, Hank Gowdy, Randy Hundley, Ed McFarland, Buddy Rosar, Hank Severeid, Ted Simmons, Bob Tillman, and Jack Warner.

In 1979 major league managers who had caught no-hitters were Torborg, Herman Franks, Pat Corrales, and Les Moss, who handled the bizarre Bobo Holloman effort with the St. Louis Browns.

Unrecognized Heroes: No-Hit Umpires

Larry R. Gerlach

The drama of All-Star, Championship Series, and World Series contests notwithstanding, the no-hitter remains the most intensely exciting game in baseball for spectators and participants alike. The pressure felt by a pitcher striving to realize a rare achievement that will ensure him both fame and immortality in the record books is widely appreciated. And the burden upon the catcher who devises the strategy for the masterpiece is also recognized. (See Stan Grosshandler's "Unsung Heroes: No-Hit Catchers" (page 182). But what about the other member of the strategic trio—the man in blue, who by calling balls and strikes vitally affects both the pitcher's performance and the catcher's strategy?

As with many memorable games in baseball history, the umpires who worked the plate in no-hitters are forgotten figures. Not many students of the national pastime recall that in 1956 Babe Pinelli worked Don Larsen's perfect game, the only one ever in the World Series. Fewer still know that Harry Geisel called Bob Feller's blanketing of the White Sox on April 16, 1940, the lone opening-day no-hitter in baseball history. While trivia specialists remember that on May 2, 1917, Cincinnati's Fred Toney and Chicago's Jim "Hippo" Vaughn combined to pitch a dual no-hitter for nine innings (the Reds won 1–0 in the tenth), virtually none remember former pitcher Albert Orth as the umpire in that unique contest. And probably only Harry Wendelstedt and Bill Jackowski know that they worked the first consecutive-game no-hitters in history, on September 17–18, 1968, although many people know that Gaylord Perry and Ray Washburn pitched the tandem.

It is unfortunate that umpires are not accorded some type of recognition after their role in a special achievement like a no-hit game. Babe Pinelli wound up his career of twenty-two years as the umpire-in-chief in what was perhaps the single most extraordinary game in baseball history—Larson's perfect game in the 1956 World Series. After that historic game Pinelli wept from emotion, but not a single person other than his fellow umpires—not a sportswriter, not the president of the National League, not the commissioner of baseball—came into the dressing room to congratulate him. Tom Gorman, a member of the crew that day, summed up the situation accurately: "It was a disgrace."

Umpires who work no-hit games deserve recognition for two reasons. The first is that the arbiters themselves regard such a game as a career milestone. Ed Sudol, who had three no-hitters during two decades in the National League, put it succinctly: "The highlight for any umpire working behind the plate is a no-run, no-hit game." Ask any umpire to recall the most memorable events of his career, and the no-hit game will rank with the World Series as the high points.

The second reason umpires deserve recognition is the special role they play in the unfolding of a no-hit game. In addition to the usual physical strain on the back and legs from crouching constantly and the mental exhaustion from rendering some 250 split-second decisions in two to three hours, the plate umpire in a no-hit game shoulders an enormous emotional burden, because he literally controls the pitching strategy. If the umpire is erratic in calling pitches, the pitcher and the catcher cannot achieve consistency—by making a decision that runs the ball–strike count to 3–1 instead of 2–2, the umpire has fundamentally affected the pitching strategy. Although those conditions are present in every game, the fact remains that the finer the pitching performance, the greater the precision demanded of the arbiter. The pressure stems from the simple desire to avoid making a mistake that would affect the outcome of a historic pitching performance.

The pressure rises perceptibly, of course, when a perfect game—27 batters up, 27 batters out—is at stake. Ed Sudol, who called Jim Bunning's perfect game against the Mets on June 21, 1964, later spoke of his feelings:

> I knew all along that he had a perfect game going because that mammoth scoreboard was staring right at me. That's what made me so extra tense; I wanted to be perfect, too. I

didn't want to be responsible for a blunder that would ruin a perfect game. What if on a full count, three and two, the batter doesn't swing on a pitch that could go either way? The adrenalin was really flowing. . . . I was so exhausted after the game that I left the dressing room an hour after my partners had gone. I was drenched with perspiration and exhausted by all the mental notes from that pressure-packed game.

In addition to Sudol, eight other umpires have called perfect games: Tommy Connolly (Joss, 1908), John Dwyer (Young, 1904), Dick Nallin (Robertson, 1922), Larry Napp (Hunter, 1968), Brick Owen (Shore, 1917), Pinelli (Larsen, 1956), Ed Vargo (Koufax, 1965), and Rich Garcia (Barker, 1981).

In 1959, when Harvey Haddix lost his perfect game in the thirteenth inning, umpire Vincent Smith also lost a chance to make history; neither the pitcher nor the arbiter ever recorded a genuine no-hitter. Fate was kinder to George Pipgras and Eddie Rommel, for as umpires each recorded the no-hitter that had eluded them as pitchers; Bill Dinneen is the only man who both pitched (1905) and umpired no-hit games in the major leagues.

The odds against pitching or calling a no-hitter are great, but the chances of having a double in a single season are exceedingly remote. Five pitchers have thrown two no-hitters in a single season: Johnny Vander Meer (1938), Allie Reynolds (1951), Virgil Trucks (1952), Jim Maloney (1965), and Nolan Ryan (1973). In none of these cases did one umpire call both games. The distinction of having called two no-hitters in a single season belongs to Tommy Connolly (1908), Bill Deegan (1977), Bill Dinneen (1923), Bill Jackowski (1968), Dick Nallin (1917), Larry Napp (1970), Harry Schwarts (1962), Mel Steiner (1965), Tony Venzon (1960), and Silk O'Loughlin, who did it twice (1905, 1917).

Dick Nallin recorded the first double no-hitter by an umpire. He was behind the plate in St. Louis on May 5, 1907, when Ernie Koob of the Browns no-hit the White Sox 1–0 and again the next day when Bob Groom blanked Chicago 3–0 in the second game of a doubleheader. More than a half century passed before Tony Venzon both duplicated and surpassed the feat in Cincinnati in 1969. Where Nallin had no-hitters in successive appearances behind the plate, Venzon had them in consecutive games. Venzon was umpire-in-chief on April 30 when Jim Maloney of the Reds struck out 13 Astros en route to a 10–0 no-hitter and again the next day, May 1, when Don Wilson of Houston got revenge by fanning 13 Reds in a 4–0 gem.

Calling a no-hit game is a rare honor for an umpire. Since 1901 only 90 of the nearly 350 men who have umpired in the major leagues have had the distinction of working no-hitters. For most of them it was a once-in-a-lifetime achievement; only 38 arbiters have worked more than one no-hitter, and only 20 of them have worked more than two. Hall of Famer Billy Evans had only one no-hitter; Bill McGowan, perhaps the best ball-and-strike man in AL history, saw 25 years pass between his two no-hitters (1926 and 1951).

Longevity is not an important factor in accounting for the number of no-hitters worked by umpires. It is not surprising, perhaps, that Bill Klem had 5 in 36 years or that Bill Dinneen worked 6 in 29 seasons. But how is it that Hank O'Day had only 2 in 35 years, Al Barlick 1 in 26 years, and Hank Soar none in 24 years? Conversely, how is it that Babe Pinelli had 4 no-hitters in 22 years, Tony Venzon 4 in 15 years, and Silk O'Loughlin a record 7 no-hit games in only 17 years.

Opportunity is an important consideration. Prior to the establishment in 1933 of three-man crews for all regular season games, an umpire worked 50 percent of the games behind the plate. Predictably, the three umpires with the most no-hitters to their credit worked before 1933. Since the adoption of the four-man crew in 1952, the opportunity for an umpire to have a no-hitter is about the same as for a starting pitcher—once every four games. Viewed from the perspective of opportunity, Tony Venzon had 4 no-hitters in 15 seasons for the best ratio of no-hit games per seasons worked (3.8), followed by Stan Steiner with 3 no-hitters in 12 years (4.0). But the fact that both Venzon and Steiner had 2 no-hitters in a single season significantly increases their ratios; the best ratio of no-hitters per season for an umpire who did not have a "double" belongs to Ed Vargo with 3 no-hit games in 17 years (5.7). Vargo, moreover, is the only umpire to call a no-hitter in three consecutive seasons.

Apart from greater or fewer opportunities to work no-hitters at various times in history, the central question remains: What makes one arbiter in a given era record proportionally more no-hitters than another? Is it luck or fate? Is it a matter of being a "pitcher's umpire"— having a relatively expanded strike zone? Is it the ability to handle pressure and maintain consistency in calling pitches in the late stages of the game, thereby allowing the pitcher to remain in the groove?

Whatever the reason for accumulating no-hit games—surely a combination of factors are at work—twenty umpires have called three or more no-hitters since 1901. The following table, arranged by number of games, is a list of those top twenty.

Umpire	League	Years	No-hitters	Year (Pitcher)
Frank H. O'Loughlin	AL	17	7	1905 (Henley), 1905 (Smith), 1908 (Young), 1911 (Wood), 1912 (Hamilton), 1917 (Cicotte), 1917 (Mogridge)
William H. Dinneen	AL	29	6	1910 (Bender), 1912 (Mullin), 1914 (Scott), 1918 (Leonard), 1923 (Jones), 1923 (Ehmke)
William J. Klem	NL	36	5	1907 (Maddox), 1912 (Tesreau), 1915 (Lavender), 1916 (Hughes), 1934 (P. Dean)
August J. Donatelli	NL	24	4	1956 (Erskine), 1961 (Spahn), 1964 (Johnson), 1969 (Moose)
George J. Honochick	AL	25	4	1952 (Trucks), 1962 (Kralick), 1966 (Siebert), 1968 (Phoebus)
Larry Napp	AL	24	4	1967 (Chance), 1968 (Hunter),* 1970 (Wright), 1970 (Blue)
Ralph A. Pinelli	NL	22	4	1946 (Head), 1948 (Barney), 1954 (Wilson), 1956 (Larsen)*
Anthony Venzon	NL	15	4	1960 (Cardwell), 1969 (Maloney), 1969 (Wilson), 1970 (Ellis)
Thomas H. Connolly	AL	33	4	1905 (Dinneen), 1908 (Rhoades), 1908 (Joss),* 1916 (Bush)
Robert D. Emslie	NL	35	3	1903 (Fraser), 1904 (Wicker), 1907 (Pfeffer)
Robert C. Hubbard	AL	16	3	1937 (Dietrich), 1948 (Lemon), 1951 (Reynolds)
William Jackowski	NL	17	3	1960 (Burdette), 1968 (Culver), 1968 (Washburn)
James E. Johnstone	NL	10	3	1906 (McIntire), 1908 (Rucker), 1909 (Ames)
Richard F. Nallin	AL	18	3	1917 (Koob), 1917 (Groom), 1922 (Robertson)*
John F. Sheridan	AL	14	3	1901 (Moore), 1904 (Tannehill), 1907 (Walsh)
Melvin J. Steiner	NL	12	3	1962 (Koufax), 1965 (Maloney), 1965 (Maloney)
John W. Stevens	AL	24	3	1957 (Keegan), 1967 (Barber), 1967 (Horlen)
William J. Stewart	NL	22	3	1938 (Vander Meer), 1940 (Carleton), 1944 (Tobin)
Edward Sudol	NL	20	3	1963 (Marichal), 1964 (Bunning),* 1970 (Singer)
Edward P. Vargo	NL	17	3	1963 (Nottebart), 1964 (Koufax), 1965 (Koufax)

* Perfect game

Mordecai Peter Centennial Brown

Paul C. Frisz

He had one name from the Old Testament, one from the New, and one which commemorated the fact that he was born in the centennial year of 1876. But he became better known as Three-Finger Brown because of an accident he sustained in childhood.

Considering that the Society for American Baseball Research selected Brown as the outstanding baseball personality born in 1876, a brief review of his career would be in order. First, some clarification about his accident is necessary. Although young "Miner" Brown did spend several years in the coal mines of his native Indiana, he did not lose his finger in a mining accident.

The accident took place on his uncle's farm when Brownie was only seven years old. He caught his right hand in a corn grinder and had it badly chewed up. When he was taken to the doctor, it was found necessary to amputate almost all of the forefinger. His second finger was saved but it was mangled, as shown in the accompanying drawing. The sketch also shows his little finger as being in bad shape. This was not caused by the feed grinder accident but resulted from his trying to stop a shot through the middle when he was pitching.

Brown was a good semipro player but didn't consider baseball as a serious career until he was twenty-four. He started as an infielder with Terre Haute in 1901 but soon switched to the mound. He found that

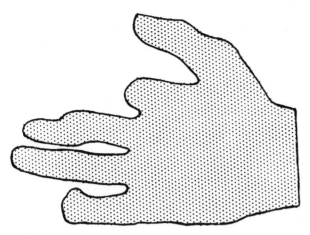

The mangled pitching hand of Mordecai Brown

he could get a good spin on the ball by releasing it off the stub of his forefinger.

The former coal miner went from Omaha in 1902 to the St. Louis Cardinals in 1903. He was twenty-six when he broke into the majors. After one year with the tail-end Cardinals, Brown was traded with catcher Jack O'Neill to the Cubs for pitcher Jack Taylor. The Cubs had not had a first-rate club in years. Brown blossomed in 1906 with a 26–6 record as Chicago racked up 116 victories, an all-time major league record. Nevertheless, the White Sox beat them in the World Series.

In 1907, Brown won 20 games, and the Cubs won the pennant and swept the Tigers in the World Series. The next year he upped his victories to 29, and the Cubs again won the Series from Detroit.

These were glory years for the Cubs, even though the Giants beat them out of the pennant in 1909. Brown nevertheless won 27 games. In 1910 he won 25, and Chicago took its fourth pennant in five years.

Brown again won more than 20 games in 1911, but the next year he missed much of the season because of injuries. He hurled for Cincinnati in 1913, and spent two moderately successful years in the Federal League in 1914–15, part of which time he served as manager. He returned to the Cubs in 1916, where he closed out his career on September 4 in a specially arranged final duel with Christy Mathewson. Matty, who had become manager of Cincinnati, beat Brown 10–8 in the final major league contest for each.

It was the twenty-fifth time the two had faced each other on the mound. They both had won 12 games, but Brown had the edge because Matty had lost 13 to his 10. Three games were credited to other Cub hurlers. One game the three-fingered ace lost was the 1–0 no-hitter that Matty pitched on June 13, 1905. After that, Brown beat him nine straight times between 1905 and the end of the 1908 season. The final win in that streak was the famous playoff game between the Cubs and the Giants in which Merkle failed to touch second base. The two teams had finished in a tie at the end of the season, and the game was scheduled for October 8. Jack Pfiester, the "Giant Killer," started for the Cubs. But Brown relieved him in the first inning when he got into trouble and won the pressure game over Matty 4–2.

Pitching under pressure was one of Brown's points. He was frequently called on to work in relief, and when he wasn't carting off the victory he was saving games for others. He is credited with 48 saves, a much higher total than any other hurler of his era. He could come in without warming up and show excellent control in spite of his mangled pitching hand. Brown, with his forefinger missing, would toss his curve ball with a straight overhand motion. The ball would drop down and away from right-handed batters, who would frequently hit it into the dirt. As a former infielder, he fielded his position well and was death on bunts.

As a reporter wrote in 1917, "Brown made his very injuries work for him. He claimed, and we believe with reason, that the loss of his first finger enabled him to get a sharper break on his curve ball than would have been possible with a complete set of fingers. Anyway, he had a beautiful curve, a fine fast ball, and amazing control. All these with a hand that looks like a veteran of the seven years war."

It was an unusual handicap for a pitcher and undoubtedly contributed to baseball lore of the period. After Brown became famous as a pitcher, and even long after he retired and operated a garage in Terre Haute, people still went out to his uncle's farm to view the feed grinder, since stored and polished, that had launched the career of Three-Finger Brown.

Schedule Changes Since 1876

Ronald G. Liebman

When expansion in the 1960s brought about an increase in major league schedules from 154 to 162 games and, later, divisional play in each league, traditionalists muttered about tampering with the schedule. Actually, the major league schedules have been changed several times since the National League was organized in 1876.

In that first season there were eight teams, with each team playing its seven rivals ten times for a total of 70 games. Each team played about three games per week. The following two years there were only six teams, playing each other twelve times for a total of only 60 games. During this early period, many teams had only one regular starting pitcher; like an infielder or outfielder, he was expected to perform in almost every game and every inning. But the avalanche of sore arms on the part of pitchers who were expected to hang in there despite injury, fatigue, or ineffectiveness resulted in very short careers for many of the early pitchers. This led to the rotation of two or more starting pitchers and later the use of relief pitchers.

After two years of six teams, the league returned to an eight-team setup in 1879 and adopted an 84-game schedule. The schedule was gradually increased to 140 games in 1888 through the periodic addition of two more games with each opposing team. The league maintained its

140-game schedule through 1891. The games usually started in late afternoon and frequently suffered the twin hazards of rain and darkness.

During the 1882–91 period, the American Association (AA) existed as a rival major league. It adopted a six-team, 98-game schedule in 1882 and matched the NL with an eight-team, 80-game arrangement in 1883. In 1884, it tried twelve teams and 110 games before reverting to eight teams in 1885. It matched the NL's 112-game plan in 1885 but raised its schedule to 140 games in 1886, two years before the NL. The AA continued the 140-game pattern until its demise in 1891. Two other leagues, the Union Association (UA) and the Players' League (PL), existed as one-year major leagues. In 1884 the UA had eight teams and 112 games, as did the NL, and in 1890 the PL followed the NL–AA arrangement of eight teams and 140 games.

After the American Association disbanded, the National League operated again as the sole major league and expanded to twelve teams in 1892. The 154-game schedule made its debut in 1892, with each team playing its eleven rivals fourteen times apiece. For the first time in major league history, the season had a first half, won by Boston, and a second half, won by Cleveland. It was not a success and was not repeated. The league cut back to 132 games in 1893–97, citing economic factors, but returned to the 154-schedule in 1898–99 when the public clamored for more baseball. However, the league was finding a twelve-team schedule to be unwieldy in that preaviation era, and they consolidated into eight teams for 1900. The league also returned to the 140-game schedule.

The American League, which had been a minor league known as the Western League, gained recognition as a major league in 1901, and the two leagues each played 140-game schedules in 1901–03. The two leagues played a World Championship Series in 1903 to determine an overall champion, with Boston AL beating Pittsburgh NL five games to three. No World Series was played in 1904, because of opposition by John McGraw, manager of the NL champion New York Giants, but the fall classic has been played annually since 1905.

The eight-team, 154-game schedule by which each team played its rivals twenty-two times was inaugurated in 1904 in both leagues and became traditional. It stayed in existence continuously from 1904 through 1960, except for 1918 and 1919. The Federal League (FL), which operated as a third major league in 1914 and 1915, used the same format. In 1918, the final year of World War I, the major league season was curtailed on September 2 (twenty-seven days early) on orders from U.S. Secretary of War Newton Baker as a means of securing greater military manpower. Each team played about 125 games, with the teams that were leading on September 2, the Boston Red Sox and the Chicago

Cubs, being given special dispensation to play in the World Series. For the 1919 season, the owners reduced the schedule to 140 games as an economy measure based on a declining interest and attendance in baseball. But with the war over and the home run hitting of Babe Ruth starting to make news, baseball enjoyed increased popularity in 1919. This resulted in a return to the 154-game schedule in 1920. President Franklin D. Roosevelt permitted the schedule to continue without a hitch during the trying period of World War II, writing a famous "green light" letter to Baseball Commissioner Kenesaw Landis in January 1942.

At their joint meeting in August 1946, the two leagues tentatively adopted a proposed 168-game schedule, the longest ever considered. This was done on the strong recommendation of Yankee executive Larry MacPhail in order to capitalize on the postwar popularity of baseball and to compensate the owners for pension benefits and other concessions granted to the players. Heavy opposition from the public and the players doomed the plan, however, and the owners voted to continue with the 154-game card at a meeting held in September 1946. Owner Tom Yawkey of the Boston Red Sox was credited with convincing the other owners that the MacPhail plan should be scrapped.

Expansion brought about the ten-team, 162-game schedule (18 games between opponents), with the American League initiating the move in 1961 and the National League following suit in 1962. The move of the Brooklyn Dodgers and New York Giants to California after the 1957 season paved the way for expansion. The NL was then lacking a team in New York City, and the AL wanted to have its own team in lucrative California. The year 1961 marked the only year that the National League and the American League played schedules of different lengths, and it was also the only year prior to 1977 that the leagues had a different number of teams. The leagues had originally considered 153 games (17 with each opponent) but settled on 162 so as to provide an equal number of home and road games with each opponent plus some additional revenue from the extra games.

The majors expanded to twelve teams each in 1969 in another radical change of pattern. In a 162-game schedule, each team was to play 18 games with five opponents and 12 games apiece with six others in a twelve-team, two-division arrangement. Under this plan, proposed by the American League, the two divisional champions in each league would meet in a Championship Series (play-offs) of 3 out of 5 games, with the winners being declared the pennant winners. These games would not count in the final standings and averages. Although this plan would not always result in the team with the league's best won-lost percentage qualifying for the World Series, it was felt that having two separate pennant races in each league and eliminating the embarrassment of teams which finished eleventh or twelfth would be a better set-up on balance. In addition there would be, of course, the added revenue and publicity to be gained by having additional postseason games. The NL had originally balked at the plan, wanting 12 teams with each team having 15 games with the eleven rivals for 165 games, but the league finally capitulated after being persuaded by San Francisco Giants' vice-president Chub Feeney (soon to become NL president).

An interesting and overlooked irony of history revolved around the placing of Cincinnati in the Western Division and St. Louis, 300 miles west of Cincinnati, in the Eastern Division. New York Mets' board chairman M. Donald Grant had been reluctant to agree to divisional play because it would mean that the Mets would play three fewer home games against the popular Dodgers and Giants than against some other NL teams. Grant was also told that neither the Dodgers nor the Giants could be put into the Eastern Division with the Mets. However, in order to placate Grant somewhat, the National League agreed to his compromise request that the St. Louis Cardinals, romping toward their second consecutive pennant and believed by many to be establishing a dynasty in the league, be placed in the NL Eastern Division. This would enable St. Louis to have three more home dates with the Mets in New York than some of the supposedly lesser teams, including Cincinnati. But the Cardinals faded after 1968, winning no championships for the next thirteen years, whereas the Reds became a strong and popular team in the NL West. The alignment has remained intact, however, with the Reds in the West and the Cardinals in the East.

The first change in the schedule pattern in the 1970s occurred in 1972, when an early-season strike by the players led to the cancellation of the first ten days of play. The owners and players could not agree on the issue of compensation for the replay of games postponed during the strike, so a compromise plan, put forth by the AL owners, was adopted which provided for cancellation of games scheduled during the strike period. A total of 86 games (43 in each league) were cancelled, and this resulted in uneven schedules of 153–156 games in the NL and 154–156 games in the AL. In the AL Eastern Division, Detroit finished with a won–lost record of 86–70 to 85–70 for Boston and was declared the division champion by ½ game.

The National League's twelve-team plan adopted in 1969 has remained in use, but the American League expanded to fourteen teams in 1977. The American League had difficulty working out a schedule pattern which utilized the now sacrosanct 162-game schedule. Their original fourteen-team plan, used in 1977 and 1978, called for each team to play 15 games with its six division rivals (90 games) and 10 games with each of the seven teams in the other division (70 games). Since this added up to only 160 games, each team was scheduled to play 1 additional game with two of the seven teams in the other division, to reach exactly 162 games. This awkward pattern was abandoned after two years when the AL Western teams complained that they had fewer home dates with the Yankees and the Red Sox, considered the best draws, than the teams in the East had. The present "balanced" schedule used in the AL was adopted in 1979 and provided for each team to play 13 games with the six rival teams in its own division (78 games) and 12 games with the seven teams in the other division (84 games).

This schedule was resumed in 1982 after a devastating players' strike, which lasted nearly two months in mid-1981. No games were played from June 12 through August 9, which resulted in two widely separated half-seasons. Total games played by clubs varied from 103 to 110 in the AL and from 103 to 111 games in the NL, and there was no even pattern of divisional play.

Schedule Changes Since 1876

Years	League(s)	Teams	Series	Games
1876	NL	8	7×10	70
1877–78	NL	6	5×12	60
1879–82	NL	8	7×12	84
1883	NL	8	7×14	98
1884–85	NL	8	7×16	112
1886–87	NL	8	7×18	126
1888–91	NL	8	7×20	140
1892	NL	12	11×14	154
1893–97	NL	12	11×12	132
1898–99	NL	12	11×14	154
1900	NL	8	7×20	140
1901–03	NL–AL	8	7×20	140
1904–17	NL–AL	8	7×22	154
1918	NL–AL	8	7×22	*
1919	NL–AL	8	7×20	140
1920–60	NL–AL	8	7×22	154
1961	NL	8	7×22	154
1961	AL	10	9×18	162

(Continued)

* Season ended on September 2, 1918, instead of September 29, by decree of U.S. Secretary of War Newton D. Baker. NL teams played 123–129 decisions and AL teams 122–128.

Years	League(s)	Teams	Series	Games
1962–68	NL–AL	10	9 × 18	162
1969–71	NL–AL	12	5 × 18	162
			6 × 12	
1972	NL–AL	12	5 × 18	†
			6 × 12	
1973–76	NL–AL	12	5 × 18	162
			6 × 12	
1977–80	NL	12	5 × 18	162
			6 × 12	
1977–78	AL	14	6 × 15	162
			5 × 10	
			2 × 11	
1979–80	AL	14	6 × 13	162
			7 × 12	‡
1981	NL–AL	12–14		

† Games scheduled on first ten days of 1972 season canceled as result of player strike. All were intradivisional games. Teams played 153–156 decisions in NL and 154–156 decisions in AL. Season opened April 15 instead of scheduled April 5–6.
‡ Players' strike in midyear resulted in loss of one-third of season. NL clubs played 103–110 games and AL clubs 103–111 games.

Rudy York,
the Big Gun of August
Tom Hufford

In 1937 most of baseball's headlines went to the slugging exploits of Joe Medwick in the National League and Lou Gehrig, Joe DiMaggio, Jimmie Foxx, and Hank Greenberg in the American League. Little attention was paid to a bench-riding rookie on the Tigers named Rudy York, at least not until he worked his way into the lineup in early August. Then the big Oklahoma Indian rewrote the slugging records right under the noses of his more publicized contemporaries.

In the course of one calendar month, August 1937, York hit 18 home runs, breaking Babe Ruth's September 1927 record of 17. He also amassed an incredible 49 runs batted in, for one of the most productive months in baseball history. As remarkable as the totals appear now, the circumstances surrounding the Chief's performance are an even more interesting story.

In the spring of 1937 there was no question that York would make the Tiger squad. He had been up briefly once before in the course of three productive minor league seasons. He had been the Most Valuable Player at Milwaukee in 1936, and while with Beaumont the year before he was the Texas League's MVP. The only problem was that the Tigers didn't have a place for him to play.

At his regular position, first base, York certainly wasn't going to beat out Hank Greenberg, who was at the peak of his career. He gave the outfield a brief trial, but he didn't work out there. At third base he was no Pie Traynor, nor even a Marv Owen, who led the league in fielding at the hot corner. So at the beginning of the season York found himself riding the bench, and it seemed as if the Bengals were making every effort, conscious or not, to keep him there.

On May 25, in a game against the Yankees, catcher-manager Mickey Cochrane was seriously beaned by pitcher Bump Hadley. His playing career was ended, and it was assumed that York would be given a shot at the backstop spot, another position he had studied in the minors. Instead, the job was split between Ray Hayworth and young Birdie Tebbetts.

After several weeks of rusting away on the bench, with only occasional fill-in action, York was shipped out to Toledo in order to get some work. Before he had a chance to don a Mud Hen uniform, however, Tiger third baseman Marv Owen suffered a broken hand, and York was recalled to take over. A funny thing happened before Rudy made it back, though. Utility man Flea Clifton moved to third, and Cliff Bolton was purchased from Washington as insurance behind the plate. York found himself back in the dugout, as frustrated as ever.

Clifton did not prove to be the answer at third, so a week later York got a chance, but his fielding was spotty and he was not used regularly by acting manager Del Baker. When Cochrane returned to the team on July 27, he huddled with York regarding his inactivity. At that time the Tigers were in dire need of pitching help. Schoolboy Rowe was out with an arm injury, and Tommy Bridges was off his regular pace. Even the controversial and colorful "Boots" Poffenberger was taking a regular turn. York, eager for action, volunteered to toe the mound in an effort to help. He actually warmed up during several contests, but he did not make it into a game.

Finally, on August 4, after the Tigers had lost six straight games, Cochrane shook up the lineup to provide more punch. After all, York had hit a dozen homers in spite of his infrequent use. York, inserted as the catcher, responded to the opportunity by rapping a home run off Harry Kelley of the A's, and he won himself a job. The Tigers then went to Washington for a series, and York collected three homers in spacious Griffith Stadium. The next week he hit three in equally spacious Comiskey Park in Chicago.

The frustration York had experienced during the first half of the season surfaced again in the midst of his August streak. In the August 19 game at Chicago, York had already hit two home runs, one of them a grand slam, and had driven in six runs when he came to bat in the seventh inning with the bases full. With Gee Walker on third, Gehringer on second, and Greenberg on first, York rapped a shot to deep center field, 440 feet away. It was described as a sure inside-the-park home run. However, Greenberg held up, thinking that the ball might be caught. When he saw the ball bounce off the wall, he could only manage to make third, and York had to settle for "the longest double ever hit in Comiskey Park."

York had visions of getting that home run, as it would have been his second grand slam of the game, and the ten RBIs would have put him only one short of the league record with two more innings to play. As it happened, however, the rains came in the bottom of the inning, and the score reverted back to what it had been in the sixth inning, thus wiping out York's long double and two RBIs. As York grumbled after the game, "Some other day it won't rain."

Rudy continued his rampage with a pinch homer against the Browns on August 22. On August 24 he hit three in a twin bill with the A's. Two came off Harry Kelley, his favorite target. On August 30 he hit one off Lefty Gomez of the Yankees, the top pitcher in the league that season. Then, just as Ruth had climaxed his great September 1927 splurge against the Senators, York closed out his record-setting month with two blasts off Pete Appleton of the Nats on August 31.

York tailed off somewhat in September, but he finished with 35 home runs in only 375 at bats. He also knocked in 103 runs in 104 games. In spite of his heroic efforts and those of Gehringer, who led the league in batting, and Greenberg, who knocked in 183 runs, the Tigers could not catch the front-running Yankees.

Yet nothing can diminish the luster of that one month's performance. York batted .360 in 30 games, with 114 at bats, 27 runs, 4 doubles, 2 triples, 18 homers, 49 RBIs, and a slugging percentage of .895. He not only exceeded Ruth's home run record of 17, but his 49 RBIs exceeded the best effort of Lou Gehrig, who had 48 in August 1935. In fact, in August 1937 Lou gave York a merry chase with 44 RBIs. Ruth had knocked in 43 runs in September 1927 when he hit his 17 round-trippers.

Moses Solomon, the Rabbi of Swat

Howard Lavelle

*For the hour will come when
Your vigor will fade,
And Fortune, ye know is a slippery jade;
The Partition's but flimsy, 'twixt
glory and shame
And Solomon like Napoleon
is now lost to fame.*

—Anonymous

Homer King Solomon ruled supreme for one brief and brilliant year. He wore the flowing purple in 1923, when he rode with the long-ball lords of the past. He hit 49 round-trippers that year for Hutchinson in the Southwestern League, the highest total ever recorded in the minor leagues up to that point.

Moses Solomon outhomered them all, the big and the small, in the width and the breadth of the land. Only one home run king in organized baseball had hit more big ones in one season than Old Hickory, and that was the greatest of them all, Babe Ruth, in 1920 (54), and 1921 (59).

The twenty-three-year-old slugging Solomon was to all appearances the answer to John McGraw's quest for a Jewish Babe Ruth. A "Jewish appeal," the mercenary McGraw figured, would help to offset the tremendous drawing power of the Babe in his new tower of babble. Ruth, the greatest money player of all time, had hit a typical Ruthian homer to open Yankee Stadium in 1923.

McGraw was anxious to compete with the Yankees in the increasingly heavily Jewish residential areas of the Bronx and upper Manhattan. Although Solomon's sensational slugging was done in the Class C Southwest League, he was a native of New York City, which only whetted McGraw's enthusiasm. The Giants paid $4,500 for the Rabbi of Swat.

Solomon was brought up to the NL by the Giants at the tail end of the 1923 season. The pennant-winning Giants were on a four-year pennant push (1921–24) and had a veteran outfield of Ross Youngs, Irish Meusel, and Casey Stengel.

Two rookies on the bench beside Solomon were Lewis Robert "Hack" Wilson, a squat, muscular home run hitting outfielder (he had led two minor leagues in homers, the Blue Ridge League in 1922 with 30 homers, and the Virginia League in 1923 with 19), and William Harold Terry, whose only claim to fame was pitching a no-hit game for Newman against Anniston in the Georgia–Florida League in 1915 when he was seventeen years old.

Each of them played in three games. Terry batted .143 and Wilson hit an even .200, while Solomon scored a fancy .375. What happened to them? Terry became the last National Leaguer to hit over .400 for a season (.401 in 1930). Wilson set the National League home run record of 56, also in 1930.

And Moses Solomon? The king abdicated. The clouting colossus of the Southwest collapsed. His fielding was atrocious. He couldn't catch a fly without flypaper. He was a hazard on defense, not only to himself but also to his teammates. The king was soon exiled to the minors, shorn of his tinsel and glamour. The Rabbi of Swat had become a rabbit of swatters; the long-ball touch was gone. He did, however, hit over .300 seven times in the minors.

In the end Solomon whacked more homers in his one year at Hutchinson than he did in the rest of his baseball career. A sadder but wiser man, he quit in 1930 at thirty years of age. Moses then moved into real estate, where he became richer and happier.

Lou *Who* Stole Home 15 Times?

Raymond J. Gonzalez

The disclosure that Lou Brock stole home only once in his 938 success-ful thefts comes as quite a surprise. Modern players are still stealing home—Rod Carew has done it more than a dozen times in his career—but Brock, one of the greatest base stealers of this century, apparently did it only once—a double steal with Billy Williams of the Cubs May 24, 1964.

Get ready for another surprise—about another Lou. Did you know that Lou Gehrig, the 210-pound slugger of the Yankees, stole home 15 times in his career? This ranks him pretty high on the all-time list, not far behind the likes of Ty Cobb, George J. Burns, Johnny Evers, Eddie Collins, Frank Frisch, and Jackie Robinson and ahead of Hans Wagner and Max Carey. But what is old Piano-Legs doing among those gazelles of bygone eras?

Gehrig was not a graceful runner, but he was not slow. In addi-tion, he was a real team player, and an aggressive one, and several times he stole in extra innings. He stole 102 bases in his career—not bad in an era known for its hitters. Twenty-three of his 102 steals were double steals with another member of the Yankees, and he was on the front end of most of those.

The double steal is not employed much anymore, but it was used

Lou Gehrig

a fair amount before World War II. The Yankees, and particularly their sturdy first baseman and captain, used it most effectively. But this strategy never really received much notice. The focus was on Babe Ruth, the home run, and Murderer's Row. But in the midst of all the thundering bats the Bronx Bombers were also stealing some bases, occasionally two at a time.

The Yankees were an excellent all-around ball club in the 1920s and 1930s, but there was so much emphasis in the press on hitting that you almost had to read between the lines to get a more balanced view. Even when Ben Chapman stole 61 bases for the New Yorkers in 1931, Ruth and Gehrig were hitting 46 homers apiece and Lou was knocking in 184 runs. Gehrig stole 17 bases that season, a career high for him. Three came on April 27 in a game against Washington. Gehrig and Chapman engineered a successful twin theft from second and third base that day. Typically the double steal is initiated with runners on first and third.

Gehrig stole his first base as a rookie on June 24, 1925. It was a steal of home, and the record books don't indicate whether any other player has ever done this on his first theft. It was a double steal with catcher Wally Schang going down to second. On July 4, 1925, he stole his second base, and it was of second base as Bob Meusel stole home. It was a double embarrassment for Philadelphia catcher Mickey Cochrane, who was the backstop during eight of Lou's career thefts.

Lou's favorite double-steal partners were Ben Chapman and Tony Lazzeri. Chapman and Gehrig, alternating positions, worked it successfully five times. He did it four times with Lazzeri, with the Iron Horse serving as the lead runner each time. But Gehrig had more famous partners. In 1926 he stole home twice, and Babe Ruth was his burglary mate on both occasions. This was a year before they became known as the "home run twins." A decade later, Lou teamed up with Joe DiMaggio in two successful double steals. This was somewhat unusual for DiMag, and it wasn't long afterward that Yankee management decided he should not take the chance of injuring his legs stealing.

As a result, the elder DiMaggio, who was a very good base runner, ended his career with a meager 30 thefts. In contrast, Gehrig kept pushing to the end. His last two steals came in the same game, on September 7, 1938, against the Red Sox. Twice he walked and twice he swiped second. He could be resourceful even without using his big bat.

Listed below are his 15 steals of home and his 8 other double steals.

Steals of Home by Gehrig

Date	Opposing Team
June 24, 1925	Washington in 7th; double steal with Wally Schang
Apr. 13, 1926	Boston in 1st; double steal with Babe Ruth
July 24, 1926	Chicago in 3rd; double steal with Babe Ruth
June 11, 1927	Cleveland in 5th; double steal with Tony Lazzeri
June 29, 1927	Boston in 8th; double steal with Bob Meusel
July 30, 1927 (1)*	Cleveland in 3rd; double steal with Bob Meusel
July 19, 1929 (1)	Cleveland in 2nd; double steal with Cedric Durst
June 7, 1930	St. Louis in 6th; double steal with Bill Dickey
Apr. 15, 1931	Boston in 8th; double steal with Tony Lazzeri
July 28, 1931	Chicago in 5th; double steal with Ben Chapman
Apr. 12, 1932	Philadelphia in 9th; double steal with Ben Chapman
June 20, 1933	Chicago in 6th; double steal with Tony Lazzeri
June 28, 1933	Detroit in 9th; double steal with Ben Chapman
June 2, 1934	Philadelphia in 1st; double steal with Jack Saltzgaver
May 15, 1935	Detroit in 7th; double steal with Tony Lazzeri

* Numbers in parentheses indicate first or second game of a doubleheader

Other Double Steals by Gehrig

Date	Opposing Team
July 4, 1925 (2)	Philadelphia in 1st; Gehrig to second, Bob Meusel home
Sept. 9, 1926	Boston in 4th; Gehrig to second, Earle Combs home
Sept. 13, 1930 (2)	Detroit in 1st; Gehrig to second, Earle Combs home
Apr. 27, 1931	Washington in 5th; Gehrig to third, Ben Chapman home
July 23, 1933 (2)	Cleveland in 5th; Ben Chapman to second, Gehrig to third
Aug. 31, 1933	Boston in 1st; Gehrig to second, Dixie Walker home
July 18, 1936 (2)	St. Louis in 3rd; Gehrig to second, Joe DiMaggio home
July 18, 1937	Cleveland in 3rd; Gehrig to second, Joe DiMaggio third

On-Base Average
Pete Palmer

There are two main objectives for the hitter. The first is to not make an out, and the second is to hit for distance. Long-ball hitting is normally measured by slugging average. Not making an out can be expressed in terms of on-base average (OBA), where:

$$\text{OBA} = \frac{\text{hits} + \text{walks} + \text{hit-by-pitch}}{\text{at bats} + \text{walks} + \text{hit-by-pitch}}$$

For example, if we were figuring out Frank Robinson's career on-base average, it would be compiled like this: 2,943 hits + 1,420 walks + 198 hit-by-pitch (4,561), divided by 10,006 at bats + 1,420 walks + 198 HBP (11,624). His OBA is .392, which happens to be one of the higher figures of recent years but does not compare very well with players of the past. Sacrifice hits are ignored in this calculation.

On-base average can be quite different from batting average. Take, for example, Joe DiMaggio and Roy Cullenbine, once outfield teammates for the Yankees. DiMag had a lifetime batting average of .325 and Cullenbine one of .276. But Roy was walked much more frequently than Joe and made fewer outs; he had an OBA of .408 compared to .398 for the Yankee Clipper.

In calculating OBA, the Macmillan *Baseball Encyclopedia* was used for hits, at bats, and bases on balls. Hit-by-pitch data are from official averages back to 1920 in the American League and 1917 in the National League. Figures back to 1909 have been compiled by Alex Haas from newspaper box scores. Some data before then come from Haas, John Tattersall, and Bob Davids. Additional information is available in some of the old newspapers but has not yet been compiled. Players with incomplete totals are credited with HBPs at the known rate from available data for those unknown appearances. In the NL prior to 1887 a batter was not awarded first base when hit by a pitch. In the American Association, HBP was started in 1884.

Who is the all-time leader in on-base average? It is Ted Williams, with a spectacular .483 mark. Not surprisingly, Babe Ruth is second, with .474. It is no secret that Williams and Ruth were both exceptionally good hitters as well as being among those frequently walked. It was not unusual for them to get on base 300 times a season. Ranking third on the all-time list is John McGraw, who was elected to the Hall of Fame as a manager but who also was a fine hitter. In addition, he was adept at getting on base by walks and HBPs. He holds the all-time NL record for OBA—both lifetime and season. Billy Hamilton, the stolen base king, and Lou Gehrig are next in line, followed by such big names as Rogers Hornsby, Ty Cobb, Jimmie Foxx, and Tris Speaker. Rounding out the top ten is Ferris Fain, former first baseman of the A's, who quietly attained a very high OBA to go with his two batting titles.

Some players who many fans might not think of as among the leaders in OBA are Max Bishop, second baseman of the A's last super teams of 1929–31, Clarence "Cupid" Childs, Cleveland second sacker in the 1890s, Roy Thomas, Phil center fielder at the turn of the century, and Joe Cunningham, who played with the Cardinals and White Sox in the 1950s and 1960s. On the other hand, some of the famous hitters of baseball are not included in the accompanying list of players with lifetime on-base averages of .400 or better. Missing are such stars as Willie Keeler, Bill Terry, George Sisler, Nap Lajoie, Al Simmons, Hans Wagner, Cap Anson, Joe DiMaggio, and Roberto Clemente.

Most of the players in the .400 list are either outfielders or first basemen. When you look at OBA data by position, you find that there are many unheralded players near the top of their respective lists. Wally Schang, for example, played for a number of AL clubs in the teens and twenties; he is second among catchers, with an OBA of .393. Elmer Valo, another Connie Mack product, ranks sixth in right field.

There is only one active player with OBA of .400 or better and only a few among the leaders by position. The level of OBA in the majors is presently quite low. This could be attributed to many factors, such as improved pitching (bigger and stronger pitchers throwing from the unchanged distance of 60 feet 6 inches, more use of relief pitchers, and the widespread use of the slider as an extra pitch), larger ball parks, and increased emphasis on hitting home runs.

The surprise leader among players active in 1982 is Mike Hargrove of the Indians, who annually receives a high total of bases on balls. His OBA percentage is .405, a half dozen points ahead of Joe Morgan. Another surprise among the leaders is Gene Tenace, with a career batting average of only .242—but he gets almost as many walks as hits. The top ten among players active in 1982 with at least 1,000 career games include:

Mike Hargrove	.405	Mike Schmidt	.386
Joe Morgan	.398	Carl Yastrzemski	.383
Rod Carew	.397	Fred Lynn	.382
Ken Singleton	.396	Bill Madlock	.380
Gene Tenace	.391	Pete Rose	.380
Keith Hernandez	.390		

Mike Schmidt was the season leader in 1982 with a .407 mark. Dwight Evans led in the AL with a modest .403 figure. These season averages are far below the top season marks of the past, which are dominated by Ted Williams and Ruth. Here is the list of top season OBA performers with averages of .500 or more.

Ted Williams, 1941	.551	Babe Ruth, 1926	.516
John McGraw, 1899	.546	Mickey Mantle, 1957	.515
Babe Ruth, 1923	.545	Babe Ruth, 1924	.513
Babe Ruth, 1920	.530	Babe Ruth, 1921	.512
Ted Williams, 1957	.528	Rogers Hornsby, 1924	.508
Billy Hamilton, 1894	.521	Joe Kelley, 1894	.502
Ted Williams, 1954	.516	Hugh Duffy, 1894	.501

Ted Williams led the league in OBA every year he qualified except for his rookie season, and he had a higher OBA than the leader in three of his four seasons shortened by injury. Those leading the league most often in OBA are:

American League		National League	
Ted Williams	12	Rogers Hornsby	8
Babe Ruth	10	Stan Musial	6
Ty Cobb	6	Billy Hamilton	5
Lou Gehrig	5	Joe Morgan	5
Carl Yastrzemski	5	Richie Ashburn	4
Rod Carew	4	Mel Ott	4
		Honus Wagner	4

It is important to remember that OBA is only one component of hitting and that slugging is equally valuable. Of course, the best long-ball hitters usually rank high in both departments because they are generally walked more frequently. One thing the OBA does is give percentage recognition to the player's ability to get on via the walk and the HBP as well as the hit. He has saved his team an out, and he is in a good position to score a run.

On-Base Average Leaders, Career
(1,000 games, through 1980)

Player	Years	AB	BH	BB	HBP	OBA
Ted Williams	1939–60	7706	2654	2018	39	.483
Babe Ruth	1914–35	8399	2873	2056	42	.474
John McGraw	1891–06	3924	1309	836	116	.464
Billy Hamilton	1888–01	6268	2158	1187	93*	.455
Lou Gehrig	1923–39	8001	2721	1508	45	.447
Rogers Hornsby	1915–37	8173	2930	1038	48	.434
Ty Cobb	1905–28	11437	4192	1249	92	.433
Jimmie Foxx	1926–45	8134	2646	1452	13	.430
Tris Speaker	1907–28	10205	3514	1381	101	.427
Ferris Fain	1947–55	3930	1139	903	18	.425
Eddie Collins	1906–30	9949	3310	1503	77	.424
Joe Jackson	1908–20	4981	1774	519	59	.423
Max Bishop	1924–35	4494	1216	1153	31	.423
Mickey Mantle	1951–68	8102	2415	1734	13	.423
Dan Brouthers	1879–04	6711	2296	840	105	.423
Mickey Cochrane	1925–37	5169	1652	857	29	.419
Stan Musial	1941–63	10972	3630	1599	53	.418

(Continued)

* Hit by pitch estimated from partial career totals

On-Base Average Leaders, Career
(1,000 games, through 1980)

Player	Years	AB	BH	BB	HBP	OBA
Clarence Childs	1890–01	5615	1720	990	66*	.416
Jesse Burkett	1890–05	8421	2850	1029	70*	.415
Melvin Ott	1926–47	9456	2876	1708	64	.414
Ed Delahanty	1888–03	7505	2597	741	95*	.412
Hank Greenberg	1930–47	5193	1628	852	16	.412
Roy Thomas	1899–11	5296	1537	1042	42*	.411
Charlie Keller	1939–52	3790	1085	784	10	.410
Harry Heilmann	1914–32	7787	2660	856	40	.410
Jackie Robinson	1947–56	4877	1518	740	72	.410
Eddie Stanky	1943–53	4301	1154	996	34	.410
Roy Cullenbine	1938–47	3879	1072	852	11	.408
Joe Cunningham	1954–66	3362	980	599	49	.406
Riggs Stephenson	1921–34	4508	1515	494	40	.406
Denny Lyons	1885–97	4294	1333	621	70*	.406
Arky Vaughan	1932–48	6622	2103	937	46	.406
Mike Hargrove	1974–82	4459	1305	795	48	.405
Paul Waner	1926–45	9459	3152	1091	38	.404
Charlie Gehringer	1924–42	8858	2839	1185	51	.404
Joe Kelley	1891–08	6977	2213	910	86*	.402
Lu Blue	1921–33	5904	1696	1092	43	.402
Pete Browning	1882–94	4820	1646	466	24*	.402

* Hit by pitch estimated from partial career totals

The Youngest Boy Manager

Eugene Murdock

Bucky Harris and Lou Boudreau have been traditionally acclaimed as baseball's boy managers. Harris was elevated to lead the Washington Senators in 1924 at the age of twenty-seven, and he guided them to two American League pennants and one World Series title. Boudreau became Cleveland's manager after the 1941 season at the age of twenty-four. But what baseball history has forgotten is that there was another ballplayer who actually took over a major league club when only twenty-three years old, four years the junior of Harris and one year younger than Boudreau when they assumed command.

The youngest boy manager honor goes to Roger Peckinpaugh, who became manager of the New York Yankees in mid-September 1914 and handled the team for the remainder of the season. He led the Yanks in 17 games, winning 9 and losing 8. Although he was replaced by Bill Donovan in 1915 after the Ruppert–Huston group purchased the club, his brief tenure assures him a page in baseball's book of unique honors.

In 1975 the former shortstop, then 83, recalled with precision and humor the circumstances that led to his appointment. (Peckinpaugh died in 1977.) Frank Chance, the New York manager, had become irritated with the club ownership in 1914 and decided to quit. In the process of telling Yankee Frank Farrell what he thought of the whole business, Chance said it might be a good idea to name young Peckinpaugh his successor.

Chance confided to Peck that he had recommended him and urged him to demand more money if he was offered the job. Farrell, too, had been impressed by his shortstop and followed Chance's advice, tendering him the post. No mention was made of money.

"I was tickled to death to be offered the position," Peck recalled, "but I never would have thought of asking for more money if Frank hadn't told me to. And they never would have volunteered to give me any more," he chuckled. "But I finally asked for another $500, and after a little bargaining I got it."

Peck's lengthy career began when he signed with Cleveland in 1909, straight from the Cleveland sandlots, and was shipped to New Haven in the Connecticut League for the 1910 season. He was brought up to the parent club at the tail end of the 1910 season and played there until 1913, when he was traded to the Yankees.

In 1921 the Yankees won their first pennant in history. It was a great year for Peck and his teammates, even though they lost the Series in eight games to the Giants. One can imagine Peckinpaugh's chagrin, therefore, when he read in the newspaper that winter that he had been traded to Washington.

"That hurt," Peckinpaugh remembered, "and it hurt more because it was not my fault. We had just come off a beautiful year, and there was no reason to trade me. The trouble was that Babe Ruth had been openly knocking manager Miller Huggins and boosting me to be manager. Since they weren't going to get rid of Ruth, baseball's greatest drawing card, they had to get rid of me, even though I had nothing to do with the matter. Yes, that one hurt."

Although Peck lost out on two pennants in New York in 1922 and 1923, he picked up two others in Washington in 1924 and 1925. The Senators won the World Series from the Giants in 1924, and Peck was the leading hitter with an average of .417. The 1925 season was his best: he led Washington to another pennant, and he won the AL's most valuable player award.

But things did not go well in the World Series with the Pittsburgh Pirates. Not only did the Pirates win, but it was Peck's darkest hour. "It is lucky they picked the most valuable player before the World Series began, or I might not have gotten it afterwards." The reason was that Peckinpaugh set a record that still stands—eight errors by a shortstop.

"It upset me then, and it still does today. Because after my long career, the first thing people ask is, 'What about that 1925 World Series?' They don't ask about the 1924 World Series, or any of the other things that went well, but only that 1925 World Series. Well, to begin with, it was not nearly as bad as it sounds. We were playing on some pretty wet ballfields then, and they used the same muddy, soggy ball until somebody knocked it out of the lot.

"About four of these errors were low throws to first base which Joe Judge would normally have eaten up. Every time I see Max Carey [the Pirate captain in the 1925 Series] at the Hall of Fame game in Bradenton, Florida, he asks me, 'How could they give you an error on that fifth hit of mine? They should have given me a hit, not you an error. Five hits off Walter Johnson could have meant thousands of dollars.' "

"I told Max," Peck continued, "that the reason for it was simply that Pittsburgh's Honus Wagner held the World Series record of six errors by a shortstop, and that was one record the Pittsburgh scorers did not want Wagner to have. So I wound up with eight errors and broke Wagner's record."

Peckinpaugh finished his playing career with the White Sox in 1927 and was then brought to Cleveland to manage the Indians in 1928. He held that post until early in the 1933 season when Walter Johnson—a close friend from his Washington days—succeeded him. Peck was restored to the Cleveland spot in 1941 but managed only that year before moving upstairs to the vice-presidency. He was succeeded by the boy manager, Lou Boudreau.

Sewell and Fox—
The Hardest to Fan
L. Robert Davids

There is some irony in the fact that baseball record keepers maintain a list of the annual leaders in most strikeouts by a batter. This is a negative category, yet for years these tabulations have been carried right along with the annual leaders in home runs, batting, and so on.

A much more positive and meaningful listing would be the season leader with fewest strikeouts per at bat. In other words, a batter with 15 strikeouts in 600 at bats would get recognition over someone who fanned 12 times in 400 at bats, because his percentage would be better.

What is the significance of a batter who whiffs, say, 20 times a season rather than 100? The player who fans 100 times is making no contribution; he is freezing the action on each of those occasions. The player who fans 80 fewer times is keeping the ball in play. Even by making an infield out he could be advancing runners, possibly even scoring a run.

A review of the batters with fewest strikeouts over the past 70 years indicates that the totals have gone up and down by era. There was a fair amount of whiffing in the teens, but with the introduction of the lively ball in 1920, there was a general reduction which lasted until about World War II. In the late 1940s and in the 1950s the totals were up a little; in the 1960s and even in the present period strikeouts per at bat have been higher than ever before.

In spite of these ups and downs, there are two players who stand out in their respective eras. They are Joe Sewell in the period 1920–33, when there were the fewest strikeouts, and Nellie Fox, 1947–65, who played in an era of increasing numbers of strikeouts. Fox led his league 11 times, while Sewell held the title 9 times. Although Sewell's yearly totals were about half those of Fox, the two were nearly comparable for their eras.

These two players clearly dominated in their particular specialty. Some say Willie Keeler would be in the same category, but strikeout records for batters were not really kept during most of his career. Consequently, there is no sound basis for a statistical comparison. In spite of published reports that in the 1890s Keeler once went a full season with the Orioles without striking out, recent research has proved that inaccurate. Even with incomplete data, at least two strikeouts have been found for each of those seasons.

The death of Nellie Fox in 1975 prevented an interview with him on the subject of his few strikeouts. However, we were able to talk with Joe Sewell at his home in Tuscaloosa, Alabama, after a detailed analysis was made of each of Sewell's strikeouts. First the date of each whiff was copied from the game record, and the opposing pitcher was singled out from the play-by-play account. This was done primarily to find out which pitcher fanned Sewell the most times, but the close scrutiny resulted in another interesting discovery.

By checking the dates of each of Sewell's 114 career strikeouts, we found that on May 17, 1929, Sewell was fanned in the third inning by George Blaeholder of the Browns. He was not victimized again until Danny MacFayden of the Red Sox set him down in the sixth inning on September 20, 1929. In the interim he played in 115 games and went to bat 442 times without whiffing. Heretofore, Fox has been credited with going a record 98 consecutive games without striking out.

By analyzing the pitchers who were able to strike him out, we found that Sewell, who batted left-handed, was fanned by southpaws 44 times and by right-handers 70 times. On two occasions he was fanned twice in the same game. The first time was on May 13, 1923, and Wally Warmoth, a rookie southpaw for the Senators, set him down both times. The next time was May 26, 1930, and Lefty Pat Caraway of the White Sox did it twice then.

By that time Sewell was notorious for being tough to strike out, and Caraway's feat received some notice. Joe recalls that it was the white shirts in the center field bleachers that threw him off. Anyway, he fanned only three times in 1930, and two of them came in the same game. Joe was so irked he went the rest of the season, from May 26 on, without fanning.

Playing for the Yankees the next season, Sewell recalls that in one game he was again batting against George Blaeholder, who was supposed to have invented the slider. "Bill McGowan was the umpire and the count was 3 and 2. The next pitch was a fast ball right even with my cap bill. McGowan hollered, 'Strike three—Oh, my God, I missed it.' All this in one breath. I looked at him but did not say a word. The next day he came over before the game and apologized for missing the third strike in the previous game. He was a good umpire, very capable, and I never held it against him."

In his fourteen years of play, Sewell was never fanned by any pitcher more than four times. Nine different pitchers accomplished that. They included Blaeholder, Bob Shawkey, Walter Johnson, Urban Shocker, Waite Hoyt, and Earl Whitehill, all long-service hurlers, and three short-time lefties, Billy Bayne, Mike Cvengros, and Ed Wells. Yet Sewell says it was none of these who gave him the most trouble. "The hardest pitcher for me was Hubert 'Dutch' Leonard of Detroit. He was a left-handed spitball pitcher, and he was mean with it. I had real good luck against both Lefty Grove [who fanned him only one time] and Walter Johnson. I am almost certain I had better than a .300 average against both of them. I got 5 for 5 one day off of Lefty Grove, the last one a home run in Yankee Stadium."

Unlike Keeler or Fox, Sewell did not really choke up on the bat. At 5 feet 6½ inches and only 155 pounds, he was smaller than Fox, but he hit more homers and doubles. He usually swung away, and therefore his record for fewest strikeouts is all the more remarkable. He didn't start off particularly well, fanning 17 times in 1921 and 20 in 1922. By 1925 he was down to 4 strikeouts, and he never got into double figures again. He had the five best season marks in recorded history: 3, 3, 4, 4, and 4. Those five seasons are balanced on the other end of the strikeout spectrum by free swingers of another era—Bobby Bonds, 189 and 187; Mike Schmidt, 180; Dave Nicholson, 175; and Gorman Thomas, 175.

There follows a list by year of the players with the fewest strikeouts on a frequency basis with a minimum of 350 at bats for a 154-game schedule and 400 at bats for 162 games.

	National League		American League	
1910	John Evers, Chi.	18		
1911	Fred Tenney, Bos.	17		
1912	John Evers, Chi.	18		
1913	John Evers, Chi.	14	Nap Lajoie, Clev.	17
1914	Bill Sweeney, Chi.	15	Nap Lajoie, Clev.	15
1915	Gus Getz, Bkn.	14	Tris Speaker, Bos.	14
1916	Larry Doyle, N.Y.	23	Tris Speaker, Clev.	20
1917	Ivy Wingo, Cin.	13	Tris Speaker, Clev.	14
1918	Edd Roush, Cin.	10	Tris Speaker, Clev.	9
1919	Ivy Olson, Bkn.	12	Joe Jackson, Chi.	10
1920	George Cutshaw, Pitt.	10	Tris Speaker, Clev.	13
1921	Edd Roush, Cin.	8	Stuffy McInnis, Bos.	9
1922	Chas. Hollocher, Chi.	5	Stuffy McInnis, Bos.	5
1923	Frank Frisch, N.Y.	12	Eddie Collins, Chi.	8
1924	Stuffy McInnis, Bos.	6	John Tobin, StL.	12
1925	Billy Southworth, N.Y.	11	Joe Sewell, Clev.	4
1926	Andy High, Bos.	9	Joe Sewell, Clev.	7
1927	Frank Frisch, StL.	10	Joe Sewell, Clev.	7
1928	Pie Traynor, Pitt.	10	Joe Sewell, Clev.	9
1929	Pie Traynor, Pitt.	7	Joe Sewell, Clev.	4
1930	Frank Frisch, StL.	16	Joe Sewell, Clev.	3
1931	Edd Roush, Cin.	5	Joe Sewell, N.Y.	8
1932	Lloyd Waner, Pitt.	11	Joe Sewell, N.Y.	3
1933	Lloyd Waner, Pitt.	8	Joe Sewell, N.Y.	4
1934	Frank Frisch, StL.	10	Joe Vosmik, Clev.	10
1935	Lloyd Waner, Pitt.	10	Bill Dickey, N.Y.	11
1936	Lloyd Waner, Pitt.	5	Rip Radcliff, Chi.	12
1937	Lloyd Waner, Pitt.	12	Roger Cramer, Bos.	14
1938	Lloyd Waner, Pitt.	11	Billy Sullivan, StL.	10
1939	Johnny Cooney, Bos.	8	Roger Cramer, Bos.	17
1940	Debs Garms, Pitt.	6	Charlie Gehringer, Det.	17
1941	Frank McCormick, Cin.	13	Roger Cramer, Wash.	15
1942	Jimmy Brown, StL.	11	Stan Spence, Wash.	16
1943	Arky Vaughan, Bkn.	13	Roger Cramer, Det.	13
1944	Tommy Holmes, Bos.	11	Ralph Hodgin, Chi.	14
1945	Tommy Holmes, Bos.	9	Ed Busch, Phil.	9
1946	Tommy Holmes, Bos.	14	Lou Boudreau, Clev.	14
1947	Emil Verban, Phil.	8	Lou Boudreau, Clev.	10

(Continued)

	National League		American League	
1948	Eddie Waitkus, Chi.	19	Lou Boudreau, Clev.	9
1949	Tommy Holmes, Bos.	6	Dale Mitchell, Clev.	11
1950	Eddie Waitkus, Phil.	29	Yogi Berra, N.Y.	12
1951	Don Mueller, N.Y.	13	Nelson Fox, Chi.	11
1952	Peanuts Lowrey, StL.	13	Dale Mitchell, Clev.	9
1953	Don Mueller, N.Y.	13	Billy Goodman, Bos.	11
1954	Don Mueller, N.Y.	17	Clint Courtney, Balt.	7
1955	Don Mueller, N.Y.	12	Nelson Fox, Chi.	15
1956	Don Mueller, N.Y.	7	Nelson Fox, Chi.	14
1957	Red Schoendienst, Mil.-N.Y.	15	Nelson Fox, Chi.	13
1958	Frank Torre, Mil.	14	Nelson Fox, Chi.	11
1959	Smoky Burgess, Pitt.	16	Nelson Fox, Chi.	13
1960	Jim Gilliam, L.A.	28	Nelson Fox, Chi.	13
1961	Harvey Kuenn, S.F.	34	Nelson Fox, Chi.	12
1962	Bob Lillis, Hous.	23	Nelson Fox, Chi.	12
1963	Jim Gilliam, L.A.	28	Nelson Fox, Chi.	17
1964	Nelson Fox, Hous.	13	Bobby Richardson, N.Y.	36
1965	Bob Lillis, Hous.	10	Bobby Richardson, N.Y.	39
1966	Glenn Beckert, Chi.	36	Bobby Richardson, N.Y.	28
1967	Glenn Beckert, Chi.	25	Luis Aparicio, Balt.	44
1968	Glenn Beckert, Chi.	20	Cesar Tovar, Minn.	41
1969	Glenn Beckert, Chi.	24	Luis Aparicio, Chi.	29
1970	Matty Alou, Pitt.	18	Horace Clarke, N.Y.	35
1971	Felix Millan, Atl.	22	Felipe Alou, N.Y.	24
1972	Glenn Beckert, Chi.	17	Buddy Bell, Clev.	29
1973	Felix Millan, N.Y.	22	Luis Aparicio, Bos.	33
1974	Felix Millan, N.Y.	14	Buddy Bell, Clev.	29
1975	Felix Millan, N.Y.	28	Dan Meyer, Det.	25
1976	Dave Cash, Phil.	13	George Brett, K.C.	36
1977	Tim Foli, Mon.-S.F.	20	George Brett, K.C.	24
1978	Bill Buckner, Chi.	17	Bob Bailor, Tor.	21
1979	Tim Foli, N.Y.-Pitt.	14	George Brett, K.C.	36
1980	Bill Buckner, Chi.	18	Rich Dauer, Balt.	19
1981	Tim Foli, Pitt.	10	Mike Hargrove, Clev.	16
1982	Bill Buckner, Chi.	26	Tim Foli, Cal.	22

Batters Most Difficult to Strike Out, Career

Years	Player	AB	SO	AB/SO Ratio
1920–33	Joe Sewell	7132	113	63
1927–45	Lloyd Waner	7772	173	45
1947–65	Nelson Fox	9232	216	43
1942–52	Tommy Holmes	4992	122	41
1913–28	Tris Speaker	7899*	220*	36
1913–27	Stuffy McInnis	6667*	189*	35
1922–34	Andy High	4440	130	34
1919–37	Frank Frisch	9112	272	34
1915–34	Sam Rice	9269	276	33
1921–44	Johnny Cooney	3372	107	32

* Career data not complete

Home Runs vs. Strikeouts

If a batter hits 47 or 48 home runs a season, he's going for the fences, right? And if he's going for the fences, he's going to strike out a lot, right? Well, yes and no. It is primarily yes in recent years, with Dave Kingman hitting 48 homers and striking out 130 times in 1979 and Mike Schmidt having 48 homers and 119 strikeouts in 1980. But in 1971, the last year in which there were two sluggers with 47 or more homers, there was an interesting contrast.

Willie Stargell led the National League in 1971 with 48 round-trippers and 154 strikeouts. Henry Aaron was second in four-baggers with 47. However, Aaron fanned only 58 times, which is further confirmation that he had one of his best seasons ever in 1971.

The great contrast between Aaron and Stargell in strikeouts, 58 to 154, is fairly typical of the great sluggers of the past. Of those players hitting at least 47 homers—and this has happened 40 times—Stargell fanned most frequently, more than three times as often as he blasted one out of the park. This surpassed the marks of Reggie Jackson and Harmon Killebrew in their biggest home run years.

Was there ever a player who hit 47 or more homers who had fewer strikeouts than home runs? Yes, three. Johnny Mize did it once and Lou Gehrig and Ted Kluszewski each did it twice. Gehrig had the best season ratio when he hit 49 homers and fanned only 31 times in his Triple Crown season of 1934. Roger Maris came pretty close to even figures in 1961, even though he was obviously pressing for home runs. He fanned only 67 times while hitting 61 out of the park. In contrast, teammate Mickey Mantle, who hit 54 round-trippers in that expansion year, whiffed on 112 occasions.

Those players who have hit 47 or more four-baggers in a season are listed below with the number of times they struck out that season.

Year	Player	HR	SO	Year	Player	HR	SO
1961	Roger Maris	61*	67	1954	Ted Kluszewski	49*	35
1927	Babe Ruth	60*	89*	1962	Willie Mays	49*	85
1921	Babe Ruth	59*	81	1964	H. Killebrew	49*	135
1932	Jimmie Foxx	58*	96	1966	Frank Robinson	49*	90
1938	H. Greenberg	58*	92	1969	H. Killebrew	49*	84
1930	Hack Wilson	56*	84*	1933	Jimmie Foxx	48*	93*
1920	Babe Ruth	54*	80	1962	H. Killebrew	48*	142*
1928	Babe Ruth	54*	87*	1969	Frank Howard	48	96
1949	Ralph Kiner	54*	61	1971	Willie Stargell	48*	154*
1961	Mickey Mantle	54	112	1979	Dave Kingman	48*	131*
1956	Mickey Mantle	52*	99	1980	Mike Schmidt	48*	119
1965	Willie Mays	52*	71	1926	Babe Ruth	47*	76
1977	George Foster	52*	107	1927	Lou Gehrig	47	84
1947	Ralph Kiner	51*	81	1950	Ralph Kiner	47*	79
1947	Johnny Mize	51*	42	1953	Ed Mathews	47*	83
1955	Willie Mays	51*	60	1955	Ted Kluszewski	47*	40
1938	Jimmie Foxx	50	76	1958	Ernie Banks	47*	87
1930	Babe Ruth	49*	61	1964	Willie Mays	47*	72
1934	Lou Gehrig	49*	31	1969	Reggie Jackson	47	142
1936	Lou Gehrig	49*	46	1971	Henry Aaron	47	58

* Asterisk indicates league leader

Was the Federal League a Major League?
Emil H. Rothe
Assisted by Richard L. Burtt

Was the Federal League of 1914 and 1915 a major league? Baseball authorities interested in the answer have been, and still are, divided in their opinions. Could a six-team independent league in 1913, generally regarded as no better than Class D, become an eight-team organization of major league quality a year later? The odds suggest that even the thought is preposterous. And yet, the historical background suggests that we ought not reach hasty, unwarranted conclusions.

In simplest terms the historical background began in 1912. That year two attempts were made to start independent leagues without the blessings of the National Association of Professional Baseball Leagues. The United States League, composed of eight eastern cities, survived only a month, and the Columbian League, made up of cities in the Midwest, didn't even open the season.

In 1913 the United States League opened the season but folded after only three games. The Midwestern organization, rechristened the Federal League (FL), with John T. Powers as its president, not only opened as a six-team league but completed a 120-game season. Chicago, Cleveland, Covington, Indianapolis, Pittsburgh, and St. Louis had teams in that loop. When the Covington club was unable to attract the attendance that had been anticipated, the franchise was transferred to Kansas City forty-one games into the season. Competing head-to-head with major league teams in four of the six cities proved to be a serious financial strain, and there was talk of dissolving the league.

Later in the season, however, James A. Gilmore, a Chicago manufacturer, was appointed temporary president of the league when Mr. Powers was given a "vacation." Mr. Gilmore proved to be a dynamic leader and was certainly not of a mind to give up the venture. His enthusiasm convinced the owners to continue their league in 1914. He interested Charles Weeghman, a wealthy Chicago restaurateur, in the FL and with him as an ally attracted strong financial backing in other cities: Phil Ball and Otto Stifel in St. Louis; Robert B. Ward, president of the Ward Baking Company in Brooklyn; and in 1915 the multimillionaire oil tycoon Albert Sinclair. Earlier Weeghman and Ball had both sought to purchase major league franchises but had been turned down. Their eagerness to own a baseball club of stature made them even more enthusiastic when the FL proclaimed itself a major league. Initially the established leagues ignored that boast, but when the FL began to sign some of the stars of organized baseball and when eight new ball parks began to take form, the National and American Leagues realized that a baseball war was indeed in the offing.

Early in January 1914 Gilmore stated that clubs in the league would respect existing major league contracts but that players who were merely on the reserve list were fair game. The Feds quickly signed many major leaguers. The first to jump was Joe Tinker, who doubled his Cincinnati salary when he agreed to manage and play shortstop for the Chicago Feds. Following Tinker's defection, other established major league standouts, including Otto Knabe, Three-Finger Brown, Hal Chase, and Russ Ford, signed FL contracts.

In its February 7, 1914, issue, *Literary Digest* reported that the FL had 40 major league players in the fold but added jocularly that "the American and National leagues still had 250 left." The same article pointed out that the Feds sought to have at least 5 players of major league stature on each of its teams.

As the FL was evolving, another phenomenon was developing. In October 1912, David L. Fultz, a former outfielder with the Athletics and Highlanders (Yankees) and subsequently a lawyer, organized the Baseball Players' Fraternity. By 1913 he had a membership of 700, and as a consequence of that impressive number he was able to command respectful attention when he presented a set of seventeen "demands" and seventeen "requests" to the National Commission to improve conditions for those playing in the major leagues. The impact and consequences of Fultz's actions is another story, but the net results were improvements in players' rights and an improved salary structure.

On March 3, 1914, Dave Fultz stated that a league must be judged as a major league on the basis of the salaries it paid and that "the Federal Leaguers are paying unlimited salaries." He freely admitted that the Feds had done more for the players than his Fraternity or anyone else. Thus, Fultz did the FL a favor when he tacitly recognized it as a major league. However, he may have hurt the Feds as a result of being instrumental in improving pay and working conditions in the existing major leagues. It is conceivable that many more stars might have responded to offers from the Feds if those improvements had not been made. Another deterrent to jumping to the Feds was the fact that men who did sign FL contracts were blacklisted by the National Commission.

In November 1913 Charles Comiskey and John McGraw took the Chicago White Sox and the New York Giants on a world tour. The teams were actually conglomerates. Only seven had been members of the White Sox, and only five Giants made the trip. The balance of the two squads consisted of players from other teams. The tour ended in New York on March 5, 1914, and the FL was there to meet them, offering contracts to Tris Speaker, Sam Crawford, Ivy Wingo, Mickey Doolan, Steve Evans, Lee Magee, and others. The last three named accepted the offers; the others did not. Many other players of rank, among them Walter Johnson, Ty Cobb, and Christy Mathewson, were approached by agents of the FL, but they chose to stay with their clubs when their salaries were substantially upgraded.

The first legal battle of the baseball war began when the Chicago Whales obtained the signature of Bill Killifer on an FL contract on January 14, 1914, and paid him a $500 advance. Reindeer Bill had been a catcher for the Phillies since 1911 but, as of that January 14 date, was not under contract to the Philadelphia club. Less than a week later (January 20), he had second thoughts and signed a contract to play with the Philadelphia Nationals in 1914. Two clubs in different leagues now claimed his services. The FL claimed that the sanctity of a contract was the fundamental issue at law. Philadelphia lawyers took the position that the seducer of an employee should not be entitled to equity in the courts. On March 18 the Chicago Feds filed suit in the District Court of the United States for the Western District of Michigan to prevent Killifer from playing with any team other than the Chicago FL club. Judge Clarence V. Sessions was assigned to the case. Final arguments were heard on April 4.

Manager Joe Tinker of the Chicago Feds said, "We can't lose. If our contract is good, we'll have Killifer and Fred Blanding and George Kading [those two had also signed Chicago FL contracts while on the Cleveland reserve list though not under contract to that club]. If the decision is adverse, baseball contracts will no longer have validity, enabling us to offer inducements to major league stars even if they are under contract to National or American league teams."

Judge Sessions handed down his decision on April 10. He denied the FL petition on moral rather than legal grounds and castigated Killifer as one whose pledged word could not be relied upon. He ruled that the contract of January 14 with the Chicago Feds and the one of January 20 when he jumped back to the Philadelphia Phillies were both valid. Organized baseball claimed victory by virtue of the fact that the FL petition had been denied. The Feds claimed victory because the judge's ruling of "moral rather than legal" invalidated the reserve clause and declared that fans could expect open war between the rival leagues and that players from the established leagues would "jump right and left."

Following Sessions's ruling, the picture changed. Gilmore sent wires to his clubs to go after any player whether he was under contract or not. Ban Johnson, president of the AL, responded with, "I don't care a rap what the Feds do, and I would just as soon have war as not." Those were brave words considering the fact that the FL was backed by very wealthy men to the tune of $50 million (a considerable sum in those days).

While it is difficult for us today to sense the intense emotions generated by player raids and counterraids and by legal actions by both sides against organizations and players alike, we can judge the depth of feelings in those days by reading the front-page headlines of the 1914 *Sporting Life*, a weekly baseball tabloid that was considered must reading for anyone interested in baseball. From before the start of spring training in 1914 until a week before the start of the World Series between Connie Mack's Philadelphia Athletics and Boston's Miracle Braves, *every* page-one banner headline contained a reference to the baseball war, to the exclusion of any other event of interest that might have occurred in baseball the preceding week. The headline of the March 14, 1914, issue illustrates the extent and intensity of the confrontation: FEDERAL WAR PLANS—The Independent Stirred into Reprisals by Personal Attacks—Prepare to Prosecute the War Vigorously—By Legal Proceedings, Establishment of Minor Alliances, and Wholesale Capture of Players. Similar "war" announcements appeared *each* week until World Series time.

Just before teams headed south for spring training, *Sporting Life* opined that the NL and AL would not know the full extent of the FL inroads until players actually reported. When, on April 1, the FL published the 1914 rosters for its clubs, they showed that 59 players had jumped—39 from the NL and 20 from the AL. The Feds had made good their threat to have at least 5 major leaguers on each of their clubs; they averaged a little better than 7 per team. Of the 39 NL defectors, Philadelphia lost 9 men, while Brooklyn lost only 2. AL losses ranged from 1 (Danny Murphy of Philadelphia) to 4 from the New York Yankees. The original jumpers were augmented by additional deserters all through the 1914 season. More major leaguers made the crossover for the 1915 season.

In 1914 and 1915, the two years of its existence as a self-appraised major league, a total of 286 men appeared on the rosters of the FL. It is reasonable to assume that to qualify as a major league, a baseball organization must put on the field men who are recognized as having major league talent. What is that talent if it is not the skill to perform for teams in the NL or AL? If that assumption is valid, the next logical step is to analyze the rosters of the Feds. Almost 60 percent of the FL players had had previous NL or AL service—172 players by actual count.

Many of those, it is true, sensed that their major league careers might soon come to an end, and they welcomed the generous FL offers, as well as a chance to extend their playing days at top dollar. At the other end of the scale were those who had played only a year or two as fringe hangers-on.

Those who deserted their teams in organized baseball for a fling with the Feds varied in big league experience—from the fourteen years that Danny Murphy had, mainly with the Athletics in the first decade of the century, to the one inning that Estey Chaney had as a pitcher for the Boston Red Sox in 1913. Incidentally, Chaney didn't do much more for the Brooklyn Feds in 1914 (one game—four innings).

All in all, 101 men who had worn uniforms of an NL or AL team and had then jumped to the outlaw league ended their days as major leaguers with the FL. When the FL died, so did their careers as major leaguers.

Other players that attracted the attention of the FL were those who had already called it quits as big league performers, voluntarily or by request, before the 1913 season. Sixty-one men were lured out of retirement to don again a baseball uniform with a major league logo on the shirt. Thirty of them had last played in the bigs in 1912; eight had closed their careers in 1911; seven dated from 1910 and seven more from 1909. The Feds even signed four from the retirement class of

1908 and four from the year before that. Charlie Carr, who had last played for Cincinnati in 1906, was resurrected to play 115 games at first base for the Indianapolis Federals in 1914.

For 71 of those 172 with previous major league experience, the time they spent in the FL proved to be merely an interlude. When the terms of settlement went into effect dissolving the renegade league, they included the canceling of the blacklist that had been established for those who had deserted. The 71 were able to return to the sites of their former employment. Most of them returned in time for the 1916 season. When the United States entered World War I, major league clubs lost some men to the draft or by enlistment. Those vacancies were filled by another 24 players who had not been signed in 1916 but were called back—7 in 1917 and 17 in 1918. For some the return was hardly worth the bother. Fred Jacklitsch, with ten years in the big time and two more with the Feds, got into only one game with the Boston Braves in 1917 and didn't even get to bat. Benny Meyer, who had played the outfield in 309 games in 1913–15, didn't appear in a major league lineup again until 1925, and then it was for only one game with the Phillies. He did get one at bat—he hit a double and is in the records with a batting average of 1.000 for that year.

Of all the men who ever appeared in a FL game, only 89 of them never played with a NL or AL club. The FL did unearth some rookies who demonstrated enough ability to attract the attention of the big league clubs. Twenty-five men who had their rookie experience with the FL later signed on with the surviving major organizations. Twelve made it in 1916, while the others surfaced during the following three years. Pitcher Dave Black had to wait until 1923, when he landed employment with the Red Sox. For one FL rookie, Frank "Sugar" Kane, the return was for only one game for the Yankees in 1919.

A summary of the foregoing might be useful.

286—Played in the FL in 1914 and/or 1915
172—Had previous major league experience
101—Had played in the majors before and ended their careers with the FL
  71—Played in the majors both before and after their FL sojourn
  89—Never played in the majors before or after their FL days
  25—Were FL rookies who later signed with major league clubs

Four leagues and triple occupancy in two cities made FL scheduling difficult. The Chicago Whales and the St. Louis Terriers each faced competition from two major league clubs. The Brooklyn Tip Tops and the Pittsburgh Rebels had NL rivals. The Kansas City Packers and the Indianapolis Federals (sometimes called the Hoosiers) were confronted by established American Association (AA) clubs. And the Buffalo BufFeds and the Baltimore Terrapins had firmly entrenched International League (IL) teams to contend with.

The two major leagues and two minor leagues announced their schedules well before the FL published its dates. There were 264 game conflicts with organized baseball. The greatest problem was in St. Louis, where a total of 70 conflicts was discovered. The Whales in Chicago were home on the same dates as the White Sox 24 times and were attendance rivals with the Cubs on 28 occasions. In Pittsburgh there were 27 days when the Pirates and Rebels were in town the same days. The Brooklyn Feds were head to head with the Brooklyn Nationals 21 times; if the Giants and Yankees' schedules were included, the entire season would have found two and sometimes three games in greater New York each day of the baseball year. The American Association was in conflict on 34 dates in Kansas City and 20 in Indianapolis. The International and Federal schedules clashed in Baltimore and Buffalo on 20 dates in each city.

In mid-May, John Tener, president of the NL, announced that the FL was not hurting any city in his league except Chicago, where the Whales of Joe Tinker were more popular than the Cubs of Hank O'Day.

By the end of June, Buffalo and Baltimore of the IL were in trouble and appealed to the National Commission for financial assistance and suspension of the draft rule to enable them to compete with their FL rivals for the baseball fan dollar. Both appeals were denied. Ban Johnson, AL president, proposed consideration of another major league composed of the better cities in the IL and the AA. The idea was applauded by both of those organizations, but the Pacific Coast League objected to any change in status that did not include it. Their position was based on the Organized Baseball Agreement of 1903. NL president Tener remained noncommittal, and FL prexy James Gilmore said, "We're too busy planning to obtain more players to worry about another major league." By July the idea had lost appeal, although *Sporting Life* reasoned that eventually there would be a third and maybe a fourth major league regardless of what might happen to the Feds. As we now know, the expansion that *Sporting Life* foresaw took the form of more teams in the two existing leagues rather than more leagues.

Indianapolis won the 1914 FL championship. Chicago finished second, a game and a half out. In June, President Gilmore had said there would be a "world series"—the winner to play an all-star team selected from the other seven teams—but that event never materialized. Benny Kauff of Indianapolis was the batting champ with .370. The Feds led the other two leagues in homers with 295, and Dutch Zwilling of the

Whales was the individual leader with 16. The Nationals managed 266, with Cactus Cravath of the Phillies hitting 19 for top honors. The Americans fell far short with only 148, and the best individual record was 8. Late in April, Otto Knabe, manager of the Brooklyn Tip Tops, had predicted heavy hitting in the FL. "I told President Gilmore that our ball was too lively, but Joe Tinker said it wasn't lively enough, so nobody listened to me. In spring training I noticed how our guys hit the ball. I had trained on the same grounds when I was with the Phillies. My boys were hitting 25–30 yards farther than Art Wilson, Dode Paskert, and other long-distance Philadelphia hitters."

Russell Ford of the BufFeds posted a 21–6 won–lost mark. Claude Hendrix, Chicago's standout mound ace, won 29 games. Ed Lafitte pitched the only FL no-hitter that year. He beat Kansas City 6–2 on September 19. The two runs were the result of his own wildness. Indianapolis amassed 24 hits in a 21–6 conquest of Pittsburgh, and the Hoosiers also ran up a consecutive win streak of 15 games.

With all teams in the three leagues suffering financially, August Herrmann, chairman of the National Commission, offered to meet a representative of the FL early in November. Charlie Weeghman represented the Feds. They met for two days, with Ban Johnson and James Gilmore also on hand. The meetings proved to be fruitless, and early in December the Feds called a halt to further proceedings.

In January 1915 the FL instituted an antitrust suit in the U.S. District Court in Chicago before Judge Kenesaw Mountain Landis. Judge Landis endeared himself to organized baseball when he successfully "sat" on the case by means of legal delays until the following December, when the suit was dropped because by that time there no longer was a FL.

In February, Gilmore announced that the FL would put a team in the Bronx or in Newark for the 1915 season. He had Pat Powers and Harry Sinclair poised to buy the Kansas City franchise and move it to the New York area. Later that month Kansas City obtained an injunction to prevent such a move. At a peace meeting in New York, arrangements were made to move the Indianapolis franchise instead. Newark was selected as the site for the new FL member.

The 1915 season was played with continued animosity between organized baseball and the FL. While some of the action was still conducted in the courts, there was not nearly as much legal maneuvering as in 1914. The FL antitrust suit was still pending; Benny Kauff sued the New York Giants for a promised $5,000 bonus; and the St. Louis Terriers won the Armando Marsans case. (The Cincinnati Reds claimed that Marsans ran out on a contract, but the judge ruled the document was not binding.)

Outfielder Benny Kauff was the outstanding player of the Federal League in 1914–15; playing for Indianapolis and Brooklyn, he led the league in batting average and stolen bases for both seasons, as well as hits, doubles, and runs scored in 1914 and slugging percentage in 1915

All three leagues enjoyed unusually close races in 1915. Almost all the teams except the Athletics (Connie Mack had dismembered his AL champs) had early season pennant fever. Three teams battled for the AL championship almost to the last week. The NL was so well balanced that the ultimate pennant winner had the lowest ever winning percentage and the team in last place had the best won–lost record ever achieved by an eighth-place club. The FL had six teams in the fight. In the last series of the season the title was still on the line and the first four teams were in head-to-head competition, Chicago vs. Pittsburgh and Kansas City vs. St. Louis. In the very last games of the season the Chicago Whales defeated Pittsburgh while the St. Louis Terriers beat the K.C. Packers. Chicago claimed the flag. St. Louis finished second and Pittsburgh third, with only five percentage points separating the trio.

Besides an exciting 1915 race, the Feds had four no-hit games. Frank Allen of Pittsburgh posted the first on April 24 against St. Louis. Three weeks later, on May 15, Chicago's Claude Hendrix made Pittsburgh the victim. On August 16, Alex Main of Kansas City pitched one against Buffalo. Dave Davenport of St. Louis hurled the fourth in a game with Chicago on September 7.

Kauff repeated as the batting champ with a .342 mark, and Hal Chase, Buffalo first baseman, captured the home run crown with 17. Eddie Plank had a solid 2.08 ERA and a won–lost mark of 21–11. Chicago's George McConnell won 24 and lost 10.

In spite of the close races, only three NL clubs showed even a small profit; four teams in the AL posted heavy losses; and in the FL only two clubs ended in the black—just barely. The exciting pennant races should have been profitable but weren't. Schedule conflicts that placed two teams in the same city on too many days hurt. Economic depression threatened; the cost of living was on the rise; our relations with Mexico were unstable; the war in Europe was a grave concern; and there was other competition for surplus dollars—movies, the automobile, and other sports like golf and tennis. But the main problem was the persistent challenge from the FL. Continuing the war was senseless.

President Tener of the NL initiated conferences with representatives from the Feds in the fall of 1915. Other conferences followed without progress, until in mid-November the Federals announced that they intended to place a team in Manhattan. That stirred Tener to renewed activity, and his league and the FL finally reached a tentative agreement in mid-December. It was presented to the AL, which promptly approved it, and a committee was set up to work out details. In Cincinnati, on December 22, the most costly baseball war came to an end. The main issues of the settlement included reinstatement of all players who had been blacklisted. Charles Weeghman, owner of the Chicago Whales, was permitted to buy the Chicago NL club, and Phil Ball, owner of the St. Louis Feds, was allowed to purchase the St. Louis Browns. FL players except those from Chicago or St. Louis were to be sold to the highest bidder. The FL withdrew its antitrust suit. While there were other stipulations, these are the main ones that ended the conflict.

From the 1915 rosters of the Feds, the NL teams selected 39 men for the 1916 season and the AL 20. The Chicago Cubs, in effect, were half Cubs and half Whales, with 17 of the latter. The St. Louis Browns and the Terriers also became a single unit (12 Feds were included). For one reason or another, the St. Louis Cardinals did not add one player from the dissolved league. Three AL teams, Boston, Chicago, and Philadelphia, also passed up the opportunity.

With all the movement of players between the three different leagues during the two-year FL interlude, only two men in all baseball history can claim to have played in three different leagues in the same city. And both names start with Z! Rollie Zeider, an infielder, and Dutch Zwilling, an outfielder, each started with the Chicago (AL) White Sox in 1910, joined the Chicago (FL) Whales in 1914, and, finally, in 1916 played for the Chicago (NL) Cubs.

It must be noted that six Federal Leaguers were eventually inducted into the Baseball Hall of Fame. Not, of course, on what they accomplished during their FL stints, but one or two of their baseball years *were* spent with the Feds. The selectees included three pitchers, Chief Bender, Mordecai Brown, and Eddie Plank, and Bill McKechnie, Edd Roush, and Joe Tinker.

If the FL was not a major league, there is room for conjecture that in 1914 and 1915, with the drain of quality players from the established leagues, maybe, in those days at least, there existed three high-level minor league organizations instead.

The Last Tripleheader
A. D. Suehsdorf

Only one tripleheader has been played in the majors in this century, and that was more than sixty years ago. Considering that in this age of television nine innings can take three or more hours to play, it is unlikely that we shall soon see another one.

The last tripleheader was played on October 2, in the final week of the 1920 season. The Brooklyn Robins were leading the National League comfortably. The Giants were second, no threat but well enough ahead of the Reds, the fading World Champions, who had won 80 and lost 69 and were 3½ games ahead of the Pirates.

Cincinnati was at Pittsburgh for a three-game series, after which the season would end with single games: the Pirates at Chicago and the Cardinals at Cincinnati. The Pirates' chances were slim, but four wins and four Red losses would put them in third place by half a game. Aside from the honor of nosing out the old champs, there would be the tangible reward of the third-place players' share of World Series receipts. Divided among some twenty-five men, this would not be an impressive amount by current standards, but it would exceed the fourth-place team's share, which was nothing.

Unluckily, the Friday game was rained out. Now 3½ behind with three to play, and no makeup dates available, the Pirates' hopes were dead.

Not so fast! Supposing the teams played a tripleheader on Saturday? Barney Dreyfuss, the Pirates' energetic owner, proposed this to Pat Moran, the Reds' manager, who sensibly, if not sportingly, refused. Undaunted, Dreyfuss got in touch with John A. Heydler, the NL president, in New York. As has happened once or twice before in baseball, the owner got his way. Heydler telegraphed Moran to play the three games.

Saturday the weather cleared. The first game began at noon. Moran pitched right-hander Ray Fisher, who was 10–10 on the season and at the end of a modest career spent mostly with the Yankees. George Gibson, the old catcher, long a Pittsburgh favorite and now in his first season as manager, picked his ace, lefty Wilbur Cooper, winner of 24 games, his career high.

The Reds went to bat with the lineup that had served them for two years: Morrie Rath, second base, Jake Daubert, first base, Heinie Groh, third base, the excellent Edd Roush, center field, Pat Duncan, left field, Larry Kopf, shortstop, and Earl "Greasy" Neale, right field. (Neale would soon find a new career in football and eventually serve several seasons as coach of the NFL's Philadelphia Eagles.) Second-stringer Bill Rariden caught Fisher.

The Pirates had stumbled since the glory days of Fred Clarke, even to the extent of finishing eighth in 1917, but were on the way back. There was a World Series triumph not too far ahead, in 1925, and three players who would help make it happen were already on hand: Max Carey, the skillful outfielder and base stealer, and two rookies, Clyde Barnhart at third and Pie Traynor at short. Carson Bigbee was in left field and Billy Southworth, later a fine and patient manager of the Cards and Braves, in right. Charlie Grimm was at first and another rookie, Cotton Tierney, at second. Walter Schmidt caught Cooper.

It was no contest. The great Cooper didn't have a thing. The Reds bombed him for ten hits and eight runs in 2⅔ innings and went on to win 13–4. Kopf had two triples, Roush two doubles, and the Reds stole seven bases on Schmidt. A susceptibility to theft ran in the family. Walter was the younger brother of Boss Schmidt, Detroit's principal catcher in its losing Series of 1907–08–09, when the Cubs and Pirates stole 49 bases in 16 games!

Young Traynor, playing his sixteenth game for Pittsburgh, went one for four, handled nine chances, including a double play, and made two bobbles at short. He would later switch to third base.

Despite all the hits and runs, the rout was completed in two hours and three minutes, and the Reds, four and one-half ahead with three to play, were definitely the champions of third place.

Moran sat most of his regulars down for the second game and

started a lineup with four pitchers in it. In addition to Buck Brenton on the mound, Dutch Ruether was at first, Fritz Coumbe in center, and Rube Bressler in right. This was the transitional year for the Rube. After winning 26 and losing 31 in seven years as a pitcher for the A's and Reds, he was switching to the outfield (and first base) and would swing a big bat for the Reds and Dodgers until 1932.

The Pirates made a few changes but kept a predominantly right-handed lineup against Brenton. They didn't play the right–left percentage much in those days. Traynor was benched.

The game was close for six innings. In the seventh the Reds exploded for seven runs and won easily, 7–3. Brenton's win was his second of the season. The Pirates' Jimmy Zinn was pounded for 14 hits, including 3 by Hod Eller, Cincinnati's best pitcher, who was having fun subbing at second and first.

Time: one hour and fifty-six minutes—18 full innings in one minute under four hours.

Though it was now late in the afternoon, game 3 got under way. Pittsburgh batted first this time, with Cincinnati technically becoming the home team. The Pirates scored three in the first and three in the sixth, while Jughandle Johnny Morrison, making the only start of his rookie year, shut out the same makeshift Reds lineup with four hits. At the end of the sixth, darkness was descending on the Smoky City, and the game was called. Pittsburgh 6, Cincinnati 0. The umpires were Peter Harrison, behind the plate for all three games, and the famous Hank O'Day, chief umpire the day of Fred Merkle's never to be forgotten base-running error in 1908.

Traynor got no hits, had five chances, and no errors. He was still a year away from becoming the Pirates' nonpareil third baseman.

The time of the game was one hour and one minute—24 innings of play in precisely five hours.

Cincinnati went home four and one-half ahead of the Pirates. The Reds lost to the Cards and Wee Willie Sherdel in 12 innings on Sunday, while the Pirates were beating Lefty Tyler in Chicago. So the season ended with Cincinnati 82–71 and Pittsburgh 79–75. As third-place winners the Reds earned a total of $10,744.14. For fourth place the Pirates won zilch.

In an initial burst of enthusiasm the press reported that this was the first tripleheader in major league history. From a purist's point of view this is probably correct. However, there were two other occasions when three games were played in one day. On both occasions there was a morning game, followed by a break in the action and then an afternoon doubleheader. There were two admissions; such was not the case with the 1920 trio of games.

A search of the records revealed that the Brooklyn Bridegrooms of the NL won three games at home on Labor Day, September 1, 1890. And whom did they beat? Pittsburgh, then known as the Innocents. (They became the Pirates a year later after pirating a player incautiously left off another team's reserve list.)

Why three games? Probably because of crosstown competition. This was the one year of existence for the Players' League and an opposition Brooklyn club, led by the popular Monte Ward, was playing a doubleheader against Buffalo. Since the NL had altered its schedule to assure that its teams would be playing in brotherhood towns on the same day, the Bridegrooms' three games probably offered a better attraction than the upstarts' two. Actually, morning game attendance was light, with only 915 showing up.

Brooklyn, managed by Bill "Gunner" McGunnigle, was a fine team, about to win the flag in its first season in the NL. The Innocents, riddled by nine desertions to the Pittsburgh entry in the PL, were dreadful. They would finish the season in eighth place, with a 23–113 record, 66½ games behind Brooklyn.

The first game—begun at 10:30 A.M.—looked like a runaway for the Bridegrooms. However, in the top of the ninth, with Brooklyn leading 10–0, the Innocents came alive. They scored six runs and filled the bases with "two hands out" and third baseman Doggie Miller up. He rapped a hit deep to left field, a triple at least, possibly an inside-the-park home run. The three base runners scored and Doggie was carrying the mail around second as center fielder Darby O'Brien caught up with the ball and threw to Germany Smith, who had run out from short to take the long throw. "O'Brien and Smith handled the ball very cleverly," reported the *New York Times*. Germany whirled, and as fine shortstops have been doing for ninety years since, made the classic throw to the plate to nail the desperate Doggie "by a few inches." Brooklyn 10, Pittsburgh 9.

Game 2 was also tight, with Brooklyn winning 3–2. Game 3 was one of the iron man performances so typical of baseball's early days. Dave Anderson, who lost game 2, returned to try again for the Innocents. He pitched the distance but lost to the Bridegrooms 8–4. Adonis Bill Terry, who had played left field for Brooklyn in the first two games, pitched the victory. His place in left field was taken by pitcher Bobby Caruthers, who had won the first game.

The other three-game marathon took place in Baltimore on September 7, 1896, and was also a Labor Day affair. Doggie Miller and Gunner McGunnigle were again involved, this time with the Louisville Colonels—McGunnigle as manager and Doggie as a utility player in his last year—and also as an umpire in the afternoon contests. They lost to the Orioles 4–3, 9–1, and 12–1.

The Colonels were almost as bad as the Innocents, lying dead last in a 12-team league and finishing 53 games behind the Orioles, then at their peak. These were Ned Hanlon's incomparables—McGraw, Keeler, Jennings, Kelley, and so on. Keeler, for example, had seven hits and five stolen bases for the day. Wilbert Robinson was lauded for catching all three games without a flaw of any type.

After a reasonably close first game, won by Dr. Arlie Pond, the Orioles put on their hitting shoes and rapped a total of 30 hits, good for 21 runs, in the two afternoon games off Louisville's Art Herman and Bert Cunningham, neither of whom was relieved. After eight innings of the third game, the teams agreed to quit. It was getting dark, and enough was enough. The *Baltimore Sun* told the story in banked headlines:

Baseball to Burn

Louisville on the Fire
In Three Successive Games

Warmed Up in the Forenoon

And Done Brown on Both Sides
On a Pretty Afternoon

Scoring Every Inning
Robert E. Jones

The structure of baseball provides the potential for a rare performance that can secure any game's place in baseball history. No one will forget having seen a no-hit game or a perfect game, a high-strikeout game, or a batter going 6 for 6 or hitting four home runs. Nor will it be forgotten who made these singular achievements. But there is a team feat which is probably the most unusual occurrence in baseball and is probably the least appreciated of baseball's rarities: scoring in every inning. It is unusual because of the incredible combinations of team play needed to pull it off, and it is less appreciated because no heroic efforts are required of any one player. The only result of the game is an interesting line score.

Consider that most of baseball's rules operate to prevent runs from being scored. The offensive team does not control the ball. Most of the time, the game is played by nine players against one; at most, nine against four. Of the nine offensive opportunities a team has, scoring in only one of them is often sufficient to win a game. In the majority of games, the winning team scores in only two or three of their allotted times at bat.

Since 1900, only two teams have managed to score in each of nine innings of a game. On June 1, 1923, the New York Giants did it against the Philadelphia Phillies, winning 22–8. On September 13, 1964, the St. Louis Cardinals beat the Chicago Cubs 15–2, likewise never giving the opposing pitchers an inning to be proud of.

How did the Giants and Cardinals manage their scoring binges? Simple. They had a day when hitters could do no wrong and opposing pitchers could do no right. In addition, a more than moderate amount of luck was thrown in. Let's look at these games in detail, starting with the New York–Philadelphia game in 1923.

The Giants entered Baker Bowl in Philadelphia on June 1 solidly in first place, 5½ games ahead of Pittsburgh and 17½ games ahead of the day's opponent.

New York scored quickly in the first. Dave Bancroft and Heinie Groh both singled. After Frankie Frisch flied out, Irish Meusel walked to set up Ross Youngs's bases-clearing triple to right center. Walter Holke then dropped George Kelly's fly to short right, and Youngs scored.

In the second, Bancroft hit a one-out single to left and scored on Groh's double to right center. Following an out, Groh went to third on a passed ball. Meusel walked, and Groh scored on Youngs's single.

The Giants scored only one run in both the third and fourth innings. In the third, walks to Jimmy O'Connell and Claude Jonnard, who had replaced Rosie Ryan on the mound, were followed by Groh's two-out single to score O'Connell. In the fourth O'Connell's solo home run, the only homer of the game, put across another Giants run.

After four innings, the game was still close, 8–6 in favor of New York. However, the next two innings saw the Giants pull away for good. They sent nine batters to the plate each inning and scored five runs each time. Bancroft opened the fifth with a walk, and Groh was safe on Russ Wrightstone's error. Then Frisch doubled, scoring Bancroft and Groh, and Meusel singled, scoring Frisch. Youngs singled, and one out later O'Connell doubled, scoring Meusel. Youngs stopped at third, only to score on Earl Smith's infield out.

Bancroft, Groh, and Frisch led off the sixth with consecutive singles. Meusel's out was only a breather. Youngs doubled, scoring Bancroft and Groh. Kelly singled, scoring Frisch. O'Connell doubled, with Kelly stopping at third. Heinie Sand's error on Smith's grounder allowed Kelly to score with the fifth run.

With the score 18–7 after six innings, the only matter to settle was whether the Giants could continue their magic. Groh punched a one-out single in the seventh but was forced by Frisch. Freddie Maguire ran for Frisch. Following Meusel's third free pass of the game, Maguire scored on Youngs's single.

In the eighth, O'Connell led off with a single. Alex Gaston, who had taken over for Smith behind the plate, walked. Jonnard sacrificed both runners along, and O'Connell scored on Wrightstone's second error of the day. Gaston moved to third on the error and scored when O'Connell was forced at second.

It looked as though the scoring streak would end in the ninth when Maguire and Bill Cunningham, playing for Meusel, both made quick outs. But Youngs tripled and Kelly's double to left center scored him to set the record.

The Giants were clearly in offensive control that day, sending 63 men to the plate. Three batters—Groh, Youngs, and O'Connell—had five hits each, and Youngs had seven RBIs. O'Connell's five hits included three doubles and one home run. Only once, in the ninth, did the first run of the inning score with two out. Only once, in the eighth, did the first run score by the aid of an error.

New York	ab	r	h	bi	Philadelphia	ab	r	h	bi
Bancroft, ss	5	4	3	0	Mokan, lf	4	2	2	1
Jackson, ss	1	0	0	0	Wr'stone, 3b	5	3	3	3
Groh, 3b	7	4	5	2	Williams, cf	4	0	2	1
Frisch, 2b	5	2	2	2	Leach, cf	1	0	1	0
Maguire, 2b	1	1	0	0	Walker, rf	4	0	2	3
Meusel, lf	3	2	1	1	Tierney, 2b	5	0	0	0
Cun'ham, lf	1	0	0	0	Holke, 1b	5	1	3	0
Youngs, rf	6	3	5	7	Sand, ss	3	2	1	0
Kelly, 1b	7	2	2	2	Parkinson, ph	1	0	0	0
O'Connell, cf	6	3	5	4	Wilson, c	3	0	0	0
Smith, c	5	0	0	1	O'Brien, c	2	0	0	0
Gaston, c	0	1	0	0	Head, p	0	0	0	0
Ryan, p	1	0	0	0	Behan, p	1	0	0	0
Jonnard, p	4	0	0	1	Winters, p	1	0	0	0
					Bishop, p	1	0	0	0
					Rapp, ph	1	0	1	0
Totals	52	22	23	20	Totals	41	8	15	8

New York .... 4 2 1 1 5 5 1 2 1 — 22
Philadelphia .... 1 4 0 1 1 0 0 1 0 — 8

New York	IP	H	R	ER	BB	SO
Ryan	1⅔	4	4	4	2	0
Jonnard (W)	7⅓	11	4	4	2	4

Philadelphia	IP	H	R	ER	BB	SO
Head (L)	1⅔	6	6	5	2	0
Behan	2⅓	4	2	2	5	2
Winters	2	8	10	9	0	3
Bishop	3	5	4	3	2	1

E—Maguire, Mokan, Wrightstone 2, Holke, Sand 2, O'Brien. DP—New York 1, Philadelphia 1. LOB—New York 14, Philadelphia 11. 2B—O'Connell 3, Frisch, Groh, Holke 2, Williams. 3B—Youngs, Kelly, Wrightstone. HR—O'Connell. SB—O'Connell, Frisch. SH—Jonnard, Behan. HBP—By Bishop (Gaston). WP—Winters, Bishop. PB—Wilson, Smith. T—2:47.

Forty-one years later the St. Louis Cardinals matched the Giants inning for inning as they played the Cubs in cozy Wrigley Field.

Curt Flood led off the Cardinal first with a single. After Lou Brock struck out, Dick Groat singled, with Flood taking third. Ken Boyer's infield hit scored Flood, and Groat took third on Cub pitcher Dick Ellsworth's error. Groat scored on Bill White's grounder to second.

The Cardinal run in the second inning scored on Julian Javier's leadoff home run.

In the third inning, Groat led off with a single to center and was joined on base by Boyer, who drew a walk. White sacrificed, but all runners were safe when a force play failed. Mike Shannon then singled, driving in Groat and Boyer.

Lou Brock, blossoming with the Cardinals after having been acquired from the Cubs earlier in the season, opened the scoring in the fourth inning with a leadoff home run. Two outs later, Boyer was safe on Joe Amalfitano's error, taking second on the play. Boyer scored on an error by Andre Rodgers off White's bat.

With one out in the fifth, Bob Uecker stroked a single to left, his only hit of the day. Curt Simmons, the Cardinal pitcher, who was breezing along with a 7–1 lead, bunted Uecker to second but was safe himself on Don Elston's error. Flood sacrificed Uecker and Simmons to third and second, respectively. Groat singled, scoring Uecker, and Simmons continued home on Amalfitano's second error of the day.

Shannon's solo home run with one out in the sixth kept the Cardinal scoring string alive.

In the seventh, with Sterling Slaughter pitching for the Cubs, the top of the potent Cardinal batting order struck again. In quick succession, Flood singled, Brock doubled, and Groat doubled, scoring Flood and Brock. Dal Maxvill, running for Groat, scored on Boyer's single.

That was all for Slaughter, but that was all for St. Louis, too, as John Flavin took over on the mound and retired the side.

Javier hit a leadoff double in the eighth inning and advanced to third on Simmons's grounder to Ron Campbell, who had replaced Amalfitano at second. Flood singled Javier home, thereby setting up the record-tying ninth inning.

With one out in the ninth, Boyer was safe on Campbell's error. White singled Boyer to third, and Shannon scored Boyer with a sacrifice fly.

The key to the Cardinals' success was making the most of the opportunities they had. Each player, except Ray Washburn, who did not bat, scored, knocked in a run, or kept a rally alive for a subsequent run. Cardinal players reached base 25 times. All except two, Uecker in the third (walk) and Javier in the sixth (double), figured in the scoring.

Both New York in 1923 and St. Louis in 1964 went on to win pennants, the Giants in a slaughter, and St. Louis with the help of the famous Philadelphia collapse. Both teams beat the New York Yankees in the World Series, the Giants in six games and the Cardinals in seven.

St. Louis	ab	r	h	bi	Chicago	ab	r	h	bi
Flood, cf	5	2	3	1	Amalfitano, 2b	3	1	1	0
Brock, lf	6	2	2	1	Slaughter, p	0	0	0	0
Groat, ss	5	2	4	3	Flavin, p	0	0	0	0
Maxvill, ss	1	1	0	0	Stewart, ph	1	0	0	0
Boyer, 3b	5	3	2	2	Gregory, p	0	0	0	0
White, 1b	5	0	1	1	Burton, rf	5	0	1	1
Shannon, rf	5	1	2	4	Williams, lf	4	0	0	0
Javier, 2b	6	2	3	1	Santo, 3b	4	0	1	1
Uecker, c	4	1	1	0	Banks, 1b	3	0	0	0
Simmons, p	4	1	0	0	Cowan, cf	4	0	0	0
Washburn, p	0	0	0	0	Rodgers, ss	3	1	3	0
					Campbell, 2b	1	0	1	0
					Schaffer, c	3	0	1	0
					Ellsworth, p	1	0	0	0
					F. Burdette, p	0	0	0	0
					Burke, ph	1	0	0	0
					Elston, p	0	0	0	0
					Kessinger, ss	2	0	0	0
Totals	46	15	18	13	Totals	35	2	8	2

St. Louis .... 2 1 2   2 2 1   3 1 1 — 15
Chicago .... 1 0 0   0 0 1   0 0 0 — 2

St. Louis	IP	H	R	ER	BB	SO
Simmons (W)	8	8	2	2	5	7
Washburn	1	0	0	0	1	0

Chicago	IP	H	R	ER	BB	SO
Ellsworth (L)	3⅔	7	7	6	2	2
F. Burdette	⅓	0	0	0	0	0
Elston	2	4	3	1	0	1
Slaughter*	0	4	3	3	0	0
Flavin	2	2	1	1	0	3
Gregory	1	1	1	0	0	0

* Pitched to four batters in seventh

E—Brock, Ellsworth, Rodgers 2, Amalfitano 2, Elston, Campbell. DP—Chicago 1. LOB—St. Louis 10, Chicago 12. 2B—Santo, Rogers, Javier 2, Brock, Groat. HR—Javier, Brock, Shannon. SH—White, Simmons, Flood. SF—Shannon. T—2:46.

Ruth Makes War on Warhop

Al Kermisch

On May 7, 1915, a German submarine sank the Cunard liner *Lusitania* off the coast of Ireland with a loss of 1,198 lives. This was one of the biggest news stories of the twentieth century. The day before, however, a young pitcher with the Boston Red Sox lost a tough 5–3, 13-inning game to the Yankees at the Polo Grounds in New York, making baseball history, although it would take a few years before the significance of the event would be realized. For on that afternoon—Thursday, May 6, 1915—Babe Ruth, the 20-year-old Boston southpaw, hit the first of his grand total of 714 regular-season major league home runs.

Ruth's first home run came in the third inning off Jack Warhop, the starting Yankee right-hander. He led off the inning, and he hit Warhop's first pitch into the second tier of the right field grandstand. The ball, a prodigious wallop, landed in Seat 26 of Section 3. Although Ruth had been with the Red Sox for a few games in 1914, his first home run came on only his 18th time at bat in the majors. He went to bat 10 times in 1914, and this was his eighth time up in 1915. It was his fifth major league hit, his other hits up to that time included three doubles and a single.

Among the gathering of 8,000 who witnessed Ruth's first circuit clout were Ban Johnson, president of the American League; Joseph Lannin, owner of the Red Sox; and two baseball reporters who later

hit it big in the literary field after graduating from the sports desk—
Damon Runyon and Heywood Broun.

Runyon, who covered the game for the *New York American,*
wrote, "Fanning this Ruth is not as easy as the name and occupation
might indicate. In the third inning Ruth knocked the slant out of one
of Jack Warhop's underhand subterfuges, and put the baseball in the
right field stands for a home run. Ruth was discovered by Jack Dunn
in a Baltimore school a year ago where he had not attained his left-
handed majority, and was adopted and adapted by Jack for use of the
Orioles. He is now quite a demon pitcher and demon hitter—when
he connects."

Broun penned the following for the *New York Tribune*:

> Pitted against Pieh was Babe Ruth, the remarkable
> young player discovered by Jack Dunn in a reform school
> last year. Ruth was put in the school at an early age, but
> seemingly he quit too soon to be completely reformed. He is
> still flagrantly left-handed. Babe (he was christened George)
> deserved something better than a defeat. It was his home run
> into the second tier of the grandstand which gave the Red
> Sox their first run of the game, and later he singled twice. He
> missed a chance to strike a telling blow in the eleventh inning
> for, with a runner on first and third with only one out, he was
> fanned by Pieh.

Broun also added this humorous note: "Nobody can take a mark
of distinction away from Ruth. He is practically the only left-handed
pitcher in the country not called Rube."

Another famous baseball writer who was on hand for Ruth's first
four-base blow was Fred Lieb. His story in the *New York Press* contained the following:

> George Ruth, the sensational kid who set the Interna-
> tional League grass on fire last season, went the entire
> thirteen rounds for the crimson hose and but for his support
> would have registered a win in regulation rounds. Bill
> Carrigan failed to hold the Yank runners and they kept on
> swiping bases on Chet Thomas who succeeded him. Warhop
> cooled off in the second and then Paul Shannon (reporter
> for the Boston *Post*) began to lecture on Babe Ruth's ability
> as a smitter. It was an illustrated lecture, as Babe illustrated
> Paul's remarks by lifting the pill far up in the upstairs section
> of the right field stands for a merry-go-round trip.

Wilmot E. Giffin, who wrote under the pseudonym of "Right Cross" in the *New York Evening Journal*, was also inspired by Ruth's first blast:

This Ruthless Ruth, the stem-winder, is some hurler. A pitcher who is so versatile that he can not only shoot all sorts of deliveries from the port turret, but can besides all this hit a home run, and a couple of incidental singles in one game is some asset, ladies and gentlemen, some asset indeed. When he is not pitching they can use him for an outfielder or pinch hitter. In these days of efficiency he is the ideal player. It was a genuine home run that Ruth swatted the first time up, landing in the upper tier of the south grandstand with a thump. Mr. Warhop of the Yankees looked reproachfully at the opposing pitcher who was so unclubby as to do a thing like that to one of his own trade. But Ruthless Ruth seemed to think that all was fair in the matter of fattening a batting average.

Ruth's home run lingered in the mind of "Right Cross" into the next day, when he added a little poetry entitled "A Social Error":

When a pitcher meets a pitcher,
    Should a pitcher clout?
When a pitcher meets a pitcher,
    Shouldn't he fan out?
When a pitcher slams a pitcher
    Lifts it from the lot,
You would call the gink unclubby,
    Very, would you not?

To this he added the comment, "Pitcher Warhop has not yet recovered from the great mental anguish he suffered when a player in the same line of endeavor took one of his nicest twists and just naturally lifted it out of the lot. Warhop probably will appeal to the other pitchers to ostracize Ruth over the violation of etiquette."

Just about four weeks later, the Red Sox played a return engagement at the Polo Grounds. On Wednesday, June 2, it was Ruth against Warhop again. And once again on his first time up—in the second inning with two out and Chet Thomas on first—the Babe slammed one of Warhop's pitches far into the right field stands. The ball landed on top of Seat 31 in Section 3, more than 10 feet farther than the previous one. This time the mighty Ruth was not denied. He won handily, 7–1, setting the Yanks down on five hits. The Babe was now on his way, gaining respect both as a star moundsman and a dangerous batsman, and in a few years he was destined to forsake the pitcher's box to fulfill his destiny as the greatest slugger of all time.

Babe Ruth as a Right-Handed Batter

If some old-timer tells you that he saw Babe Ruth at the plate at Yankee Stadium batting from the right side, you can take his word for it. The Babe changed over several times in 1923. The pitchers were walking him so often that year, he changed his position at the bat just to keep things interesting. On August 1, he crossed up the Indians by starting in to bat right-handed against Sherrod Smith in the ninth inning. He took one strike and then jumped back to the left side, which necessitated the entire rearrangement of the Cleveland defense (clubs were shifting against Ruth as early as 1920). Hardly was the shift completed when Smith pitched and Ruth swung. There was the well-known crack, and the ball was on its way far into the right field bleachers for Babe's 25th homer of the season. Smith, however, defeated the Yankees 5–3. Four days later against the St. Louis Browns, again at Yankee Stadium, Ruth batted right-handed twice when he saw that Elam Vangilder, who was pitching in relief for the Browns, intended to walk him, the first time with two on in the eleventh inning. He also did the same thing in the thirteenth inning when he was again passed intentionally to fill the bases. But this time Bob Meusel singled in Waite Hoyt to give the Yanks a 9 to 8 victory. The Browns were taking no chances with Ruth in the extra innings, for earlier in the contest he had hit his 26th and 27th home runs off Ray Kolp.

Al Kermisch

The Henry Aaron Home Run Analysis
John C. Tattersall

It has been several years since Henry Aaron closed out his illustrious career and there still is no home run hitter of note around to challenge his record. That provides a good opportunity to sum up his contributions in the context of an overall home run review.

As practically every baseball fan knows, Aaron closed out with 755 round-trippers. He hit 385 on the road, and 370 at home, both of which are new career records he took over from Babe Ruth. The key to his overall performance was consistency over a long period. He hit 341 homers in his twenties (trailing only Jimmie Foxx, Eddie Mathews, and Mickey Mantle); he hit 372 in his thirties (trailing only Ruth and ahead of Willie Mays); and he hit 42 in his forties (trailing only Stan Musial and Ted Williams). Note that except for Aaron, the cast changes in each decade. He hit 10 or more for 23 consecutive years, easily a record.

Aaron's chief home run victim was Don Drysdale of the Dodgers, who was reached for 17 round-trippers. This number is not a record, as Ruth hit 18 off Rube Walberg, Mays 18 off Warren Spahn, and Foxx 18 off both Red Ruffing and Al Crowder.

Henry hit extra-inning homers 13 times but trails several players in that department. Mays hit 22 after the ninth inning, Ruth and Frank Robinson 16, Foxx and Mantle 14. (Williams, like Aaron, hit 13.)

With his 755 home runs, Aaron knocked in 1,240 runs, a record. This averages out to 1.64 runs per homer, compared to 1.69 for Ruth. As might be expected, Aaron hit the most home runs with the bases empty, 399, compared to 365 for Mays and 350 for Ruth. When it came to belting with Braves and Brewers on base, Henry could not quite get out of the shadow cast by the Bambino. The Babe edged him in two-run homers, 249 to 243, and in three-run blasts, 99 to 97. In terms of grand slams Aaron and Ruth are locked in fifth place with 16 each. Ruth's slugging mate Lou Gehrig is out in front with 23.

A review of the career records of the top 60 or so home run hitters reveals that round-tripper run production by Ruth and Aaron was pretty typical of their different eras. Great power hitters of the 1920s and 1930s usually hit more than 50 percent of their four-baggers with one or more runners on base. Sluggers of the past 25 or so years usually hit less than 50 percent of their homers with bases occupied. The main reason for that disparity is that there were more base runners and fewer homers hit in the 1920s and 1930s. The reverse has been true in the last generation.

There are exceptions in both eras, and I suppose clutch hitting on an individual basis might be one of the factors. Batting third or fourth would also make a difference over a career in the number of runs batted in with homers. And then certain teams have a higher on-base average.

In regard to the exceptions, it might come as a surprise that Rogers Hornsby, a central figure in the heavy-hitting era, hit slightly fewer than 50 percent of his homers with men on. Bob Johnson of the Athletics, a good RBI man on a weak team, was another who hit more than one-half of his round-trippers with the bases empty. Gabby Hartnett and Dolph Camilli are two more from that era.

Since Williams retired in 1960, there have been very few sluggers who could connect 50 percent of the time with someone on base. Yogi Berra and Vic Wertz, who hit their last homers in 1963, did it, and Wertz was particularly productive. The 1960s, the decade of the pitchers, were quite rough on run production. Two batters who got through in pretty good shape were Harmon Killebrew and Boog Powell, neither of whom hit much for average but connected with men on base. Killebrew was the most consistent of all sluggers in hitting 2-run homers. I don't know whether it was Tony Oliva or Rod Carew who was getting on base for the Twins, but Harmon hit 223, or 39 percent of his 573 homers with one man on.

Among veteran players active in 1982, only three have connected 50 percent of the time with teammates on base—Willie Stargell, Tony Perez, and George Foster. Foster is easily the best at producing runs on homers, averaging out to 1.75 per round-tripper. In fact, Foster and Dave Kingman, both criticized for their poor play with the Mets in 1982, are the career leaders among active players.

At the end is a breakdown of the home runs hit by the top career leaders through the 1982 season. As it is not very meaningful to compare totals when you have a spread of nearly 500 home runs—from 755 for Aaron to 261 for Foster—it would be best to summarize on a percentage basis the top and bottom figures. For example, it might be interesting to know that among the players considered, Ted Williams connected most frequently with men on—whether it was 1, 2, or 3. Conversely, only 44.5 percent of his 521 homers came with the bases empty. At the other end of the run-producing spectrum are Jimmy Wynn and Reggie Smith, who have connected 58 percent of the time with no one on base. But Wynn and Smith are only the modern reflection of a "bases empty" syndrome which includes such names as Reggie Jackson, Norm Cash, Mickey Mantle, Willie Mays, Frank Robinson, Orlando Cepeda, and Al Kaline.

Kaline hit the fewest grand slams, only 3 out of 399, while Gehrig hit 23 out of 493, or 5 percent. Rudy York was next with 12 out of 277 (4.3 percent). On three-run homers, York and Jimmie Foxx top the list with 18 percent while Norm Cash was down to 8 percent. On two-run homers, Killebrew leads with 39 percent, followed by Del Ennis, Tony Perez, and Ted Williams. Orlando Cepeda hit only 27 percent of his homers with one man on.

On overall run production with home runs, Vic Wertz averaged 1.80 RBIs per homer, York 1.78, and Gehrig 1.77. At the other end, Reggie Smith averaged 1.54, and George Scott and Ted Kluszewski 1.55. Henry Aaron is in the midrange with 1.64. Here is the full list.

	Total homers	Bases empty	One on	Two on	Grand slam	RBIs on homers	RBIs/ homer
Henry Aaron	755	399	243	97	16	1240	1.64
Babe Ruth	714	350	249	99	16	1209	1.69
Willie Mays	660	365	219	68	8	1039	1.57
Frank Robinson	586	325	184	70	7	931	1.59
Harmon Killebrew	573	275	223	64	11	957	1.67
Mickey Mantle	536	297	162	68	9	861	1.60
Jimmie Foxx	534	254	167	96	17	944	1.76
Ted Williams	521	233	197	74	17	917	1.76
Willie McCovey	521	280	156	67	18	865	1.66
Ed Mathews	512	271	182	51	8	820	1.60
Ernie Banks	512	262	160	78	12	864	1.69

	Total homers	Bases empty	One on	Two on	Grand slam	RBIs on homers	RBIs/ homer
Melvin Ott	511	235	187	82	7	883	1.73
Lou Gehrig	493	231	166	73	23	874	1.77
Stan Musial	475	230	181	55	9	793	1.67
Willie Stargell	475	236	162	66	11	802	1.69
Reggie Jackson	464	263	135	57	9	740	1.59
Carl Yastrzemski	442	234	149	52	7	716	1.62
Billy Williams	426	216	162	40	8	692	1.62
Duke Snider	407	219	140	43	5	648	1.59
Al Kaline	399	220	136	40	3	624	1.56
Frank Howard	382	202	133	42	5	614	1.61
Orlando Cepeda	379	209	103	48	9	595	1.57
Johnny Bench	377	199	112	55	11	632	1.68
Norman Cash	377	213	123	33	8	590	1.56
Rocky Colavito	374	192	116	59	7	629	1.68
Gil Hodges	370	196	105	55	14	627	1.69
Ralph Kiner	369	188	121	47	13	623	1.69
Tony Perez	363	180	138	40	5	596	1.64
Joe DiMaggio	361	170	119	59	13	635	1.76
Johnny Mize	359	172	125	56	6	614	1.72
Yogi Berra	358	169	129	51	9	616	1.72
Lee May	354	193	108	42	11	579	1.64
Richie Allen	351	183	121	39	8	574	1.64
Mike Schmidt	349	180	110	54	5	582	1.67
Ron Santo	342	180	112	44	6	560	1.64
Boog Powell	339	160	130	42	7	574	1.69
Joe Adcock	336	182	106	38	10	558	1.66
Bobby Bonds	332	185	99	41	7	534	1.61
Hank Greenberg	331	160	109	51	11	575	1.74
Dave Kingman	329	167	99	52	11	565	1.72
Willie Horton	325	164	101	51	9	555	1.71
Roy Sievers	318	163	99	46	10	539	1.69
Reggie Smith	314	181	98	32	3	485	1.54
Graig Nettles	313	178	98	34	3	488	1.56
Al Simmons	307	144	109	44	10	534	1.74
Rogers Hornsby	301	152	92	45	12	519	1.72
Chuck Klein	300	140	108	45	7	519	1.73
Jimmy Wynn	291	169	85	33	4	454	1.56
Bob Johnson	288	148	93	39	8	483	1.68
Del Ennis	288	130	111	41	6	499	1.74

(Continued)

	Total homers	Bases empty	One on	Two on	Grand slam	RBIs on homers	RBIs/ homer
Hank Sauer	288	154	91	39	4	469	1.63
Rusty Staub	287	156	88	34	9	470	1.64
Frank Thomas	286	160	92	30	4	450	1.57
Ken Boyer	282	159	92	24	7	443	1.57
Ted Kluzsewski	279	156	95	25	3	433	1.55
Rudy York	277	133	81	51	12	496	1.78
Roger Maris	275	148	90	32	5	444	1.61
George Scott	271	153	89	26	3	421	1.55
Brooks Robinson	268	154	74	35	6	428	1.60
Vic Wertz	266	120	88	48	10	480	1.80
Bobby Thomson	264	142	88	26	8	428	1.62
Greg Luzinski	262	143	87	27	5	418	1.60
George Foster	261	130	76	46	9	456	1.75

A Short Cup of Coffee
Leon Uzarowski

There is an expression in baseball that refers to a player "having a cup of coffee" in the majors. The inference is that he was with a team such a short time about all he had time for was a cup of coffee.

In that parlance, the shortest cup of coffee is an appearance in one official box score. This happened to no fewer than 588 players in the period 1900 to 1973, and some interesting circumstances are involved in a number of these one-game appearances.

Probably the most recognizable of these one-time wonders is Walter Alston, the highly successful manager of the Los Angeles Dodgers. On September 27, 1936, he was a late-inning substitute at first base for Johnny Mize of the Cardinals. He made one error in two chances and was fanned by Lon Warneke of the Cubs in his only time at bat.

Cal Ermer, who managed the 1967–68 Twins, also played in just one game. He went to bat three times, with no luck, as a member of the 1947 Washington Senators.

The most publicized one-game performer was Eddie Gaedel, the famed midget batter signed by Bill Veeck. In celebration of the fiftieth anniversary of the American League, Veeck hired the 3'7", 65 lb. Gaedel for $100 and insured him for $1 million. Although he entered

257

a major league contest strictly for publicity purposes, Gaedel is probably the most famous player from the inept 1951 St. Louis Browns.

Eddie was, however, not the only nonprofessional to achieve instant big league status. In 1912, Ty Cobb was suspended prior to a game between Detroit and Philadelphia. In protest the Tiger players staged a strike, refusing to play the scheduled game. Faced with the possibility of forfeiting the contest, which would also have resulted in a $1,000 AL fine, Tiger manager Hugh Jennings had contracts drawn for eight players from St. Joseph's College of Philadelphia and one sandlotter to replace the regular Tiger team. The game was a mockery, naturally, as the A's pounded the one-day pros with a lopsided 24–2 score. Al Travers, throwing for Detroit, gave up 14 earned runs, 10 unearned runs, 26 hits, and 7 walks. Somehow he managed to register 1 strikeout.

Inept pitching has a way of magnifying itself when confined to a single game. Marty Walker, a native of Philadelphia who was starting his first game for the 1928 Phillies, promptly gave up two hits and three walks and then walked to the showers and hasn't been heard from since.

In 1918, Harry Heitman, a twenty-year-old right-hander for Brooklyn, gave up four hits, retiring just one batter in his initial major league start. After the game he ran down to the recruiting station and enlisted in the U.S. Navy.

Elmer Hamann was brought in as a relief thrower for the 1922 Cleveland Indians. Six batters later his major league career came to a close. Elmer's pitching statistics—three hits and three walks.

Some moundsmen stayed around longer but wished they hadn't. Joe Cleary of the 1945 Washington Senators struck out one batter for his only out. He was reached for five hits and three bases on balls, to produce a gaudy 189.00 career ERA.

And those who dared to linger longer than one inning were tortured more severely. Hanson Horsey, a classic baseball name, couldn't make a career of it. Pitching for the Reds on April 27, 1912, Horsey was belted by the Pirates for 14 hits in four innings. One of those hits was a triple by Chief Wilson, who went on to hit a record 36 that season.

Similarly, Hank Hulvey was given a chance by Connie Mack to face the Yankees on September 5, 1923. The minor league veteran pitched seven innings, and his only claim to fame was that he gave up Babe Ruth's 230th career home run.

Another one-time hurler used by Connie Mack was Arliss Taylor, an obscure left-hander from Pennsylvania. Taylor started against the

Indians on September 15, 1921. He gave up seven hits in two innings, but he did fan one batter. The name of the victim was Joe Sewell, the toughest batter to strike out in major league history.

Monty Swartz of the 1920 Cincinnati Reds had the unusual distinction of pitching in only one game, but it went 12 innings. He pitched the complete game, and lost.

Of course, not all one-game hurlers lost. Dave Skeels, a seventeen-year-old starting pitcher for the 1910 Tigers, gave up eight runs but managed to record a win. Doc McMahon yielded 14 hits in nine innings but was victorious for the Red Sox in 1908. And Ray Brown of the 1909 Cubs pitched a five-hit, nine-inning win and then disappeared from the league scene.

There was also a lack of hitting prowess in these one-game appearances. Most batters struck out in their only major league at bat. Tommy Patton of the 1957 Baltimore Orioles, on the other hand, struck out twice, and Chris Haughey, a seventeen-year-old pitcher for the 1943 Brooklyn Dodgers, fanned three times in three plate appearances. Chris wasn't much better on the mound, as he walked ten batters in the game.

None of the one-time wonders ever slammed a home run, but Ed Irwin, the famed sandlotter of the 1912 strike-struck Tigers, ran out two triples in that game against Philadelphia.

Fred Lindstrom's son Charlie, in one at bat for the White Sox in 1958, knocked in a run with a triple, for a 3.000 slugging average.

There have been more than twenty batters who have achieved a perfect 1.000 lifetime batting average. Most of them had one hit in one at-bat, but John Paciorek, an eighteen-year-old strong boy from Michigan, went three for three in the final game of the 1963 season for the Houston Colts. Paciorek also drew a pair of walks. John scored four of the five times he was on base, as the Colts galloped to a 13–4 triumph over the New York Mets.

After that game Gus Maucuso wrote in the *Houston Press,* "Paciorek should be a cinch to make it as a big leaguer. He shows promise of becoming a great hitter. He swings the bat with authority and shows good speed in the outfield and on the bases, too."

But in 1964 Paciorek was back in the minors, where he remained until a back operation in 1967 ended his hope of ever appearing in the big leagues a second time. His younger brother Tom broke in with the Dodgers in 1970.

Twenty-year-old Ray Jansen of the 1910 St. Louis Browns also hit impressively. He went four for five. All his hits were singles, and he retired with an .800 lifetime major league batting mark.

Pitcher John Kull, hurling for the 1909 Philadelphia A's, achieved a 1.000 career batting average and a 1.000 pitching percentage. He then quit while he was ahead. No sense improving perfection.

It's easy to see why they call Philadelphia the city of Brotherly Love; 92 out of the 588 one-game major leaguers appeared for either the A's or the Phillies. They believed in giving everyone at least one chance. Washington was the most hospitable team in the AL, getting 55 players into a box score once.

Some one-day players had brothers of a more lasting quality. Note the following career games played on the major league level by these brother combinations:

Games	Name	Games	Name
1	Frank Cross	2275	Lafayette Cross
1	Tommy Sewell	1902	Joe Sewell
		1630	Luke Sewell
1	Ralph Miller	1820	Bing Miller
1	Joe Evers	1762	Johnny Evers
1	Jim Westlake	958	Wally Westlake
1	Ralph Gagliano	656	Phil Gagliano
1	Dave Bennett	182	Dennis Bennett

Most of the 588 one-game players between 1900 and 1973 made it to the big leagues the hard way. They labored several years in the minors to get that cup of coffee. More than one-half made it as pitchers (316). There were also 66 catchers, 12 first basemen, 11 second basemen, 26 third basemen, 17 shortstops, 44 outfielders, and 96 pinch hitters or pinch runners.

The oldest one-game player was Art Jacobs, a thirty-seven-year-old pitcher making his debut with the 1939 Reds. He hurled one inning and injured his shoulder. Bill Bradford, thirty-five, appeared for the 1956 Kansas City A's.

There were several who were seventeen when they made their singular appearance. Skeels and Haughey have already been mentioned. Jay Dahl, killed in an auto accident two years later, pitched in an all-rookie lineup for Houston on September 27, 1963. Mike Loan was seventeen when he caught and singled in a game for the Phils on September 18, 1917.

Average Batting Skill
Richard D. Cramer

Is the American or the National the tougher league in which to hit .300? How well would Babe Ruth, Ty Cobb, or Cap Anson hit in the 1980s? What effects did World War II or league expansion or racial integration have on the caliber of major league hitting? Here are definitive answers on this type of question.

The answers come from a universally accepted yardstick of batting competitiveness, the comparing of the performances of the same player in different seasons. For example, we all conclude that the National League is tougher than the International because the average of most batters drops upon promotion. Of course, factors other than the level of competition affect batting averages. Consider how low were the batting averages of the following future major leaguers in the 1971 Eastern League (EL):

	BA, EL (1971)	BA, majors (through 1979)
Bill Madlock	.234	.320
Mike Schmidt	.211	.255
Bob Boone	.265	.268
Andre Thornton	.267	.252
Bob Coluccio	.208	.220
Pepe Frias	.240	.239

Double A seems a bit tougher than the major leagues from these data because (1) this player sample is biased: most Eastern Leaguers don't reach the majors, and I haven't shown all the 1971 players who did, and (2) large and poorly lighted parks made the 1971 EL tough for any hitter, as shown by its .234 league average. My study tries to avoid these pitfalls, minimizing bias by using all available data for each season-to-season comparison, and avoiding most "environmental factors," such as ball resilience or rule changes that affect players equally, by subtracting league averages before making a comparison. Of course, direct comparisons cannot be made for seasons more than twenty years apart; few played much in both periods, say, 1950 and 1970. But these seasons can be compared indirectly, by comparing 1950 to 1955 to 1960, and so on and adding the results.

There are many measures of batting performance. In the quest for a single accurate measure of overall batting effectiveness, I have developed the "batter's win average" (BWA) as a "relative to league average." Its value rests on the finding that the scoring of major league teams is predicted from the BWAs of its individual players with an error of ± 21 runs (standard deviation) when all data are available (SB, CS, HBP, and GDP as well as AB, H, TB, and BB) and about ± 30 runs otherwise.

A property useful in visualizing the BWA in terms of conventional statistics is its roughly 1 : 1 equivalence with batting average, provided that differences among players arise only from singles. To make this point more clearly by an example, Fred Lynn's $+.120$ BWA led the majors in 1979. His value to the Red Sox was the same as that of a hitter who obtained walks, extra bases, and all other statistical oddments at the league average but who hit enough extra singles to have an average .120 above the league, that is, a BA of .390. The difference between .390 and Lynn's actual .333 is an expression mostly of his robust extra-base slugging.

The first stage in this study was a labor of love, using an HP67 calculator to obtain BWAs for every nonpitcher season batting record having at least 20 BFPs (batter facing pitcher) in major league history. The second stage was merely labor, typing all those BFPs and BWAs into a computer and checking the entries for accuracy by comparing player BFP sums with those in the Macmillan *Baseball Encyclopedia*. The final stage, performing all possible season-to-season comparisons player to player, took ninety minutes on a PDP10 computer. A season-season comparison involves the sum of the difference in BWAs for every player appearing in the two seasons, weighted by his smaller number of BFPs. Other weighting schemes that were tried seemed to add nothing to the results but complexity.

Any measurement is uncertain, and if this uncertainty is unknown the measure is almost useless. The subsequent treatment of these season to season comparisons is too involved for concise description, but it allowed five completely independent assessments of the level of batting skill in any given AL or NL season, relative to their respective 1979 levels. The standard deviation of any set of five measurements from their mean was ±.007, ranging from .002 to .011. This implies that the "true" average batting skill in a season has a 2 in 3 chance of being within ±.007 of the value computed and a 19 in 20 chance of being within ±.014, provided that errors in my values arise only from random factors, such as individual player streaks and slumps that don't cancel. However, no study can be guaranteed free of systematic error. To cite an example of a systematic error that was identified and corrected: if a player's career spans only two seasons, it is likely, irrespective of the level of competition, that his second season was worse than his first. (If he had improved, he was likely to have kept his job for at least a third season.) Another possible source of error which proved unimportant was the supposed tendency for batters to weaken with age (the actual tendency appears to be fewer hits but more walks). It appears that overall systematic error is less than 20 percent of the total differences in average levels. One check is that the 1972 to 1973 AL difference is attributable entirely to the calculable effect of excluding pitchers from batting, plus a general rising trend in AL skill in the 1970s.

As might be expected, assessment of the relative strength of the major leagues comes from players changing leagues. Results again were consistent and showed no dependence on the direction of the change. Results from the two eras of extensive interleague player movement, 1901 to 1905 and post-1960, agreed well also.

The results of my study are easiest to visualize from the graphical presentation on the next page. (Because few readers will be familiar with the BWA units, I have not tabulated the individual numbers but later convert them to relative BAs and SPcts.) Theories on the whys and wherefores of changes in average batting skill I leave to others with greater personal and historical knowledge of the game. But the major trends are clear:

(1) The average level of batting skill has improved steadily and substantially since 1876. The .120-point difference implies that a batter with 1979-average skills would in 1876 have had the value of an otherwise 1876-average batter who hit enough extra singles for a .385 BA.

(2) The AL and NL were closely matched in average batting

Corrections Applied to a Player's Batting Average and Slugging Percentage in a Particular Season to Equate Them with 1976 NL Play

	American		National			American		National	
	BA	**SPct**	**BA**	**SPct**		**BA**	**SPct**	**BA**	**SPct**
1979	+.003	−.029	−.001	−.017	1965	+.001	−.021	+.003	−.016
1978	+.011	−.007	+.005	−.004	1964	−.006	−.035	−.003	−.017
1977	+.002	−.031	−.004	−.033	1963	−.009	−.036	+.003	−.010
1976	+.016	+.017	(.000)	(.000)	1962	−.017	−.050	−.014	−.040
1975	+.009	−.006	.000	−.006	1961	−.022	−.055	−.012	−.049
1974	+.007	−.001	+.002	−.004 ·	1960	−.017	−.044	−.004	−.031
1973	+.005	−.011	+.002	−.014	1959	−.018	−.043	−.009	−.043
1972	+.013	+.015	+.005	−.007	1958	−.019	−.042	−.011	−.048
1971	+.001	−.010	.000	−.008	1957	−.024	−.045	−.011	−.045
1970	−.004	−.027	−.007	−.035	1956	−.028	−.056	−.007	−.046
1969	−.002	−.019	−.003	−.016	1955	−.029	−.046	−.015	−.057
1968	+.016	+.013	+.010	+.018	1954	−.029	−.039	−.023	−.059
1967	+.008	−.001	+.003	−.005	1953	−.035	−.050	−.027	−.066
1966	+.004	−.019	−.002	−.024	1952	−.026	−.032	−.012	−.027

BA and SPct, continued

	American		National				American		National	
	BA	SPct	BA	SPct			BA	SPct	BA	SPct
1951	−.030	−.043	−.018	−.024		1913	−.078	−.052	−.077	−.063
1950	−.043	−.068	−.020	−.054		1912	−.085	−.062	−.089	−.080
1949	−.034	−.034	−.021	−.042		1911	−.094	−.073	−.082	−.072
1948	−.036	−.046	−.018	−.034		1910	−.064	−.029	−.078	−.054
1947	−.023	−.025	−.026	−.045		1909	−.065	−.024	−.065	−.029
1946	−.030	−.032	−.018	−.011		1908	−.060	−.019	−.059	−.020
1945	−.045	−.030	−.040	−.033		1907	−.069	−.026	−.067	−.027
1944	−.051	−.038	−.034	−.030		1906	−.075	−.038	−.070	−.030
1943	−.026	−.012	−.024	−.007		1905	−.070	−.037	−.082	−.053
1942	−.032	−.026	−.013	−.001		1904	−.075	−.046	−.075	−.042
1941	−.042	−.059	−.025	−.022		1903	−.078	−.072	−.103	−.076
1940	−.047	−.077	−.034	−.040		1902	−.108	−.096	−.096	−.050
1939	−.055	−.077	−.046	−.054		1901	−.117	−.105	−.077	−.065
1938	−.059	−.087	−.037	−.040		1900			−.090	−.071
1937	−.062	−.090	−.050	−.054		1899			−.108	−.086
1936	−.074	−.100	−.057	−.059		1898			−.097	−.067
1935	−.060	−.076	−.055	−.063		1897			−.123	−.111
1934	−.063	−.077	−.056	−.065		1896			−.124	−.115
1933	−.058	−.069	−.042	−.032		1895			−.132	−.129
1932	−.068	−.089	−.057	−.071		1894			−.145	−.165
1931	−.072	−.084	−.064	−.068		1893			−.103	−.109
1930	−.081	−.108	−.095	−.134		1892	Amer.	Assoc.	−.082	−.042
1929	−.064	−.081	−.087	−.113		1891	−.127	−.110	−.091	−.075
1928	−.081	−.091	−.076	−.086		1890	−.132	−.105	−.104	−.086
1927	−.084	−.092	−.076	−.074		1889	−.112	−.098	−.107	−.096
1926	−.082	−.087	−.076	−.076		1888	−.092	−.063	−.088	−.068
1925	−.092	−.101	−.095	−.111		1887	−.124	−.112	−.117	−.123
1924	−.091	−.091	−.086	−.089		1886	−.096	−.070	−.107	−.092
1923	−.090	−.090	−.093	−.096		1885	−.107	−.083	−.095	−.070
1922	−.106	−.101	−.102	−.108		1884	−.111	−.090	−.102	−.089
1921	−.101	−.111	−.099	−.101		1883	−.124	−.097	−.111	−.103
1920	−.093	−.091	−.079	−.070		1882	−.127	−.089	−.096	−.082
1919	−.079	−.064	−.069	−.042		1881			−.107	−.079
1918	−.064	−.027	−.064	−.032		1880			−.089	−.058
1917	−.058	−.024	−.059	−.032		1879			−.106	−.074
1916	−.061	−.031	−.060	−.035		1878			−.111	−.065
1915	−.061	−.033	−.059	−.036		1877			−.131	−.092
1914	−.067	−.036	−.063	−.040		1876			−.123	−.073

	Federal League	
1915	−.090	−.069
1914	−.110	−.096

	Union 1884		Players 1890	
	−.146	−.111	−.108	−.106

strength for the first four decades (although not in number of superstars—the AL usually had many more). About 1938 the NL began to pull ahead of the AL, reaching its peak superiority in the early 1960s. A resurgence during the 1970s makes the AL somewhat the tougher today, mainly because of the DH rule.

(3) The recent and also the earliest expansions had only slight and short-lived effects on batting competitiveness. However, the blip around 1900 shows the substantial effect on competition that changing the number of teams from 12 to 8 to 16 had.

(4) World War II greatly affected competitiveness in 1944 and 1945.

Many baseball fans, myself included, like to imagine how a Ruth or a Wagner would do today. To help in these fantasies, I have compiled a table of batting average and slugging percentage corrections, based again on forcing differences in league batting skill overall into changes in the frequency of singles only. However, league batting averages and slugging percentages have been added back in to reflect differences in playing conditions as well as in the competition. To convert a player's record in year A to an equivalent performance in season B, one should first add to his year A batting and slugging averages the corrections tabulated for season A and then subtract the corrections shown for season B. The frequency of such other events as walks or stolen bases then can, optionally, be corrected for any difference in league frequencies between seasons A and B.

One interesting illustration might start with Honus Wagner's great 1908 season (BWA $= +.145$). What might Wagner have done in the 1979 American League, given a livelier ball but tougher competition? The table yields a batting average correction of $-.059 - (+.003) = -.062$ and a slugging correction of $-.020 - (-0.29) = +.009$, which applied to Wagner's 1908 stats gives a 1979 BA of .292 and SPct of .551. (In 600 ABs, he would have, say, 30 home runs, 10 triples, 35 doubles). Wagner's stolen base crown and tenth-place tie in walks translate directly to similar positions in the 1979 stats. That's impressive batting production for any shortstop, and a "1979 Honus Wagner" would doubtless be an All-Star Game starter.

These results are fairly typical. Any twentieth-century superstar would be a star today. Indeed, a young Babe Ruth or Ted Williams would outbat any of today's stars. But, of course, any of today's stars—Parker, Schmidt, Rice, Carew—would before 1955 have been a legendary superstar. Perhaps they almost deserve their heroic salaries.

Facts are often hard on legends, and many may prefer to believe veterans belittling the technical competence of today's baseball as compared, say, to pre–World War II. Indeed, little things may have been executed better by the average 1939 player. However, so great is the improvement in batting that if all other aspects of play were held constant, a lineup of average 1939 hitters would finish 20 to 30 games behind a lineup of average 1979 hitters, by scoring 200 to 300 fewer runs. This should hardly surprise an objective observer. Today's players are certainly taller and heavier, are drawn from a larger population, including more countries and races, and are more carefully taught at all levels of play. If a host of new Olympic track and field records established every four years are any indication, they can run faster and farther. Why shouldn't they hit a lot better?

Spottswood Poles
John Holway

They used to call Spottswood Poles the black Ty Cobb. He was a Negro League contemporary of the Detroit outfielder who excelled at hitting and running. Paul Robeson, the famous singer, who was a football star of the 1918–22 period, considered Poles one of the greatest black athletes of all times, grouping him with Jesse Owens, Jack Johnson, and Joe Louis.

It's just possible that Poles may indeed have been one of the finest hitters and base runners in black baseball history. We may never know for sure. His best years were some seventy years ago, back before World War I, and there are not many left who saw him at his peak. Black baseball statistics, thin even in later years, were even more rare back then. What few batting averages we do have for him are stunning: .440, .364, and .487. We can only guess what he might have hit in the missing years.

And we can only guess what he might have hit in the major leagues. The hints we do have are eye-popping, to say the least. In ten games against the best white big leaguers of his day, Poles came to bat an estimated 41 times and drilled 25 hits, for an average of .610.

If Poles could hit like Cobb, he could also run like Cobb. Stolen bases were counted in only four of his games against the big leaguers, but in those four games he stole five bases. Against black (and probably some white) opponents in 1911, he swiped 41 bases in 60 games.

Poles could still fly twelve years later, when pitcher Sam Streeter saw him. Streeter had heard of Poles's reputation on the bases, but he wasn't prepared for the performance the little thirty-six-year-old left-hander put on the first time they met. "He hit that ball on one hop right back to me," Streeter says. "It was straight, just like a line drive. I turned to throw to first, and he crossed first before the ball got there! I said, 'Well, I won't play around with *you* anymore!' "

Streeter, who saw them both, insists that Poles was even faster than Cool Papa Bell, usually called the fastest man ever to play baseball. "If Poles hits to third base or shortstop," Streeter says, "there was no question about it, he was going to be there safe."

The bowlegged Poles hardly looked like a speed merchant. He was born in Winchester, Virginia, in 1887 and died in Harrisburg, Pennsylvania, in 1962. He once reminisced, "I played baseball since I was six years old, using a broomstick and a tennis ball." At the age of nineteen, in 1906, Poles joined the Harrisburg Colored Giants in the Pennsylvania capital. "I looked like my name," he used to laugh, "a bean pole."

Three years later Spot moved to the black big time, to the renowned Philadelphia Giants team founded by Sol White, who had developed such stars as Rube Foster, Pop Lloyd, and Pete Hill. When White moved to the Lincoln Giants in New York in 1911, Poles moved with him. He enjoyed his finest years with them as a lead-off hitter and centerfielder, playing alongside such stars as pitcher Smoky Joe Williams, catcher Louis Santop, and outfielder Blainey Hall. In his very first year, Spot led the Lincolns with a .440 mark.

"We trained in Florida in those days," Poles later told sportswriter Al Clark of Harrisburg. "On Washington's Birthday, there was no game. All the players used to go to Palm Beach for a track meet, and one year I ran one hundred yards in less than ten seconds. They tell me that was pretty close to the world record at that time."

Poles spent the winter of 1912 in Cuba, hitting .364. The following autumn, in 1913, he joined the Lincolns in a postseason series against the Philadelphia Phils and their great pitcher Grover Cleveland Alexander. Poles stung Alex for three straight hits in a 9–2 victory, then slashed five hits against George Chalmers of the Phils in a 7–3 win.

The next recorded batting average we have for Poles was for the 1914 season, and it's a beauty: .487. In the autumn of that year, Poles was again playing against major league stars. He collected four hits off

Andy Coakley, former pitcher of the Athletics, in a 5–3 victory. Chief Bender came closest to stopping the pesky Spottswood, holding him to only one single. But he didn't hold him enough: Poles scored the winning run in the ninth to beat the Chief 4–3.

Poles's career was suddenly interrupted in 1917 by World War I. He enlisted at the age of thirty in the 369th Infantry, which was attached to the French army. Spot earned five battle stars and a Purple Heart in France. "I was proud then," he used to say. Mustered out, he returned to the Lincolns and later the Brooklyn Royal Giants.

At last in 1923 Poles called it a career. "I was still batting above .300 when I quit," he said. "The only thing was that I got tired of all the train travel and carrying those bags around all the time. So I got out of baseball and bought myself five taxi cabs."

Poles was in retirement in Harrisburg in 1945 when Jackie Robinson signed with the Dodgers. A few years later Poles took a promising young pitcher named Brooks Lawrence under his wing and sent him up to the St. Louis Cardinals, where he won 15 and lost 6 in 1954. "I'm proud, real proud, of Brooksie," he beamed.

How did Poles feel about missing the big time? "Maybe old Poles was born before his time," he once shrugged. "I never had a chance." Lapsing into a Pennsylvania Dutch proverb, he added, "Old Poles grew too soon old. But I came close. Mrs. John McGraw was going through her husband's stuff a little while after John died. He had a notation about us—Pop Lloyd, Joe Williams, Dick Redding, and me. If they would let us in the majors, John said we would be the ones he would pick."

Baseball Rhyme Time
Eddie Gold

Rod Carew, Vida Blue, and Big Klu,
Connie Mack, Stan Hack, Max Flack,
Guy Bush, Emil Kush, Heinie Manush,
Joe Rudi, Lyle Judy, and Howdy Doody.

Ty Cobb, Scotty Robb, Rusty Staub,
Rip Sewell, Bob Buhl, Joe Kuhel,
Hank Bauer, Vic Power, Hank Sauer,
Tris Speaker, Roy Meeker, and a streaker.

Lyn Lary, Charlie Berry, Gaylord Perry,
Jimmy Foxx, Johnny Knox, Billy Cox,
Bill Terry, Max Carey, and Larry Sherry,
Mel Ott, Dick Drott, and I forgot.

Tommy Tucker, Earl Brucker, Johnny Rucker,
George Case, ElRoy Face, Hal Chase,
Ernie Koy, Dummy Hoy, and Nap Lajoie,
Or is it La-sho-aye and Bordagaray.

Gene Dale, Larry McPhail, Bad News Hale,
Ray Narleski, Hank Majeski, Johnny Pesky,
Bucky Harris, Dave Ferris, Roger Maris,
Dick Sharon, Henry Aaron, and Red Barron.

Boccabella, Campanella, and Dan Gardella,
Ferris Fain, Sugar Cain, Johnny Sain,
Alvin Dark, Fred Clarke, Dolly Stark,
Poffenberger, Raffensberger, Wally Berger.

Pete Rose, Billy Loes, Mike de la Hoz,
Boots Day, Carlos May, Pete Gray,
Herman Franks, Howard Shanks, Ernie Banks,
Bunny Brief, George Strief, and good grief.

Lou Brock, Wes Stock, and Ray Kroc,
Buddy Myer, Eddie Dyer, Jim McGuire,
Wally Post, Lou Tost, Eddie Yost,
Gus Bell, George Kell, and William Tell.

Ford Frick, Sammy Vick, Elmer Flick,
Dick Hall, Gabe Paul, Chick Stahl,
Bobby Doerr, Ernie Shore, Herb Score,
Alex the Great, Bennie Tate, and Watergate.

Dizzy Dean, Dick Green, Harvey Kuenn,
George Dauss, Les Moss, and Buck Ross,
Don Baylor, Rollie Naylor, Dummy Taylor,
Henry Sage, Satchel Paige, and old age.

Tom Seaver, Buck Weaver, Sam Leever,
Walter Johnson, Stan Bahnsen, Evar Swanson,
Ralph Garr, Jim Barr, Ray Starr,
Billy Sunday, Rick Monday, and Tuesday Weld.

Bobby Tolan, Gary Nolan, Cozy Dolan,
Norm Cash, Billy Nash, Herb Hash,
Harry Brecheen, Frank Gustine, Claude Osteen,
Joe Lutz, Clyde Kluttz, and aw nuts.

Billy Southworth, Jimmy Bloodworth, Jim Duckworth,
Bob Feller, Hod Eller, King Kong Keller,
Frank Hayes, Willie Mays, and Van Robays,
Dom DiMaggio, Vince DiMaggio, and the other one.

Mordecai Brown, Turk Lown, Clyde Shoun,
Bill Veeck, Dave Schneck, Boom Boom Beck,
Boog Powell, Dixie Howell, Bama Rowell,
Branch Rickey, Bill Dickey, and Mantle Mickey.

George Halas, Pat Corrales, Jerry Morales,
Hank Schenz, Joe Benz, Jewell Ens,
Cot Deal, Bob Veale, Greasy Neale,
Duke Snider, Rollie Zeider, and apple cider.

Wally Pipp, Ewell the Whip, Leo the Lip,
Tony Piet, George Myatt, Whitlow Wyatt,
Jake Atz, Matt Batts, Jigger Statz,
Vinegar Bend, and this is the End!

Joe Corbett Quit Old Orioles after Great Year

To become a 20-game winner in the majors is the goal of most pitchers. Many never attain it, and Milt Pappas even became a 200-game winner without ever annexing 20 games in a season. On the other hand, Joe Corbett, younger brother of heavyweight champion James J. Corbett, won 24 games in his only full major league season. He was 24 and 8 for the old Orioles of the National League in 1897, but, disenchanted with the Baltimore offer for 1898, he remained at his home in San Francisco and never pitched for the Orioles again. He eventually came back to pitch in the Pacific Coast League, and in 1904 tried a comeback with the St. Louis Cardinals but did not finish the season. With a disappointing record of 5 wins and 9 losses he was released by the Cardinals at his own request on August 1, 1904.

"Gentleman Jim" Corbett was the guiding light behind Joe's baseball career. An excellent baseball player himself, champion Jim often made personal appearances at minor league ball parks and as part of the promotion would usually play first base for the home team. In the early part of the 1895 season, nineteen-year-old Joe would often accompany Jim on these tours and several times played shortstop in the same infield with his famous brother. With the heavyweight champion of the world to guide him, Joe got a tryout with the Washington Senators during the latter part of 1895. Jim was also instrumental in getting Joe a trial with the champion Orioles in 1896, even guaranteeing Manager Ned Hanlon that he would pay Joe's expenses if he didn't make good. Joe spent most of 1896 as an Oriole farmhand but won three games in the short time he was with the Birds. In 1897 Joe came into his own and led the Oriole staff with his 24 victories.

The Orioles were hit with a rash of holdouts in 1898, but all finally came back to the fold except Joe Corbett. His absence caused quite a stir at first but was quickly eased when the Orioles picked up an inexpensive replacement who became an instant success. James Hughes broke into the majors in a sensational fashion. His first game was a two-hit, 9–0 victory over Washington, and four days later he blanked the champion Boston club 8–0 on a no-hitter. Hughes was 21–11 for Baltimore in 1898, and the following year, when Hanlon and most of the Oriole stars transferred to Brooklyn, he led the pennant-winning Superbas with a superb 28–6 record. Not only was Joe Corbett forgotten, but brother Jim had lost his heavyweight title to Bob Fitzsimmons.

Al Kermisch